P-127 & 128

450
019

B

# THE
# FOUNDING
# FATHERS

# THE
# FOUNDING
# FATHERS
## AN EXAMINATION OF CONSCIENCE

Edward J. Melvin, C.M.

OUR SUNDAY VISITOR, Inc.
NOLL PLAZA, HUNTINGTON, IN 46750

# ACKNOWLEDGMENTS

The author is grateful to the following publishers and authors for permission to reprint copyrighted material which appeared in the following:

*Abortion and Social Justice,* edited by Thomas W. Hilgers and Dennis J. Horan, Copyright, 1972, by Sheed and Ward, Inc.

*America* magazine, Copyright, 1973, by America Press.

*Crisis in the Classroom: The Remaking of American Education,* by Charles E. Silberman, Copyright, 1973, by Random House, Inc.

*How True: A Skeptic's Guide to Believing the News,* by Thomas Griffith, Copyright, 1974, by Thomas Griffith, by permission of Little, Brown and Co., in association with The Atlantic Monthly Press.

*Man-Made Morals: Four Philosophies That Shaped America,* by William Marnell, Copyright, 1966, by William Marnell, by permission of Doubleday & Co., Inc.

*Nine Men,* by Fred Rodell, Copyright, 1955, by Fred Rodell, published by Random House, Inc.

*Seven Who Shaped Our Destiny,* by Richard B. Morris, Copyright, 1973, by Harper & Row, Publishers, Inc.

*Philadelphia Inquirer & Daily News,* Copyright, 1974, by Philadelphia Newspapers, Inc.

*The New York Times,* Copyright, 1974/1973, by The New York Times Co.

*The Occasions of Justice,* Charles L. Black, Jr., Copyright, 1963, by Charles L. Black, Jr., published by The Macmillan Co.

*We Hold These Truths,* by John Courtney Murray, Copyright, 1960, by Sheed and Ward, Inc.

*ISBN: 0-87973-890-1*
*Library of Congress Catalog Card Number: 76-379*

*Cover Design by James E. McIlrath*

*Published, printed and bound in the U.S.A. by*
*Our Sunday Visitor, Inc.*
*Noll Plaza*
*Huntington, Indiana 46750*
*890*

# CONTENTS

# AUTHOR'S FOREWORD

*The Founding Fathers: An Examination of Conscience* was ready for the printers when two newspaper accounts which I think show the need of the book were published. The first appeared in *The (Philadelphia) Sunday Bulletin,* on October 5, 1975. Written under the byline of Lou Antosh it was headlined BILLY PENN A CON MAN? NEW TEXTS BEND HALOS. Mr. Antosh's story indicates that the current trend in teaching American history is diametrically opposed to a proper understanding of the Founding Fathers as outlined in this book.

Put into context of education already deficient in the basics of mathematics and English (the Scholastic Aptitude Tests show a nationwide downward trend in ability since 1963) and defective or nonexistent moral training, the country now faces an undermining of the teaching of history and social science necessary for good citizenship. Mr Antosh's article underlines the importance of taking the Founding Fathers seriously in this Bicentennial year; it underscores that America must examine its conscience on the treatment the Founding Fathers receive in the schools. Following are excerpts* from *The Sunday Bulletin* account, headlined BILLY PENN A CON MAN? NEW TEXTS BEND HALOS, with the subhead, PAPERBACK HISTORY SERIES USED IN SOME PHILADELPHIA SCHOOLS:

"William Penn's 'walking purchase' is an example of how Indians were tricked into giving up their land.

"Penn's agent bought a piece of Indian land in Pennsylvania equal in length to 'as far as a man can go in a day and a half.' The agent hired the three best runners in the colony and started them off at dawn. One runner quit; another fell in a creek; but the third kept going a full 36 hours. Everyone thought it was a good trick and the Penn family was a million acres richer."

It must first be noted that this is false history. The notorious

---

*Reprinted with permission from *The Sunday Bulletin.*

7

"Walking Purchase" took place some twenty years after William Penn's death, under the proprietorship of Thomas Penn, his son. But the approach to the teaching of history indicated by the false Penn story is even more pernicious than its untruthfulness. Mr. Antosh's account continues:

"The social studies department head at Abington High in Montgomery County says his teachers have no problem telling students that Jefferson had a slave mistress; it shows his human condition. . . .

"The old-style history is dead, replaced by wide-reaching American and World Culture courses stressing concepts rather than dates and facts.

"Pupils are being taught 'critical thinking,' how to explore differing and conflicting versions of a past event to come up with their own conclusion. Thus, a new viewpoint on William Penn is possible. . . .

"The 'critical-thinking' approach encourages children to sniff out bias and inconsistencies in historical information and to form their own conclusions. Kids in a complex world are learning that the past was also complex. This means understanding the Founding Fathers, for instance, as humans and not as one-dimensional legends. . . .

"Penn comes off in most other school texts as the ever-kind Quaker who treated Indians as 'equal and brother.'

"Yet, there's no telling what falls from the lips of the classroom teacher when he expounds on Penn, or any of the other guiding lights of the past.

" 'It used to be that students were told certain facts and the emphasis was on patriotism,' explained Charles Clarke, social studies department head at Dobbins Tech. 'All these founders were tremendous people, with Washington chopping down the cherry tree and the whole bit.

" 'But in the '60s the students and teachers started thinking maybe it wasn't all so wonderful. The Vietnam thing put more emphasis on mistakes in the past and there is more and more emphasis on trying to look at people in human terms.' "

The problems with this type of history teaching have of course not gone totally unnoticed:

" 'Now when we teach Washington and Jefferson, it usually does come out that these people were slave-holders. Usually the kids (Dobbins is a predominantly black school) get very cynical about this. But you've got to have a discussion on this and put it into perspective and discuss those times.'

"All men have multiple dimensions and must be presented that way, said Abington High's Rorison.

" 'You have to explore it with the kids. Yes, Jefferson had slaves; yes, Jefferson had a slave mistress. Yet Jefferson wrote the Declaration of Independence. How do you fathom such a man? It's difficult.

" 'What the community is looking for is an honest approach to the history of the country, not a whitewash. They want to raise thoughtful citizens, not just memorizers. The way to do that is to make available different points of view.' . . .

"Although some conservatives have railed against the new approach to history (notably Patrick Buchanan, a speech writer for former President Nixon), most teachers see critical thinking as the new goal. There are dangers, however.

" 'Some teachers try to ingratiate themselves with the students by debunking everyone,' said Lincoln's Brown. 'But to give the sewer side of American history is bad history. You have to teach a balance and teach people as complex figures.' . . ."

According to Mr. Antosh's article the culture-history method is very official in Pennsylvania; without doubt it is the prescribed approach in other states as well.

"The modern stress on 'culture' rather than history alone, is required by the Pennsylvania Department of Education, which has dropped the label 'history' from its social-studies requirements for youngsters in grades seven to 12.

"In that grade range, the state requires two units (years) of World Culture and two units of American Culture, the latter de-

9

scribed as an 'interdisciplinary' study combining history, sociology, economics, geography, anthropology and others."

It is important to bypass labels — conservative vs. liberal — to achieve an intelligent and commonsense estimate of the "wide-reaching American and World Culture courses." Also, what is being pointed out in these paragraphs must be added to the criticism of the American history texts actually in use in our schools which occurs in Chapter 7 of this book.

These observations are justified:

1. Our children are being cheated of their heritage. They have a right to know their origin, the great men who gave us our country, the struggle which gave birth to the nation, the philosophy placed as a foundation under the American way of life and upon which we built our greatness.

2. These shallow "culture" courses at best are inadequate, at worst are false history. A child or an adolescent who studies that Jefferson had a slave mistress, given the immaturity of the pupil and the brevity of time that can be given to a great man like Jefferson, can end only with a false concept.

3. Adolescents have need of heroes; they are being robbed of their heroes and their ideals. It is false education to turn them into cynics, to destroy the natural idealism of youth. How much greater is the possibility that the young student will achieve his or her fulfillment if the emphasis is on the facts that Thomas Jefferson was a patriot who risked his life and fortune for his country, a sincere man who hated slavery and did his best to turn his country toward slavery's extinction, a genius who developed all his talents and used them for self and others, a political philosopher whose principles were written into our legal structure and have contributed to American freedom and happiness for 200 years, a politician who had great faith in the people and democratic process — than that he had a slave mistress!

Jefferson's character had its flaws; at the proper time and in a balanced way this should be taught. The same would be true of Washington, Adams, Hamilton, all our Founding Fathers, and in proportion our other great historical leaders. But their greatness is being chipped at by little minds, by shallow textbook authors, by unbalanced criticism; and teachers who follow this current fad are untruthful historians as well as inadequate educators.

4. America has something to give the world. The American form of government of the people, by the people, for the people, historically based on solid moral and philosophical principles, has insured the freest, most prosperous society in history. To the extent that these principles — often spelled out and always implicit in our national and state constitutions — have been carried out, we have had a just society.

We can learn from other nations; we should be sympathetic with other cultures. But we are the leading nation of the Western world, the inheritor of the best in Western and Judeo-Christian civilization. The other world power is based on a philosophy intrinsically evil, degrading, unjust, inhuman — a system never voted in freely by any nation and from which people flee in terror. Are we to inundate our youth with a superabundance of detail from other cultures, plus "American culture" — an "interdisciplinary" course "combining history, sociology, economics, geography, anthropology and others"?

What can be expected but confused minds devoid of American principles which could help lead the world to better things? That American leaders since the Founding Fathers have diluted and sometimes prostituted the Founders' principles is sadly true; *The Founding Fathers* tries to show what happened to their philosophy during the past hundred years, and what is happening today. This is what *An Examination of Conscience* is all about. But without definite ideals and the traditional American principles, we inevitably surrender leadership to a system which is evil and cruel but know exactly where it wants to go: Communism.

We are witnessing one more example that the American crisis today is a crisis attributable to leadership, not the people. That professional educators could produce such shallow and harmful social-studies courses and adulterate the concrete facts of what is noble in our history, bypass the principles upon which a just and free society can be built, is incredible if it were not happening.

The American people did not ask for the new teaching. Ameri-

11

can parents still want their children to be good and to have high ideals. The American public in its well-nigh universal reaction to Watergate shows that it craves what is morally and politically good; there are other evidences, too, that evil is not taken for granted. What is lacking is the leadership which can voice the ideals in words and has the stamina to take the practical means to encourage our people in the right direction.

But one can never be a leader unless there are absolutes in his (or her) moral code that tell him where he must go. George Washington was such a leader. Washington knew the type of education needed to guide society toward justice and happiness; his farewell address is still profoundly true in its analysis of what sound education requires. Were he a professional educator today he would be leading: the American people would know for what he stood and where he was directing the generation under his charge. How silly becomes that statement which sums up the new system: "Pupils are being taught 'critical thinking,' how to explore differing and conflicting versions of a past event to come up with their own conclusion. . . ." Children and adolescents are not in a position to have reliable conclusions. The obvious fact is that the educators today are not leaders because they stand on no moral absolutes which lead to firm conclusions; the children are leading.

Several weeks before *The Sunday Bulletin* article on the new approach to American history, the news services carried a second news story which indicated a more direct, but more subtle, attack on the American tradition than the educators' dereliction of responsibility. The date was September 17, 1975; the attack was a vote by the Senate Judiciary Committee's subcommittee on constitutional amendments, under the chairmanship of Senator Birch Bayh of Indiana, against four proposed amendments which would have counteracted the 1973 Blackmun permissive abortion ruling of the Supreme Court.

Until the late 1960s, state laws had with virtual unanimity protected unborn human lives. The right to life proclaimed as inalienable for all men in the Declaration of Independence had included unborn as well as born human beings until the recent pro-abortion drive had loosened state protection in a minority of jurisdictions.

12

Although there was incontrovertible evidence that the permissive-abortion drive was meeting nationwide opposition and being checked in various states the Blackmun decision struck down protective laws in all states. The Court had bypassed the democratic process. Now Senator Bayh's subcommittee was doing the same thing: it was blocking pro-life amendments.

Senator Bayh's actions during the hearings and his vote against each of the four amendments suggested by other senators are an example of the vacuum of political leadership outlined in this book. He is one among other presidential candidates who stand in sharp contrast to Washington, Adams and Jefferson, the Presidents who risked life and fortune to give us a morality-based country just as the Justices who voted with Blackmun are in naked contrast to Marshall, Wilson and Story, Supreme Court Justices who developed our constitutional law.

The Declaration of Independence outlines the political and legal philosophy of the Founders, the philosophy they codified by the specifics of the Constitution. In two sentences the Declaration proclaimed their philosophy and enunciated the principles upon which they built a nation: "We hold these truths to be self-evident, that all men are created equal, that they are endowed by their Creator with certain unalienable Rights, that among them are Life, Liberty and the pursuit of Happiness. That to secure these rights, Governments are instituted among Men, deriving their just powers from the consent of the governed, . . . ."

Senator Bayh and his colleagues cut off the possibility of the governed giving their consent through the ordinary democratic process: the amendments are not to be considered by the Senate or passed on by the people in their states.

But the vacuum is more abysmal. The Founders held certain absolutes, inalienable rights which belong to men as human beings, for which they were willing to fight, and eventually did. The right to life was first, liberty next, and the right of each individual to pursue his own way of happiness so long as he did not infringe on God's laws and other men's rights summed up the third great principle.

The right to life of all human beings was the primordial American right. Concerning this, Senator Bayh indicates he misunder-

13

stands the nature of government itself. In 1974 Senator Bayh stated publicly before the State Convention of Indiana Right to Life that he was "personally opposed to abortion . . ." and "the unborn child is a human individual. . . ." To reporters, according to a UPI story, when his committee voted down the amendments on September 17, 1975, he said that he "believes we're talking about life," but that he is "unwilling to impose their view (anti-abortionists) and mine on other people who differ." Saying the issue of abortion is "the most intimate area of personal rights" and that women "have the right to make the most intimate decision without government intervention," he reiterates, "I personally feel we'd be very wrong to impose one senator's view on abortion on others whose views were different."

The Founding Fathers, as leaders, fought a war to establish a nation on the concept that inalienable rights must be protected by government, that this is the essence of government. Their leadership could be decisive because they held certain moral absolutes, among which is that all human beings are equal and each has an inalienable right to life. It would be absurd to these men that the right to privacy of anyone could supersede the right to life of another human being, notwithstanding Senator Bayh or the Supreme Court.

The American people have a right to know what concept of government is held by any politician. Senator Bayh is one of many, including presidential aspirants, who have never revealed to the people whether they have a philosophy of government at all, whether they even understand the foundation principles of the government of which they are a part.

Glib clichés and poll watching are no substitutes for leadership. Honesty requires of politicians during this Bicentennial time that they tell the American people how many and what principles of the Founding Fathers they adhere to and use as standards to make their own political decisions. If they think they have better principles let these be stated.

I hope *The Founding Fathers: An Examination of Conscience* will contribute to the clarification of these issues.

# part one: the founding fathers

# chapter 1

## 1776-1976

On July 4, 1976, the United States of America will mark its 200th birthday. As the date approaches, preparations to make the anniversary meaningful multiply. More than 2,000 projects have been listed with the Bicentennial Administration in Washington, including cultural events, historical pageants, civic improvements and buildings newly built or restored.

Some anniversary plans bespeak the joy of a birthday party. One newspaper columnist gives a token listing of the various projects. "In New York: To counter a botanical display called '200 Years of Flower and Vegetable Hybridization' in the Bronx, Brooklyn will have 'an American musical play delineating the history, major events and people of Brooklyn.' Not to be outdone Long Island will have its Puppet Guild putting on a show called 'Long Island Sounds Off,' which will illustrate Long Island's fight for independence. And upstate, there'll be a 'workshop for teenagers to paint portable murals depicting the history of . . . Peekskill.' "

In South Carolina, besides planting all those crepe myrtle shrubs, that state also wants to form "the American Patriot Reading Club of South Carolina." Louisiana has its own approach: The City of Shreveport wants to build a "Bicentennial reflecting pool." It also submitted a program to have a big Fourth of July celebration in the city, complete with fireworks. The town of Oil City wants to rebuild the first oil derrick ever constructed there — for historical purposes, of course. And Baton Rouge wants to establish a municipal program to help it "set priorities for goals." South Dakota is ambitious and practical in submitting for approval perhaps more Bicentennial projects than any other state, and typical of them is the one to provide for "a general cleanup of Hill City that includes crushing and moving out abandoned cars." Wisconsin: "A community out there has made a big pitch for the 'restoration of the basement of Wisconsin's oldest standing synagogue.' "[1]

But a nation lives in the hearts of its people, in the justice of its laws, in the vitality of its freedoms, in its self-control, in its dedication to true and noble principles. The real criterion to measure the significance of the date is to compare the generation living in 1976 with the men who fought to give us our nation in 1776; the meaningful comparison is made between our social and legal institutions as they support and influence our people today in contrast to the men and institutions which gave birth to our country. Materially and in wealth we have grown beyond the imagination of the founding generation. Our population has increased a hundredfold, from 2,000,000 to 210,000,000. But are we a better nation? Has our progress been merely material while the spirit decayed? The Founding Fathers gave us an inheritance; have we wasted it or have we made it grow?

If this 200th anniversary is to be more than a birthday party with a veneer of patriotism, a toasting to our material success with speeches to gloss over an ailing society or a corroded government, a national examination of conscience is in order. In particular the examination should begin with our handling of the principles written in the great document which announced our birth to the world: the Declaration of Independence. It was for these principles that the founding generation bled and died; it was upon these principles they built a nation. They knew exactly what they were doing. John Hancock, President of Congress, in sending copies of the Declaration to colonial officials now become officers of thirteen independent states, wrote in a covering letter: "The important consequences to the American States from this Declaration of Independence, considered as the Ground and Foundation of a future government, will naturally suggest the propriety of proclaiming it in such a manner, that the people may be universally informed of it."

The Declaration is the "Ground and Foundation" of the Constitution. Have the generations since the Constitution was adopted plowed under the ground, weakened the foundation, ignored or abandoned any of the principles in interpreting the Constitution? Has the way we have interpreted the Constitution made for a healthier society and a government ever more of the people, by the people, for the people? Are we a better people than was the founding generation? Do we still believe in God, in rights that are inalienable because they come from Him in human dignity which we have from our humanness and not by concession of government? In this examination of conscience we owe it to the Founding Fathers, to ourselves, to our posterity, to let honesty lead where it will, let the chips fall where they may, when asking ourselves what we have done with the principles of the Declaration of Independence and the constitutional government set up to implement these principles. If this generation thinks it better not to be hung up on these principles, let that be said, too.

There seems to be total unanimity among historians that the quality of leadership the nation had at its birth was unique: "There is no more impressive paradox in all American history, and none more firmly rooted in the truth, than this: never since the United States came into being has it been as experienced and mature as it was at the hour of its birth. It was the unique good fortune of the United States to have presiding over the foundation an extraordinarily wise, experienced, dedicated, and unselfish group of statesmen."[2]

Richard B. Morris, Professor of History at Columbia University, had this to say about our Founding Fathers in an interview with *U.S. News & World Report:*

"Q. Which of the Revolutionary War leaders would you nominate as the very best?"

"A. My choices are Benjamin Franklin, George Washington, John Adams, Thomas Jefferson, John Jay, Alexander Hamilton and James Madison.

"I pick these men with all deference to other important leaders like Samuel Adams, James Wilson, Thomas Paine and others. But

19

the seven men I mentioned first were there from the start and stayed to the finish. They not only had an impact on the War of the Revolution, but they were the seminal leaders in the development of both the Confederation and the National Governments.

"There is no other team that one could pick in that particular period of time who held so many high offices of state and contributed so much to constitutional and legal change, as well as to the writing and drafting of the great state papers. They were not only intellectual leaders but also, to some extent, both the leaders of propaganda and the political leaders around whom most of the forces were organized."[3]

Another question *U.S. News & World Report* asked Professor Morris during the interview was:

"Q. Has this country ever had anything to equal that group since the Revolution?"

"A. No. Even the galaxy of Henry Clay, Daniel Webster and John Calhoun, I would say, would dim by comparison. Since 1850, we've never had a galaxy of leaders. We've had individual figures of the type of Abraham Lincoln and Woodrow Wilson and Franklin D. Roosevelt, but never a collection of great leaders comparable to these early seven."[4]

It is not just that these men were charismatic leaders. Three are considered great political philosophers, men who knew the long-range implication of all they did, who consciously and patiently struggled to place the best principles into our civil structure, men far above the day-to-day politician who leads successfully, but not always in the right direction. These three were Thomas Jefferson, John Adams and James Madison. (Alexander Hamilton, James Wilson and John Marshall were following closely.) Their learning of history and the philosophy of government dims by comparison our present-day political leadership. In the course of 200 years only two succeeding Presidents have been mentioned who realized fully and were willing to suffer heroically for such profound political and human principles: Abraham Lincoln certainly, and to a lesser extent, Woodrow Wilson.

To use such superlatives is not to degrade the successors of all these men. Nations do not produce great men every generation. It is rather that in the infancy of our republic, we were blessed with many more than our share. What we must do is to face ourselves honestly: if these men were greater than their successors, if their leadership were more secure and ennobling for the nation, and if lesser men have perhaps unwittingly substituted other principles and turned us into a different direction, is not this the time for this generation to assert itself and turn back to a wiser course? It is the height of pride to think the current ways are better than past practices just because they are modern; it is the depth of foolishness not to learn from history. And it sometimes means a choice between Washington, Jefferson, Lincoln and some of our present leaders.

But if honesty requires that we look up to the Founding Fathers in comparison to current leaders, honesty also requires that we compare the founding generation with ourselves who prepare for 1976. In the realm of political philosophy, in the understanding of the principles of government and the way human nature works through government to achieve the "general welfare" of the people, the members of the generation from 1760 to 1800 were so far ahead of their descendants today that even with all our advances in science, technology, psychology and accumulation of factual knowledge, we stand shamed. Perhaps it is because they had no autos, no good roads, no TV's, no radios, no movies, no campers or motorboats, no inexpensive jet travel to everywhere to take their minds from the fundamental political problems they faced, the struggle to place their human dignity and rights on a foundation which would stand the erosion of time.

When the growing season was ended they had long days and nights to ponder the nature of their struggle with Great Britain, and they concentrated on it. They heard preached from the pulpit the doctrine that human rights came from God and were inalienable; they read about the same doctrine in pamphlet and newspaper; in tavern and town meeting they discussed what Britain was doing to their basic human rights. They knew what were the obligations of a good government toward its citizens; they knew where the dividing line was between tyranny and merely a firm government. They pondered why men needed government at all; they examined its origin; they studied what the ancient and modern authors said about such problems. They knew exactly why they had to fight Great Britain. They knew why constitutions without bills of rights were suspect, and so the people of Massachusetts rejected the first constitution offered them, and later widespread opposition forced a bill of rights into the U.S. Constitution when curiously omitted by the greatest leaders. And they knew bills of rights did not give human rights, but only gave civil protection to what was theirs by nature. They would have been appalled to think their rights, their human dignity, came only from a written constitution.

Their grasp of the realities of human nature, the proper working of government to check the selfishness, the weakness, the ambition of government officials, to assure domestic tranquillity and achieve the general welfare, was profound. Because they thought the problems through so well and gave such impetus in the right direction, their descendants have coasted with relatively little effort. But 1976 is a good time to ponder whether we have imperceptibly changed direction, whether the new direction will achieve more surely the growth of human dignity, whether we are heading for shoals which could sink the ship of state, whether we have introduced practices which while contradicting the Founders' principles may also gum the wheels, corrode the mechanism set up to establish justice and achieve the general welfare. In a word, we must study the political philosophy which gave us birth, the principles the founding generation considered fundamental to government and society. This becomes an examination of conscience when we compare their ideology to the ideals which guide us today and to the way the Constitution is applied in practice.

It is with deliberation that the following chapters quote the Founding Fathers at length. They speak eloquently for themselves but it is hoped that the running commentary will give context and background to their thoughts and principles and will help to bring into focus the ideology upon which America was built.

# chapter 2

## GOD

### *The Existence Of God Is The Foundation Of Society And Law*

"We are a religious people whose institutions presuppose a Supreme Being." These are the words of Justice William O. Douglas speaking for the Supreme Court when in 1952 by a 6 to 3 majority it ruled that public schools were right in cooperating with "released time" religious-education efforts. Three times in our history the Court had reiterated the same judgment: in 1815, 1892 and 1931.[1]

The American way of life has been built on God. It is impossible to truly understand our legal structure without knowing its historical foundation. The Constitution and its Bill of Rights were drafted to implement the philosophy proclaimed in the Declaration of Independence, and the Declaration bases all on God: "When in the Course of human events, it becomes necessary for one people to dissolve the political bands which have connected them with another, and to assume among the powers of the earth, the separate and equal station to which the Laws of Nature and of Nature's God entitle them, a decent respect to the opinions of mankind requires that they should declare the causes which impel them to the separation. We hold these truths to be self-evident, that all men are created equal, that they are endowed by their Creator with certain unalienable Rights, that among these are Life, Liberty and the pursuit of Happiness. That to secure these rights, Governments are instituted among Men, deriving their just powers from the consent of the governed, . . ."

Alexander Hamilton was a military aide to General Washington during the Revolutionary War, a member of the Constitutional Convention, first Secretary of the Treasury in Washington's Cabinet. With John Jay and James Madison he coauthored the Federalist Papers to explain to the people the Constitution he and Madison had helped to draft. Less well-known is his work as a pamphleteer during the Revolutionary War. It is from his pamphlet entitled *The Farmer Refuted* that the following quotation is taken. Hamilton is answering the Tory Seabury, and says that it is Seabury's claim that in a state of nature the weak must submit to the strong, that naturally there is no government. Seabury in this bears a strong likeness to the philosopher Hobbes because he, like Hobbes, claimed that moral obligation derives from society and is therefore artificial:

. . . But the reason he (Hobbes) ran into this absurd and impious doctrine, was, that he disbelieved the existence of an intelligent superintending principle, who is the governor, and will be the final judge of the universe.

As you, sometimes, swear by HIM THAT MADE YOU, I conclude, your sentiment does not correspond with his; in that which is the basis of his doctrine, you both agree in; and this makes it impossible to imagine whence this congruity between you arises. To grant, that there is a supreme intelligence, who rules the world, and has established laws to regulate the actions of his creatures; and, still, to assert, that man, in a state of nature, may be considered as perfectly free from all restraint of LAW and GOVERNMENT, appears to common understanding, irreconcilable.

Good and wise men, in all ages, have embraced a very dissimilar theory. They have supposed, that the deity, from the relations we stand in to himself and to each other, has constituted an eternal and immutable law, which is, indispensibly, obligatory upon all mankind, prior to any human institution whatever.

This is what is called the law of nature, "which being coeval with mankind, and dictated by God himself, is, of course, superior in obligation to any other. It is binding over all the globe, in all countries, and at all times. No human laws are of any validity, if contrary to this; and such of them as are valid, derive all their authority, mediately, or immediately, from this original." (Blackstone)

Upon this law, depend the natural rights of mankind, the supreme being gave existence to man, together with the means of preserving and beautifying that existence. He endowed him with rational faculties, by the help of which, to discern and pursue such things, as were consistent with his duty and interest, and invested him with an inviolable right to personal liberty, and personal safety.

Hence, in a state of nature, no man had any MORAL power to deprive another of his life, limbs, property or liberty; nor the least authority to command, or exact obedience from him; except that which rose from ties of consanguinity.

Hence also, the origin of all civil government, justly established, must be a voluntary compact, between the rulers and the ruled; and must be liable to such limitations, as are necessary for the security of the ABSOLUTE RIGHTS of the latter; for what original title can any man or set of men have, to govern others, except their own consent? To usurp dominion over a people, in their own despite, or to grasp a more extensive power than they are willing to intrust, is to violate the law of nature, which gives every man a right to his personal liberty; and can, therefore, confer no obligation to obedience.

The principal aim of society is to protect individuals, in the enjoyment of those absolute rights, which were vested in them by the immutable laws of nature; but which could not be preserved, in peace without that mutual assistance, and intercourse, which is gained by the institution of friendly and social communities. Hence it follows, that the first and primary end of human laws, is to maintain and regulate these ABSOLUTE RIGHTS of individuals. (Blackstone)[2]

Hamilton has given a terse outline of the whole American position. He shows that the denial of God leads to the denial of human rights, and conversely, acknowledgment of an infinitely intelligent Ruler of the world indicates a moral law which guided mankind an-

25

tecedent to any civil law; from this law come the absolute, inalienable rights of men which must be respected by civil law. The first purpose of society is to protect these human rights. Government itself rests on the consent of the governed. The goal of society is to protect the dignity which men have simply because they are human.

In even briefer terms George Mason, the great author of the Virginia Bill of Rights, professes Hamilton's thesis:

Now all acts of legislation apparently [evidently] contrary to natural rights and justice are in our laws and must be in the nature of things, considered as void. The laws of nature are the laws of God, whose authority can be superseded by no power on earth. A legislature must not obstruct our obedience to Him from whose punishments they cannot protect us. All human constitutions which contradict His laws we are in conscience bound to disobey. Such has been the adjudication of our courts.[3]

Mason goes further than Hamilton in saying we must disobey immoral laws. Perhaps we can say that when they harm the common good there is a positive obligation to disobey.

The name of James Otis is almost forgotten today but he was a decisive influence in the direction of events which led to the Revolution. This Boston lawyer crystallized American thinking when in 1761 he argued in the famous Writs of Assistance Case that these writs violated the natural rights of Americans. In 1764 he published his book, *Rights of the British Colonies Asserted and Proved,* and developed his philosophy that human society and human laws have their basis in God's will. One does not have to accept all his thesis to realize that his is a profound analysis of the origin of society and law:

What shall we say then? Is not government founded on GRACE? No. Nor on FORCE? Nor on COMPACT? Nor PROPERTY? Not altogether on either. Has it ANY solid foundation? ANY chief cornerstone, but what accident, chance or confusion may lay one moment and destroy the next? I think it has an everlasting foundation in the UNCHANGEABLE WILL OF GOD,

26

the author of nature, whose laws never vary. The same omniscient, omnipotent, infinitely good and gracious Creator of the universe, who has been pleased to make it necessary that what we call matter should GRAVITATE, for the celestial bodies to roll round their axes, dance their orbits and perform their various revolutions in that beautiful order and concert, which we all admire, has made it EQUALLY necessary that from ADAM and EVE to these degenerate days, the different sexes should sweetly ATTRACT each other, form societies of SINGLE families, of which LARGER bodies and communities are as naturally, mechanically, and necessarily combined, as the dew of Heaven and the soft distilling rain is collected by the all enlivening heat of the sun. GOVERNMENT is therefore most evidently founded ON THE NECESSITIES OF OUR NATURE. It is by no means an arbitrary thing, depending merely on COMPACT or HUMAN WILL for its existence.

We come into this world forlorn and helpless; and if left alone and to ourselves at any one period of our life, we should soon die in want, despair or destraction. So kind is that hand, though little known or regarded, which feeds the rich and the poor, the blind and the naked; and provides for the safety of infants by the principle of parental love, and for that of men by GOVERNMENT! We have a KING, who neither slumbers or sleeps, but eternally watches for our good; whose rain falls on the just and on the unjust: yet while they live, move, and have their being in him, and cannot account for either, or for anything else, so stupid and wicked are some men, as to deny his existence, blaspheme his most evident government, and disgrace their nature.

Let no man think I am about to commence advocate for DESPOTISM, because I affirm that government is founded on the necessity of our natures; and that an original supreme SOVEREIGN, absolute and uncontroulable, EARTHLY power MUST exist and preside over every society; from whose final decisions there can be no appeal but directly to Heaven. It is therefore ORIGINALLY and ULTIMATELY in the people, ... and they never did in fact FREELY, nor can they RIGHTFULLY make an absolute, unlimited renunciation of this divine right. It is ever in the nature of a thing given in TRUST, and on a condition, the performance of which no mortal can dispense with; namely, that the person or persons on whom the sovereignty is conferred by the people shall INCESSANTLY consult THEIR good. Tyranny of all kinds is to be abhored, whether it be in the hands of one, or of the few, or of the many. . . .[4]

Otis was an independent thinker and indicates some disagreement with the English philosopher John Locke, usually pointed out as the most popular authority among the Americans in their attempts to give a rational solution for the origin of society and law. The quotations from Hamilton, Mason and Otis exemplify the starting point of the American ideology: it was based on the existence of an all-wise God who established laws for His creatures, laws which would guide them to justice toward each other, and when obeyed would lead to happiness. In a sense it was cold logic, a casuistry which justified action, sometimes violent action, to protect their rights while yet fulfilling the dictates of their consciences.

But it was not merely logic. These were men living in a Judeo-Christian tradition who spoke for a people with a living faith in God, a faith which convinced them that their living God would protect a righteous people. Their convictions had already driven them to arms at Concord, Lexington and Bunker Hill, and Washington had been appointed commander-in-chief of the American forces when the Second Continental Congress issued a "Declaration of the Causes and Necessity of Taking Up Arms." The committee appointed to draft the Declaration included Franklin, Jay, Rutledge, Livingston, Johnson, Jefferson and Dickinson, with the last two producing the final draft. The date was July 6, 1775. The Declaration begins with an act of faith in God, justifies their decisive actions on the law of God, proclaims their trust in God, and offers the olive branch of peace to the mother country if only their God-given rights will be respected:

If it was possible for men, who exercise their reason, to believe, that the divine Author of our existence intended a part of the human race to hold an absolute property in, and an unbounded power over others, marked out by his infinite goodness and wisdom, as the objects of a legal domination never rightfully resistible, however severe and oppressive, the inhabitants of these colonies might at least require from the parliament of Great-Britain some evidence, that this dreadful authority over them, has been granted to that body. But a reverence for our great Creator, principles of humanity, and the dictates of common sense, must convince all those who reflect on the subject, that government was instituted to promote the welfare of mankind, and ought to be administered for the attainment of that end. The legislature of Great-Britain, . . . where regard should be had to truth, law, or right, have at length, deserting those, attempted to effect their cruel and impolitic purpose of enslaving these colonies by violence, and have thereby rendered it necessary for us to close with their last appeal from reason to arms.

. . . Our cause is just. Our union is perfect. Our internal resources are great, and if necessary, foreign assistance is undoubtedly attainable. — We gratefully acknowledge, as signal instances of the Divine favour towards us, that his Providence would not permit us to be called into this severe controversy, until we were grown up to our present strength, had been previously exercised in warlike operation, and possessed of all the means of defending ourselves. With hearts fortified with these animating reflections, we most solemnly, before God and the world, declare, that, exerting the utmost energy of those powers, which our beneficent Creator hath graciously bestowed upon us, the arms we have been compelled by our enemies to assume, we will, in defiance of every hazard, with unabating firmness and perseverance, employ for the preservation of our liberties; being with one mind resolved to die freemen rather than to live slaves. . . .

With an humble confidence in the mercies of the supreme and impartial Judge and Ruler of the Universe, we most devoutly implore his divine goodness to protect us happily through this great conflict, to dispose our adversaries to reconciliation on reasonable terms, and thereby to relieve the empire from the calamities of civil war.[5]

By order of the Congress
John Hancock
President

(The parts left out include a lengthy and detailed list of the grievances with Great Britain.)

The fact that all just government derives its power from the people, and that people and government are subject to the laws of God, was brought out most clearly by the people of Massachusetts. In 1778 they were offered a new constitution; it was rejected overwhelmingly because it contained no bill of rights expressing these principles. In 1780 they adopted a constitution prefixed by a "Declaration of Rights" which elucidated their principles. That their convictions were not merely legal logic, abstractions derived from the existence of a remote deity, but rather that a living God was providing for them is brought out in the third paragraph of the preamble to the Declaration:

We, therefore, the people of Massachusetts, acknowledging with grateful hearts, the goodness of the great Legislator of the universe, in affording us, in the course of His Providence, an opportunity, deliberately and peaceably, without fraud, violence, or surprise, of entering into an original, explicit, and solemn compact with each other; and of forming a new constitution of civil government, for ourselves and posterity; and devoutly imploring His direction in so interesting a design, do agree upon, ordain, and establish, the following Declaration of Rights, and Frame of Government, as the Constitution of the Commonwealth of Massachusetts.[6]

And the Declaration of Independence:

We, therefore, the Representatives of the United States of America, in General Congress assembled, appealing to the Supreme Judge of the world for the rectitude of our intentions, . . . solemnly publish and declare, That these United Colonies are, and of right ought to be Free and Independent States; . . . And for the support of this declaration, with a firm reliance on the protection of Divine Providence, we mutually pledge to each other our lives, our fortunes and our sacred honor.

With such convictions it is not surprising that this Congress should have proclaimed four days of fast in petition to God before it announced our first national Thanksgiving Day on November 1, 1777.

Just as the God to whom the Founders turned is a living, personal God, so the religion built upon God must be a living force in personal and civic life; if it is not, the linchpin which must keep the wheels of government and civil society turning in place will be missing. Washington in his farewell address says the sanctity of the oath performs this function:

Of all the dispositions and habits which lead to political prosperity, religion and morality are indispensable supports. In vain would that man claim the tribute of patriotism who should labor to subvert these great pillars of human happiness — these firmest props of the duties of men and citizens. The mere politician, equally with the pious man, ought to respect and cherish them. A volume could not trace all their connections with private and public felicity. Let it simply be asked, Where is the security for property, for reputation, for life, if the sense of religious obligation *desert* the oaths which are the instruments of investigation in courts of justice? And let us with caution indulge the supposition that morality can be maintained withour religion. Whatever may be conceded to the influence of refined education on minds of peculiar structure, reason and experience both forbid us to expect that national morality can prevail in exclusion of religious principle.[7]

What happens when the sense of religious obligation deserts the oaths which are the instruments in courts of justice? Watergates of all sizes.

The Founding Fathers have told us in their own words that a nation, a civilization, must begin with God in theory, proceed with God's help in practice, be animated with a religious conviction of God's active presence, or be destroyed when it abandons God in theory or practice. An atheist philosophy by inference has no source of law beyond unstable human conventions. But also by inference and a paradox of truth and goodness atheists are protected by a theist philosophy, for those who believe in God must still re-

31

spect the human rights and dignity of an atheist: he is still a human being, a creature protected by the Creator's law. Another protective rule is found in Jefferson's Act for Establishing Religious Freedom, ratified in Virginia in January of 1786. The right to freedom of conscience limited the government's authority to actions, not thoughts:

That the opinions of men are not the object of civil government, nor under its jurisdiction; that to suffer the civil magistrate to intrude his powers into the field of opinion and to restrain the profession or propagation of principles on the supposition of their ill tendency is a dangerous fallacy, which at once destroys all religious liberty, because he being of course judge of that tendency will make his opinions the rule of judgment, and approve or condemn the sentiments of others only as they shall square with or differ from his own;

That it is time enough for the rightful purposes of civil government for its officers to interfere when principles break out into overt acts against peace and good order.[8]

# chapter 3

## NATURAL LAW

The emphasis of the previous chapter was on God; the existence of God was the dominant truth upon which the Founding Fathers would build society. They were certain of the existence of God. There were laws of nature all about them, so there must be a Lawgiver; there was plan and design everywhere in the universe, so there must be a Designer. Newtonian science was their modern proof that atheism was irrational. Of course, the knowledge they had of God from their Judeo-Christian background made His existence all the more vivid.

From the existence of an infinitely wise Creator there must be a law to guide His intelligent creatures in the actions which would relate them to Him and to each other. In dealing with man the problem of God's laws of nature was more subtle but no less certain. Men are not only intelligent by nature, they are also free: therefore this law must guide men through their intelligence and free wills. It was a moral law which commanded but did not force free actions. As much a law of nature as gravity, it did not have the inevitableness of a physical law; this natural law invited the spirits of men but did not impel their hands or bodies to good actions.

Where would they find this law of nature, this natural law? The Founders said in their own right-thinking consciences which recognized some moral truths to be self-evident, and from these others could be deduced. Good is to be done, evil avoided; some actions, like telling the truth, were evidently good; others, like murder or

33

stealing, evidently evil. If a fool or knave disputed them there was no room for discussion; there might be reason to bleed and die in defense of such truths. That each human being had a natural, inalienable right to his life, to his liberty, to his pursuit of happiness within God's commandments, to his honestly acquired property, were self-evident rights. That all men were created equal was self-evident; that no one had power over others without consent in some way having been given (save the natural power of parents over children) was a logical deduction from equality.

Was there any place where they could find the full content of the natural moral law, any source which would aid their consciences in the search for moral truths? They said it could be found in the Bible, in the Judeo-Christian tradition. They also found it in the great traditions of Western civilization, in the writings of men who made the European rules and laws for civilized living. The first source was theological, the second philosophical; but both would lead to the same list of human rights and duties.

In proclaiming via the Declaration of Independence their principle of the law of nature which bound all men the Founders relied on the philosophical foundation; in writing their state constitutions they often indicate the theological background by special mention of Christianity. One authority on the sources of American constitutionalism outlines these thoughts: "The main doctrines of the Declaration (of Independence) were familiar, especially so to New Englanders; in some respect they were of hoary antiquity. Dr. Sullivan, seeking beginnings, finds them long before the Christian era — the New England theologians would scarcely stop short of the Garden of Eden — and says, 'Thus, by Cicero's time (106-43 B.C.) there were three ideas of the Declaration known to the world.' (He must mean, I think, had been announced by philosophers.) These were, first, the conscious instituting of government by men, held by Protagoras, the Sophists, and the Epicureans; second, the equality of men — an idea advanced by the Stoics; and third, the idea of natural rights developed by Cicero. . . . It remained for one of the writers during the Conciliar Movement in the early part of the fifteenth century — Nicholas of Cusa — to take all of the doctrines of the Declaration and combine them into a systematic whole. 'Since all men,' he says, 'are by nature free, then government rests on the consent of the governed.' "[1]

John Adams implied that the people of Massachusetts would make use of the "wisest writers"[2] when drafting a new constitution for that state. Thomas Jefferson in describing his greatest work said the object of the Declaration of Independence was "not to find new principles, or new arguments, never before thought of, not merely to say things which had never been said before: but to place before mankind the common sense of the subject, in terms so plain and firm as to command their assent, and to justify ourselves in the independent stand we are compelled to take. Neither aiming at originality of principle or sentiment, nor yet copied from any particular and previous writing, it was intended to be an expression of the American mind, and to give that expression the proper tone and spirit called for by the occasion."[3]

To put it briefly, the American constitutional system rests on the best traditions of Western civilization, with emphasis on reason rather than on revelation, on philosophy rather than on theology. A few quotations from the "wisest writers" of that more than 2,000-year history brings out this tradition.

Antigone in the tragedy by Sophocles (496-406 B.C.) declares that her conscience is altogether clear even though she had deliberately overstepped a law of King Creon by burying her brother against the royal orders. She appeals to a law higher than any made by man:

> Because it was not Zeus who ordered it,
> Nor Justice, dweller with the Nether Gods,
> Gave such a law to man; nor did I deem
> Your ordinance of so much binding force,
> As that a mortal man could overbear
> The unchangeable unwritten code of Heaven;
> This is not of today and yesterday,
> But lives forever, having origin
> Whence no man knows: whose sanctions I were loath
> In Heaven's sight to provoke, fearing the will of any man.
>     (George Young's translation)[4]

35

The great Stoic philosopher of law, Cicero (106-43 B.C.), stated:

True law is right reason in agreement with nature; it is of universal application, unchanging and everlasting; it summons to duty by its commands, and averts from wrongdoing by its prohibitions. And it does not lay its commands or prohibitions upon good men in vain, though neither have any effect on the wicked. It is a sin to try to alter this law, nor is it allowable to attempt to repeal any part of it, and it is impossible to abolish it entirely. We cannot be freed from its obligations by senate or people, and we need not look outside ourselves for an expounder or interpreter of it. And there will not be different laws at Rome and at Athens, or different laws now and in the future, but one eternal and unchangeable law which will be valid for all nations and all times, and there will be one master and ruler, that is, God over us all, for he is the author of this law, its promulgator, and its enforcing judge. Whoever is disobedient is fleeing from himself and denying his human nature, and by reason of this very fact he will suffer the worst penalties, even if he escapes what is commonly considered punishment.[5]

Cicero is an example of one of the great ancient minds searching for the truth of justice and law. He states principles for their relationship as valid today as they were 2,000 years ago:

If the principles of Justice were founded on the decrees of peoples, the edicts of princes, or the decisions of judges, then Justice would sanction robbery and adultery and forgery of wills, in case these acts were approved by the votes or decrees of the populace. But if so great a power belongs to the decisions and decrees of fools that the laws of Nature can be changed by their votes, then why do they not ordain that what is bad and baneful shall be considered good and salutary? Or, if a law can make Justice out of Injustice, can it not also make good out of bad? But in fact we can perceive the difference between good laws and bad by referring them to no other standard than Nature: indeed, it is not merely Justice and Injustice which are distinguished by Nature, but also and without exception things which are honourable and dishonourable. For since an intelligence common to us all makes things known to us and formulates them in our minds, honourable actions are ascribed by us to virtue, and dishonourable actions to vice; and only a madman would conclude these judgements are matters of opinion, and not fixed by Nature.[6]

The Roman world empire tolerated the legal rules of subject peoples, and Roman jurists found there was a common element in the laws of these peoples favoring principles and institutions which did make for justice and peace in society. Thus marriage, the family, property, good faith, the right of self-defense, and so on, were protected by particular laws. The jurists concluded that these elements common to all nations were a reflection of the true law of nature. One of these jurists, Gaius, wrote some time after Cicero:

On Natural and Civil Law. Every people, who are governed by laws and customs, employ, partly, their own particular law, and, partly, the general law of all mankind; for that which each people determines as law for itself, is the particular law of that people and is called "Civil Law", as though to signify "the State's own particular law"; on the other hand, that which natural reason has established among all men, is uniformly observed among all peoples and is called "the Law of Nations", as though to signify "the law employed by all nations". Thus the Roman people employ, partly, their own particular law, and, partly, the general law of all mankind. . . ."[7]

The Stoic philosophy endorsed by Cicero is sometimes called the mother of Roman jurisprudence. As beautiful as are the statements of Cicero quoted above it remained for the Judeo-Christian concept to progress beyond some of its errors. A modern commentator notes: "Correct though Cicero's statements seem to be, we know from his writing that he like many Greeks and Latins identified the natural law with a blind necessitating force behind nature, as did all Stoics. His fact-finding was correct, his interpretation thereof was incorrect."[8] The Stoics were pantheists; the blind force is associated with pantheism.

37

The Christian tradition with its roots in Judaism builds on a personal God, and this is the God to whom the American Founding Fathers appealed. This is true even of those who were called deists, that is, Franklin, Jefferson and Adams. This personal God rules by active providence, not by blind force. St. Paul in his Epistle to the Romans gives a terse Christian statement acceptable to the Americans:

For it is not those who hear the law [of Moses] who are just in the sight of God; it is those who keep it who will be declared just. When Gentiles who do not have the law [of Moses] keep it as by instinct, these men although without the law [of Moses] serve as a law for themselves. They show that the demands of the law [of Moses] are written in their hearts. Their conscience bears witness together with that law, and their thoughts will accuse or defend them on the day when, in accordance with the gospel I preach, God will pass judgment on the secrets of men through Christ Jesus.[9]

St. Paul teaches that the Stoic blind force is not true — he defends the free will of men. The Apostle also indicates that even without the help of the Judeo-Christian revelation, pagans through their consciences know the natural law, the fundamental difference between morally good and morally bad acts. To put it another way, Paul teaches that the basic principles of morality are philosophy rather than revealed theology.

The commandments prohibiting murder, stealing and lying are known to men in general; these obligations, put in terms of the natural rights demanded by the Founding Fathers, are the rights to life, property, truth, etc., upon which they based our constitutional system. The Americans had a vivid realization that to respect the rights of other men was to obey the commands of their living God. The Judeo-Christian concept which permeated the society of the Founders was a much more forceful teacher of morality than was the working of man's natural conscience described by St. Paul; yet the moral truths taught belong to the order of reason and are only clarified by revelation. The Declaration of Independence appeals to natural reason rather than supernatural revelation, to philosophy rather than theology in proclaiming American principles to the world.

St. Thomas Aquinas (1224-1274) is often pointed out as the greatest theologian-philosopher in the history of Christianity. He wrote profoundly concerning law:

Now among all others, the rational creature is subject to Divine providence in the most excellent way, in so far as it takes a share of providence, by being provident both for itself and for others. Wherefore it has a share in the Eternal Reason, whereby it has a natural inclination to its proper act and end: and this participation of the eternal law in the rational creature is called the natural law. Hence the Psalmist after saying (Ps. iv 6): Offer up the *sacrifice of justice,* as though someone asked what the works of justice are, adds: *Many say, Who showeth us good things?* In answer to which question he says: *The light of Thy countenance, O Lord, is signed upon us:* thus implying that the light of natural reason, whereby we discern what is good and what is evil, which is the function of the natural law, is nothing else than an imprint on us of the Divine light. It is therefore evident that the natural law is nothing else than the rational creature's participation of the eternal law.[10]

In another place Aquinas sums it up:

Natural law is a knowledge naturally belonging to man, by which he is guided to the right performance of the actions proper to him. . . . All that renders an action unsuited to the end which nature intends as the result of any operation is said to be against the natural law.[11]

Probably the most influential of the "wisest writers" consulted by the American Founding Fathers was the English philosopher John Locke, who lived from 1632 until 1704. He was an original thinker in some areas but from the number of his quotations from previous authors we know that he also built upon the great Western and Judeo-Christian tradition of philosophy and law. Thus Locke pointed out:

39

The obligations of the law of nature cease not in society, but only in many cases are drawn closer, and have by human laws known penalties annexed to them to enforce their observation. Thus the law of nature stands as an eternal rule to all men, legislators as well as others. The rules that they make for other men's actions must, as well as their own, and other men's actions be conformable to the law of nature, i.e., to the will of God, of which that is a declaration, and the fundamental law of nature being the preservation of mankind, no human sanction can be good or valid against it.[12]

The American Founding Fathers showed continuity with the past not only in their adherence to the principles learned from the "wisest writers" but in their adherence to English common law which had natural law imbedded in it. Common law accompanied the settlers who established the colonies; it was followed by the courts in colonial days and kept after independence. "American jurists, including loyalists, were in the habit of quoting Calvin's case, of the time of Coke. In that case all the authorities had been examined, and the judges unanimously resolved, first, that the laws of nature are part of the law of England, secondly, that the laws of nature cannot be changed. . . . Plainly then, there was, at the time of the settlement of the colonies, a 'law of nature' which was not derived from Parliament, a law which Parliament could not change. Indeed Americans believed the doctrine without Calvin's case; the doctrine did not rest in 'musty records,' it was sound in itself. So in effect it was put by all the leaders — by Otis, Hopkins, Samuel Adams, John Adams, and Hamilton."[12a] Realizing that Blackstone's Commentaries was the bible of the colonial lawyer, Hamilton's statement above deserves extra attention:

Good and wise men, in all ages, have embraced a very dissimilar theory. They have supposed, that the deity, from the relations we stand in to himself and to each other, has constituted an eternal and immutable law, which is, indispensibly, obligatory upon all mankind, prior to any human institution whatsoever.

This is what is called the law of nature, "which being coeval with mankind, and dictated by God himself, is, of course, superior in obligation to any other. It is binding over all the globe, in all countries, at all times. No human laws are of any validity, if contrary to this; and such of them as are valid, derive all their authority, mediately, or immediately, from this original." (Blackstone)[13]

James Wilson is one of the great Founding Fathers whose contributions to the establishment of his adopted country are not sufficiently recognized by posterity. He came to the colonies from Scotland after receiving a thorough classical education at the Universities of St. Andrews, Glasgow and Edinburgh. He studied law in the office of John Dickinson, and, like Dickinson, became a pamphleteer in defense of the American cause. He was a signer of the Declaration of Independence. A legal philosopher in his own right, he helped draft the Constitution of Pennsylvania and was a member of the Constitutional Convention of 1787. At least one fellow delegate who helped write our national Constitution considered Wilson more capable and useful than James Madison; a higher compliment could not be paid. He was one of the first Associate Justices of the Supreme Court of the United States.

According to Wilson:

For it is true, not only that all men are equally subject to the command of their Maker; but it is true also, that the law of nature, having its foundation in the constitution and state of man, has an essential fitness for all mankind, and binds them without distinction.

The law of nature is immutable; not by the effect of an arbitrary disposition, but because of its foundation in the nature, constitution, and mutual relations of men and things.[14]

In 1768 the Massachusetts House of Representatives sent a circular letter to the other colonial Assemblies. Again the American philosophy is brought out:

(This House declares that) his Majesty's American subjects,

41

who acknowledge themselves bound by the Ties of Allegiance, have an equitable Claim to the full enjoyment of the fundamental rules of the British Constitution: That it is an essential, unalterable Right, in nature, ungrafted into the British Constitution, as a fundamental Law, & ever held sacred & irrevocable by the Subjects within the Realm, that whatever a man has honestly acquired is absolutely his own, which he may freely give, but cannot be taken from him without his consent: That the American subjects may, therefore, exclusive of any Consideration of Charter Rights, with a decent firmness, adapted to the Character of free men & subjects assert this natural and constitutional Right.[15]

The First Continental Congress met in Carpenter's Hall, Philadelphia, in October of 1774. One result of the Congress was the Declaration and Resolves drafted by delegates from the twelve colonies represented. Again the American philosophy of law:

Whereupon the deputies . . . declare: That the inhabitants of the English Colonies in North America, by the immutable laws of nature, the principles of the English constitution, and the several charters or compacts, have the following Rights:
Resolved, N.C.D.
1. That they are entitled to life, liberty, and property, & they have never ceded to any sovereign power whatever, a right to dispose of either without their consent.[16] (Ten specific resolutions follow.)

In summary, the American adherence to the existence of a natural moral law to command men's actions antecedent to civil law, a law which is also the origin of human rights, marks the summit of a more than 2,000-year development in human thought and civilization. This natural law is a standard attainable by reason, verifiable by reason, but historically it was clarified by the Judeo-Christian revelation. This does not militate against the fact that it has its base in reason rather than revelation. If it is good theology, independently it is still sound philosophy. And it was quoted in the Declaration of Independence as philosophy, not theology.

# chapter 4

## NATURAL RIGHTS

Because of their conviction that an intelligent and just God governed the actions of men the Founding Fathers concluded that they had certain inherent rights which no earthly government could justly take from them. It was because their rights were being taken away that the Americans were ready to shed their blood. From their innate sense of human dignity and equality they felt for these rights emotionally; believing in God and themselves the logic of their demand that respect be given them as human beings was proclaimed to the world as too obvious to need proof: ". . . We hold these truths to be self-evident, that all men . . . are endowed by their Creator with certain unalienable Rights, that among these are Life, Liberty and the pursuit of Happiness." It was so evident that they often seemed to bypass the natural law in between; their rights came from God, period. It clarifies our understanding of the American thesis to progress from the natural law to these rights, to examine what was said concerning natural rights as such.

Thus Otis was moved to state:

The Colonists being men, have a right to be considered as equally entitled to all the rights of nature with the Europeans, and they are not to be restrained in the exercise of any of these rights, but for the evident good of the whole community. By being or becoming members of society, they have not renounced their natural liberty to any greater degree than other good citizens, and if 'tis taken away from them without their consent, they are so far enslaved.[1]

The delegates from nine colonies who met in New York in 1765 to protest the hated Stamp Tax proclaimed:

The members of this Congress . . . esteem it our indispensible duty to make the following declarations . . . respecting the most essential rights and liberties of the colonists. . . .

II That His Majesty's liege subjects in these colonies are intitled to all the inherent rights and liberties of his natural born subjects within the kingdom of Great Britain.[2] (There follows a list of more specific grievances.)

George Mason is the author of most of the Virginia Bill of Rights and Constitution, adopted by the Convention which met in Williamsburg, in June of 1776. Its preamble was written by Thomas Jefferson; hence the similarity to the Declaration of Independence:

A declaration of rights made by the representatives of the good people of Virginia, assembled in full and free convention; which rights do pertain to them and their posterity, as the basis and foundation of government.

1. That all men are by nature equally free and independent, and have certain inherent rights of which, when they enter into a state of society, they cannot by any compact deprive or divest their posterity; namely, the enjoyment of life and liberty, with the means of acquiring and possessing property, and pursuing and obtaining happiness and safety.[3] (Sixteen specific implementations of these rights follow.)

In 1778 the people of Massachusetts rejected the first constitution offered them because it had no bill of rights. In 1780 they ratified a new one which had a bill of rights authored almost entirely by John Adams:

A Declaration of the Rights of the Inhabitants of the Commonwealth of Massachusetts,

ARTICLE I, All men are born free and equal, and have certain

44

natural, essential, and unalienable rights; among which may be reckoned the right of enjoying and defending their lives and liberties, that of acquiring, possessing and protecting property; in fine, that of seeking and obtaining their safety and happiness.[4] (There follow thirty separate articles specifying these rights, putting in legal terms how the rights and liberties were to be protected in Massachusetts law.)

What becomes very evident is that in the thought of the Founding Fathers no government gives basic rights; it merely protects them. Civil rights are the legal specification of natural rights in accordance with the traditions of a particular people. Civil law is built upon inalienable natural rights; a law which would deprive an innocent human being of life or liberty or property is simply no law. The individual comes before society, and laws are made so that individuals can live peaceably in society, with mutual respect and protection of their rights. This is the American philosophy of law as it was written into our national and state constitutions. The founding generation would be appalled at the thought that the rights to life and liberty, to the pursuit of happiness within the moral law, to honestly owned property, to justice, were merely constitutional or civil rights. This was what the Revolutionary War was all about; this is why the Constitution was drafted and accepted. After thirty years of existence as a nation under this Constitution, Jefferson would still declare:

Our legislators are not sufficiently apprised of the rightful limits of their power; that their true office is to declare and enforce only our natural rights and duties, and to take none of them from us. No man has a natural right to commit aggression on the equal rights of another; this is all from which the laws ought to restrain him; every man is under the natural duty of contributing to the necessities of the society; and this is all the laws should enforce on him; and no man having a natural right to be judge between himself and another; it is his natural duty to submit to the umpirage of an impartial third. When the laws have declared and enforced all this, they have fulfilled their function, and the idea is quite unfounded, that on entering into society we give up any natural right.[5]

In the same year, 1816, Jefferson gave something of a summary of men's rights in society:

I believe . . . that morality, compassion, generosity, are innate elements of the human constitution; that there exists a right independent of force; that a right to property is founded in our natural wants, in the means with which we are endowed to satisfy these wants, and the right to what we acquire by those means without violating the similar rights of other sensible beings; that no one has a right to obstruct another, exercising his faculties innocently for the relief of sensibilities made a part of his nature; that justice is the fundamental law of society; that the majority, oppressing an individual, is guilty of a crime, abuses its strength, and by acting on the law of the strongest breaks up the foundations of society; that actions by the citizens in person, in affairs within their reach and competence, and in all others by representatives, chosen immediately, and removable by themselves, constitutes the essence of a republic; that all governments are more or less republican in proportion as this principle enters more or less into their composition; and that a government by representation is capable of extension over a greater surface of the country than one of any other form.[6]

Remembering that Jefferson uses the word "republican" as we now use "democratic," we have a fairly good picture of what a truly democratic society is all about.

# chapter 5

## COMPACT

### *1*

### *Use Of The Compact In New England*

The progression of thought among the Founding Fathers was from the existence of an intelligent God to the natural law established by this God for the guidance of His creatures, then to the inalienable rights which come to men through this law, and finally to the existence of civil society which must be guided by that law and protect the rights of the men living under legitimate government. But how does civil society come to be? What is the origin of government? Where does government get its right to command? These are the questions answered by the compact theory held by the Americans who gave their posterity the Constitution, the civil compact under which we still live.

The origin of the compact principle is perhaps lost in history. "But one cannot seek the source of any widely held and widely used theory and be confident of the exact time and place of birth. The fact is, this compact theory was, in some of its aspects, so old, it had so many manifestations, or was so often propounded at least in pure theory, that confidence concerning origin and descent is quite undesirable."[1]

The most popular author to expound the compact among the Americans was undoubtedly the English philosopher John Locke, who lived a century before the Founding Fathers. Unfortunately, his version of the compact was not fully realistic. Locke believed that there was a time when men lived in a "state of nature," before civil society existed, ruled only by the natural law which came from God and was revealed to them through their own consciences. According to Locke, to be protected in their rights which came from natural law, men decided to yield to the community some of the freedoms and rights which belonged to them in this "state of nature." Rather than attempting to protect their property and more important rights personally, men decided to have the protection which came from the community, from society, from civil law. Of course, each one would then have to abide by the prescriptions of civil society, as voted by the majority, in the use of natural rights now become civil rights. That an idyllic "state of nature" ever existed is rejected by most scholars, and the idea was so abused later by Rousseau and his followers who caused the French Revolution that a "state of nature" foundation for political society became suspect.

But much more to the point is that the Americans never depended on Locke to the extent that his doubtful points weakened the social structure they raised partly with his help. He was only one of many historical influences. Before Locke was born, New Englanders had actually used compacts to establish their civil society; the most famous compact in history (if we exclude our national Constitution) was the Mayflower Compact of the Pilgrims, and this was followed by the establishment of many towns based on "mutual covenant," another name for the same process called "compact."

The Pilgrims were Separatists, people who believed that they could and should separate from the Church of England to form a more perfectly Christian church. Robert Browne, founder of the Separatists, taught that any group of Christians had the right to covenant with God and with each other to form a Congregation, an individual church. Browne also extended his theology to suggest the same principles for forming civil society. This partly explains the background of the Mayflower Compact accepted by the Pilgrims the night before they landed on Plymouth Rock:

Having undertaken for the glorie of God, and advancement of

the Christian faith, and honour of our king and countrie, a voyage to plant the first colonie in the Northerne parts of Virginia, doe by these presents solemnly and mutually in the presence of God, and one of another, covenant and combine ourselfes togeather into a civill body politick, for our better ordering and preservation and furtherance of the ends aforesaid; and by vertue hearof to enacte, constitute, and frame shuch just and equall lawes, ordinances, acts, constitutions, and offices, from time to time, as shall be thought most meete and convenient for the generall good of the Colonie, unto which we promise all due submission and obedience.[1a]

Theology may not be the full explanation for the Mayflower Compact. Also, the Pilgrims were Congregationalists, and this group often in pamphlets quoted as their example the English borough or municipal corporations as well as the corporations of merchants and artisans, both of which were the outcome of the Guilds of the Middle Ages.

At any rate, one town after another established by the Puritans who followed the Pilgrims in early New England was formed by covenant or compact. The colonies of Rhode Island and Connecticut were founded the same way. The settlers under Roger Williams in 1637, when establishing Rhode Island, adopted a written covenant whereby his followers subjected themselves "in active and passive obedience to all such orders and agreements as shall be made for public good of the body in an orderly way, by the major consent of the present inhabitants, masters of families incorporated together in a Towne fellowship, and others which they shall admit unto them, only in civil things."[2]

The Fundamental Articles of New Haven stated:

This convenant was called a plantation convenant "to distinguis itt from a chur. covenant which could nott att thatt time be made, [a] chur. nott being then gathered, butt was deferred till a chur. might be gathered according to God." By these Articles, which were adopted by a show of hands, the people bound themselves "to esta[blish] such civill order as might best conduce to the secureing of the purity and peace of the ordina[nces] to themselves and their posterity according to God."[3]

The Fundamental Orders of Connecticut (1638-1639), sometimes said to be the first written constitution in history, begins:

And well knowing where a people are gathered together the word of God required that to mayntayne the peace and union of such people there should be an orderly and decent Government established according to God, to order and dispose of the affayres of the people at all seasons as occation shall require; doe therefore associate and conjoyne our selves to be as one Publike State or Commonwealth; and doe, for our selves and our Successors and such as shall be adjoyned to us att any tyme hereafter, enter into Combination and Confederation together, to mayntayne and presearve the liberty and purity of the gospel. . . . As also in our Civill Affaires to be guided and governed according to such Lawes . . . as shall be made. . . .[4]

## 2

### Compact Vs. Consent Of Governed

Thus Locke's idyllic "state of nature" may never have had chronological existence, but from experience New Englanders knew there was logical thought in his theorizing. Actually, the "state of nature" as used by Americans was an ontological fact: men must have government, but men exist before government; the very thought of government presupposes the existence of men. Since men are equal and free by nature they must *consent* to the setting up of government. The key American word is *consent*, the word emphasized in the Declaration of Independence — wherein "compact" never appears.

In context, however, the terms are correlative: in the compact made by the people to set up their government certain powers are ceded to the government by the consent of the people. "To secure these (inalienable) rights, governments are instituted among men, deriving their just powers from the consent of the governed. That whenever any form of government becomes destructive of these ends, it is the right of the people to alter or abolish it, and to institute a new government, laying its powers in such form as to them shall seem most likely to effect their safety and happiness. . . ." This is exactly what the American people did in 1787-1788: "We, the people of the United States, in order to form a more perfect Union, establish justice, insure domestic tranquility, . . ."

To state it another way, according to the Declaration, the power to make laws resides ultimately in the people, who are always subject to the "laws of nature and Nature's God," to the moral law; and they transfer this power, with its natural limitations and the limitations they decree, to the government. The inalienable rights can never be ceded. In the American system the transfer of power took place nationally when the national Constitution was ratified; on a state level when the state constitutions were adopted. All the constitutions are compacts between the people themselves and between the people and the governments established by the people, set up by the consent of the people. These have never arisen from a "state of nature" which Locke describes.

In English history the origin of the necessity of the *consent* of the people for the valid exercise of governmental powers goes back far beyond the Pilgrims, beyond the use of the word "compact." Deep in the Middle Ages, in 1215, under the leadership of Stephen Langton, Archbishop of Canterbury, the barons wrested from King John the Magna Carta, the listing of the rights which religion and custom sanctioned. A little later in the same century the legal commentator Bracton wrote: "The king ought not be under man but under God and then under the Law, because the Law makes the king . . . for there is no king where will rules, not Law. . . . As the servant and vicar of God the king can do nothing on earth save that which he may lawfully do. It is no answer to say 'What the king wills has the force of law,' for . . . not everything that the will of the king rashly conceives . . . has the force of law. . . . As long as he administers justice, he is the vicar of the eternal king. . . . A king is king when he governs well, but a tyrant when he oppresses the people with violence."[5] Sir John Fortescue, Chief Justice of the King's Bench (d. 1476), distinguishes between the absolute and the constitutional monarch: "The seconde king (the constitutional monarch) may not rule his people by other laws than such as thai assenten to. And therefore he may set uppon thaim non imposicions without their consent."[6]

The Tudor and Stuart kings succeeded far too well in their efforts to become absolute monarchs between 1509 when Henry VIII began his reign and 1688 when Charles II was beheaded. A constitutional monarch, William of Orange, was then enthroned; England had changed from Catholic to Protestant, but the revolution of 1688 was in its own way a restoration of the medieval government limited by law. In 1616 Sir Edward Coke had remonstrated with the ruling Stuart, James I: "Your Majesty, the law is the golden measure to try the cases of his subjects. . . . The King cannot take any case out of his courts and give judgement upon it himself. The judgements are always given *per curiam* and the judges are sworn to execute justice according to the laws and customs of England." To which the King replied in a vein which shows how far removed he was from Bracton: "This means that I shall be under the law, which it is treason to affirm." Coke reminded him of Bracton and the medieval tradition of natural law: " 'Sire, Bracton saith that the King ought to be . . . under God and the Law.' Whereupon His Majesty fell into that high indignation as the like was not known in him. . . ."[7]

The significance of this is that government limited by law became American doctrine; Sir Edward Coke was a great authority for the Americans. In the war of ideas between 1760-1775 the Americans claimed that Parliament (with the acquiescence of George III) was violating the British constitution as embodied in these ancient laws and customs. By 1776 the Declaration of Independence lays all blame on the King, since the colonists had come to the conclusion that they had never truly given consent to the rule of Parliament over them; but the King, to whom they acknowledged allegiance, had violated his trust as king. Through it all runs the thought that no government may change without their consent a constitution which has been accepted by the people.

James Otis in his *Rights of the British Colonies* (1764) shows how American political philosophy grew out of its British background, and under God's law government requires the consent of the governed, "that the administrators of it were originally the whole people," etc.:

The sum of my argument is, that civil government is of God: that the administrators of it were originally the whole people: that they might have devolved it on whom they pleased: that this devolution is fiduciary, for the good of the whole: that by the British constitution, this devolution is on the King, lords and commons, the supreme sacred and uncontroulable legislative power, not only in the realm, but thro' the dominions: that by the abdication, the original compact was broken to pieces: that by the revolution, it was renewed, and more firmly established, and the rights and liberties of the subjects in all parts of the dominions more fully explained and confirmed: that in consequence of this establishment, and the Acts of Succession and Union, His Majesty George III is rightful king and sovereign and with his Parliament, the supreme legislative of Great Britain, France, and Ireland, and the dominions thereto belonging: that this constitution is the most free one, and by far the best, now existing on earth: that by this constitution, every man in the dominions is a free man: that no parts of His Majesty's dominions can be taxed without their consent: that every part has a right to be represented in the supreme or some subordinate legislature: that the refusal of this would seem to be a contradiction in practice to the theory of the constitution: . . .[8]

The Virginia "Stamp Act Resolution" in 1765 claims that Virginians were always governed by laws sanctioned by their own consent:

Resolved, That His Majesty's liege people of this his most ancient and loyal Colony have without interruption enjoyed the inestimable right of being governed by such laws, respecting their internal polity and taxation, as are derived from their own consent, with the approbation of their sovereign, or his substitute; and that the same hath never been forfeited or yielded up, but hath been constantly recognized by the kings and people of Great Britain.[9]

In 1768 when Massachusetts sent a "Circular Letter" to the Assemblies of the other colonies the Americans were still willing to recognize Parliament — provided Parliament acted within the British Constitution:

The House have humbly represented to the ministry, their own Sentiments that his Majesty's high Court of Parliament is the supreme legislative Power over the whole Empire; That in all free States the Constitution is fixed; & as the supreme Legislative derives its Power & Authority from the Constitution, it cannot overleap the Bounds of it without destroying its own foundation; That the constitution ascertains & limits both Sovereignity and allegiance, & therefore, his Majesty's American Subjects, who acknowledge themselves bound by the Ties of Allegiance, have an equitable Claim to the full enjoyment of the fundamental Rules of the British Constitution.[10]

In the "Declaration and Resolves" the First Continental Congress (1774) claimed all the rights of Englishmen and the benefit of common law — but said they never gave their consent to any government to exercise power destructive of their rights to life, liberty and property:

That the inhabitants of the English Colonies in North America, by the immutable laws of nature, the principles of the English Constitution, and the several charters or compacts, have the following rights:
1. That they are entitled to life, liberty and property, and they have never ceded to any sovereign power whatever, a right to dispose of either without their consent.
2. That our ancestors, who first settled these colonies, were at the time of their emigration from the mother country, entitled to all the rights, liberties, and immunities of free and natural-born subjects within the realm of England.

54

3. That by such emigration they by no means forfeited, surrendered, or lost any of those rights, but that they were, and their descendants now are entitled to the exercise and enjoyment of all such of them, as their local and other circumstances enable them to exercise and enjoy.

4. That the respective colonies are entitled to the common law of England, and more especially to the great and inestimable privilege of being tried by their peers of the vicinage, according to the course of that law.

5. That they are entitled to the benefit of such of the English statutes, as existed at the time of their colonization; and which they have, by experience, respectively found to be applicable to their several local and other circumstances.[11]

The "Instructions" Virginia gave its delegates to the First Continental Congress implied that because the Americans cannot be represented in the British Parliament they can never give consent — the asserted powers of Parliament over the Americans will never be constitutional:

It cannot admit of a doubt but that British subjects in America, are entitled to the same rights and privileges as their fellow subjects possess in Great Britain; and therefore, that the power assumed by the British parliament to bind America by their statutes, in all cases whatsoever, is unconstitutional, and the source of these unhappy differences.

The end of government would be defeated by the British parliament exercising a power over the lives, the property, and the liberty of the American subjects; who are not, and from their local circumstances cannot, be there represented. . . .[12]

## 3

## The American Constitution

The American foundation is the acceptance of compact as the basis of government whether it can be traced to the historical beginning of a particular government or rested implicitly on the consent of the governed. The British government by 1776 had definitively broken its compact with the colonists. Having won independence the problem was to establish a new compact, a Constitution, among themselves which would forever protect their God-given natural rights. To accomplish this, the Fathers of the Constitutional Convention of 1787 required first of all that once accepted by the people it could only be changed by the people themselves, and this through a difficult but democratic process. Congress, with two-thirds of both Houses concurring, could propose amendments which would become part of the Constitution when ratified by three-fourths of all the states; or if two-thirds of the state legislatures shall request it, Congress must call a constitutional convention, and its proposed amendments would become constitutional upon acceptance by three-fourths of the states.

Secondly, the Founders built into the Constitution definite divisions of powers within the government and automatic checks upon the use of these powers. The natural division into the legislative, executive and judicial branches was taught by one of the "wisest writers," the French Baron Charles Louis de Montesquieu: let no one person or group exercise all, or even more than one, of these powers; history had proven that too much power in one place corrupts the one having it and puts the rights and freedom of the people in jeopardy. And no individual person or group was to have total supremacy even in his or its own domain; built into the Constitution were the "checks and balances" — legislature, executive and courts could check each other. The executive could veto the legislature; the legislature could override a veto; the judges were appointed by the executive with the consent of the legislative power; the judges could declare laws unconstitutional or interpret how they were meant to work. The legislature would be checked by the people: after a shorter or longer period of time each legislator would have to return to the people for reelection. The executive would have to go to the people for a vote of confidence after four years.

Most responsibility for maintaining the Constitution went to the courts with their powers to declare a law invalid if it was contrary to the Constitution. It was Hamilton in Federalist Paper No.

78 who explained that this key provision was implied in the Constitution. And to protect the independence of the courts judges were to be appointed by the executive under the terms Congress shall determine for the use of this power, while the Justices of the Supreme Court were to be appointed by the President with the advice and consent of the Senate. Judges were to hold office "during good behavior," for life, and their salaries could not be reduced during their tenure; they could be impeached and removed from office only on conviction of treason, bribery, or other high crimes and misdemeanors.

It can be seen that the responsibility of the Supreme Court is awesome, standing on the summit of judicial decision-making as to the constitutionality of the acts of legislature and executive. If the Supreme Court misinterprets the Constitution, the recourse is the people themselves, by public opinion which will pressure the Justices to reverse themselves, or by amendment to the Constitution decided by the people. Public opinion is of course not mentioned; it is present in any democracy. Lest the people be led by demagogues to rashly want changes in the Constitution, the amending process was deliberately made cumbersome.

The Fathers had a healthy distrust for the weakness of human nature. As Christians, and with the variations of the different Christian churches, they had a theological source for this distrust in the doctrine of original sin. They also saw the weakness written throughout human history in the lust for power of kings, the selfishness of aristocracy, the violence of the masses. The system of checks and balances within government was essentially a device to use the weakness of human nature to control itself. James Madison in Federalist Paper No. 51 wrote:

"To what expedient then shall we finally resort, for maintaining in practice the necessary partitions of power among the several departments, as laid down in the Constitution? The only answer that can be given is, that as all these exterior provisions are found to be inadequate, the defect must be supplied, by so contriving the interior structure of the government, as that its several constituent parts may, by their mutual relations, be the means of keeping each other in their proper places. . . . Ambition must be made to counteract ambition. The interests of the man must be connected with the constitutional rights of the place. It may be a reflection on human nature, that such devices should be necessary to control the abuses of government. But what is government itself, but the greatest of all reflections on human nature? If men were angels, no government would be necessary. If angels were to govern men, neither external nor internal controls on government would be necessary. In framing a government, which is to be administered by men over men, the great difficulty lies in this: You must first enable the government to control the governed; and in the next place, oblige it to control itself. . . ."[13]

So the Founding Fathers at the Constitutional Convention laid the foundation for a government which was almost self-running and self-regulating. Almost; for ultimately the Constitution merely sets up a system of mechanics to generate the public welfare by keeping the wheels of government moving in the right direction, with the right speed, with the right smoothness. Self-interest is a powerful but negative force. The Fathers were distrustful of human nature but never despairing. They had won a war because so many had fought and bled for what they knew to be morally right. The energy to keep the wheels of government moving, its bearings free from gum, its parts from corroding, was to be a positive force. The *virtue of the people* was to be the energy, the anti-corrosive, needed in a democracy more than in any other form of government. And this was to be a government of the people, by the people, for the people.

# chapter 6

## VIRTUE

The mechanics of government are merely mechanics; the ultimate protection for the people had to be the people themselves. The Founders, the generation which they represent, were convinced that only the virtue of the people would insure the continuous protection of rights, the continued happiness of the citizens, the continued prosperity of the nation. They were sure also that virtue depended on sound education, that ethics was part of the study of reality, and that morality was based on true religion. There were varying degrees of confidence in the mass of people among the American Fathers — Hamilton perhaps with the least and therefore prone to give more responsibility and power to the well-to-do and the well-educated; Jefferson with an overwhelming confidence in the common man when adequately enlightened by proper leadership. But all were agreed: if a democratic society and government is to work the people must be enlightened and virtuous.

Jefferson held that the basic norms of morality were to be found in all Christian groups and indicates the necessity of morality for the welfare of society:

> Reading, reflection and time have convinced me that the interests of society require the observation of those moral precepts only in which all religions agree (for all forbid us to murder, steal, plunder or bear false witness) and that we should not intermeddle with the particular dogmas in which all religions differ, and which

are totally unconnected with morality. . . . The practice of morality being necessary for the well being of society, he (the Creator) has taken care to impress its precepts so indelibly on our hearts that they shall not be effaced by the subtleties of our own brain. We all agree in the obligation of the moral precepts of Jesus.[1]

The Virginia Bill of Rights (principal author: George Mason), adopted five days before the signing of the Declaration of Independence, puts it tersely:

15. That no free government, or the blessings of liberty, can be preserved to any people, but by a firm adherence to justice, moderation, temperance, frugality and virtue, and by frequent recurrence to fundamental principles.[2]

Section XIV of Pennsylvania's Bill of Rights, adopted September 28, 1776, was substantially the same as the above section (15) of Virginia's bill.[3]

Protestantism was the established religion of Massachusetts when its Bill of Rights, authored by John Adams, was adopted in 1780:

As the happiness of a people and the good order and preservation of civil government essentially depend upon piety, religion, and morality, and as these cannot be generally diffused through a community but by the institution of the public worship of God and of public instructions, in piety, religion, and morality. Therefore to promote their happiness and secure the good order and preservation of their government, the people of this commonwealth have a right to invest their legislature with power to authorize and require, and the legislature shall from time to time authorize and require, the several towns . . . and other bodies — politic or religious societies, to make suitable provision, at their own expense, for the institution of the public worship of God and the support and maintenance of public Protestant teachers of piety, religion, and morality. . . .[4]

The Constitution of New Hampshire, adopted June 2, 1784,

60

included a Bill of Rights as Part I of the document: it is substantially the same as Massachusetts':

VI. As morality and piety, rightly grounded on evangelical principles, will give the best and greatest security to government, and will lay in the hearts of men the strongest obligations to due subjection; and as the knowledge of these, is most likely to be propagated through a society by the institution of public worship of the DEITY, and of public instruction of morality and religion: therefore, to promote these important purposes, the people of this state have a right to impower, and do hereby fully impower the legislature to authorize from time to time, the several towns, parishes, bodies-corporate, or religious societies within this state, to make adequate provision at their own expense, for the support and maintenance of public protestant teachers of piety, religion and morality.[5]

Probably the most important act of the Congress under the Articles of Confederation was the Northwest Ordinance of 1787. The articles of the Ordinance were to be "considered as articles of compact between the original states and the people and states in the said territory and forever remain unalterable, unless by common consent." The Ordinance provided for not less than three or more than five states to be apportioned from the territory, and it forbade slavery. The same Congress had two years previously set aside a portion of land in each township of the territory for the maintenance of a public school; now it gives its attitude in terse words:

Religion, morality, and knowledge, being necessary to good government and the happiness of mankind, schools and the means of education shall forever be encouraged. . . .[6]

In the minds of the founding generation it was impossible to separate sound education from religion and morality.

George Washington was the "Father of his Country." After giving more than any other in the way of courage, sacrifice, ability and character to bring independence, he reluctantly left his earned retirement to serve as President of the Constitutional Convention in 1787 and then as first President of the United States. Without Washington the nation would not be. At his first inaugural address he spoke from his heart:

In these honorable qualifications I behold the surest pledges that as on one side no local prejudices or attachments, no separate views nor party animosities, will misdirect the comprehensive and equal eye which ought to watch over this great assemblage of communities and interests, so, on another, that the foundation of our national policy will be laid in the pure and immutable principles of private morality, and the pre-eminence of free government be exemplified by all the attributes which can win the affections of its citizens and command the respect of the world. I dwell on this prospect with every satisfaction which an ardent love for my country can inspire, since there is no truth more thoroughly established than that there exists in the economy and course of nature an indissoluble union between virtue and happiness; between duty and advantage; between the genuine maxims of an honest and magnanimous policy and the solid rewards of public prosperity and felicity; since we ought to be no less persuaded that the propitious smiles of Heaven can never be expected on a nation that disregards the eternal rules of order and right which Heaven itself has ordained; and since the preservation of the sacred fire of liberty and the destiny of the republican model of government are justly considered, perhaps, as *deeply* as *finally,* staked on the experiment intrusted to the hands of the American people.[7]

And eight years later, leaving the highest office in the land and soon to leave this life, in giving what might be considered his last will and testament to his beloved country, he could only reiterate the same principles. From his farewell address:

Of all the dispositions and habits which lead to political prosperity, religion and morality are indispensable supports. In vain would that man claim the tribute of patriotism who should labor to subvert these great pillars of human happiness — these firmest props of the duties of men and citizens. The mere politician, equally with the pious man, ought to respect and to cherish them. A volume could not trace all their connections with private and public felicity. Let it simply be asked, Where is the security for property, for reputation, for life, if the sense of religious obligation *desert* the oaths which are the instruments of investigation in courts of justice? And let us with caution indulge the supposition that morality can be maintained without religion. Whatever may be conceded to the influence of refined education on minds of peculiar structure, reason and experience both forbid us to expect that national morality can prevail in exclusion of religious principle.

It is substantially true that virtue or morality is a necessary spring of popular government. The rule indeed extends with more or less force to every species of free government. Who that is a sincere friend to it can look with indifference upon attempts to shake the foundation of the fabric? Promote, then, as an object of primary importance, institutions for the general diffusion of knowledge. In proportion as the structure of a government gives force to public opinion, it is essential that public opinion should be enlightened.[8]

Washington takes in every main point. The more democratic a government (with its officers coming from and chosen by the people, and public opinion a dominating influence) the more important it is that morality and virtue give it character and that these be strengthened by sound education. It is impossible that the desired foundation exist for popular government and a democratic society with merely a secular education. Washington, of course, did not speak in a vacuum; he saw the danger of education without moral or religious training; he knew the necessity for good citizenship of the moral training as it was then given in both public and private school.

The "Father of his Country" is the spokesman for the generation which gave us our nation. Brown College, Providence, Rhode Island, had as a thesis to be discussed at the 1769 graduation what amounted to the definition of ethics at the college: "The practical science of bringing happiness to man by the practice of virtue." Harvard discussed in a 1770 thesis: "The closest bond of civil society is the oath; therefore the persuasion of the existence of God is necessary for the preservation of civil society." Yale, in theses to be proven by 1797 graduates, had this to say: "Without virtue and literature no republic can exist happy and free. 10) In order that citizens may be gifted with virtue and intelligence it is necessary that they should be instructed in letters and good morals; therefore 11) such institutions being neglected a free and happy republic cannot exist."[9] But suppose the institutions exist, but the instruction "in letters and good morals" does not exist within them? What then?

# chapter 7

## IN SUMMARY

There are five principles which are evident in the American founding philosophy, each of which becomes more clear when put into the context in which they were held by the Founders' generation. They are: (1) An intelligent God exists. (2) He gave man a moral law which flows from the nature of man. (3) This natural law gives men certain inalienable rights upon which depend their freedom and happiness. (4) Among these rights is that of the people to choose the type government to which they will be subject, that in the compact whereby they set up government they must surrender to this government some powers, but never their inalienable rights. (5) No government, but especially a democracy, can ever succeed unless a people are virtuous.

In context the God in whom the Americans believe was a personal God who was interested in them and who ruled men by His providence. As a people they believed in the personal God of theism rather than in an impersonal deity. Essentially Benjamin Franklin, Thomas Jefferson and John Adams accepted deism, but most leaders and the mass of people belonged fully to the Judeo-Christian tradition in its various American manifestations. Even the type deism which influenced the three leaders mentioned, since it acknowledged the providence of a personal God, was accepted as true, insofar as it went, by their Christian fellow Americans. The three mentioned leaders could sincerely sign the Declaration of Independence along with Sam Adams, the Congregationalist; Rev.

John Witherspoon, the Presbyterian president of Princeton College; and Charles Carroll, the Roman Catholic from Maryland. Since John Adams, Jefferson and Franklin also adhered to Christian moral principles, while not accepting such great Christian dogmas as the Trinity and Redemption, they were essentially one with their Christian fellow countrymen in political philosophy, for government and civil society are founded on natural moral principles rather than on supernatural dogmas.

The moral law which is derived from man's nature and known through his conscience gives man his rights and duties. The founding generation held this natural law to be self-evident. They would fight for the existence of this law rather than argue about it, and a person who would deny its basic principles would not be worthy of trust in anything. To Hamilton moral obligation came from man's nature; good and wise men in all ages recognized an intelligent Creator exists, who could not leave men without law; only atheists could fall into the "absurd and impious doctrine" that man in a state of nature, before civil government, could justly "deprive another of his life, limbs, property or liberty." Jefferson was convinced that all religions agreed on certain moral precepts, "for all forbid us to murder, steal, plunder or bear false witness and that these precepts are impressed so indelibly on our hearts, that they shall not be effaced by the subtlety of our brain." Clinton Rossiter in his *Seed Time of the Republic* noted that the Americans identified natural law and Christian virtue, that to them the practice of virtue is simply obedience to natural law. The natural moral law governed all men — but Christians understood it more clearly than others.

From this natural law of God came their inalienable rights, their human dignity. Three are listed in the Declaration of Independence: life, liberty and the pursuit of happiness. A fourth often mentioned was the right to keep or dispose of one's own justly acquired property; taxation without representation was stealing and perhaps the main cause of aggravation with the mother country. There were, of course, other natural rights: the right to justice (which they thought best protected by trial by jury), the rights to freedom of conscience, to freedom of speech and its complement, freedom of the press, etc. These rights naturally implied the duty of recognizing the corresponding right in each other human being; the use of their rights, that is, their freedom implied liberty but not license. No inalienable right could be ceded to society; its use could be specified by law as the right to justice was specified in the English-American system by due process and trial by jury; but these specifications under no circumstances should be used to destroy the right.

Civil society is set up by compact; but no compact could be valid if it did not protect and foster basic human rights; the people were so dissatisfied with the Constitution of 1787 because it did not contain a bill of rights that Massachusetts, New York and Virginia forced a tacit understanding that one would be added after ratification. The first ten amendments, our national Bill of Rights, proposed by the first U.S. Congress and ratified quickly by the states, were legal specifications intended to protect natural rights. In the compact actually set up, the national Constitution decreed the mechanics of the American government: a threefold separation of functions (the executive, judicial, legislative branches), and determined what powers each branch and the whole government should have.

Lastly, no civil society would be happy, strong and prosperous, unless it was built on a moral and virtuous people; and no government official would be a good public servant unless he was first a good man. No democratic government would be a good government unless the people from which it came were a good people. The people also had to be enlightened; they had to be educated. The most important part of this education was moral training and religion; these two could not in practice be separated.

This is our American heritage; upon all these principles was built the American nation. To defend one of these principles, compromised when the Constitution was drafted and a constant rebuke to the national conscience for the generations which followed, a civil war was fought; the denial of the right to liberty, the institution of slavery, led to the blood-letting between the North and the South. The war reaffirmed the principle in its pristine purity; the Thirteenth, Fourteenth and Fifteenth Amendments were added to the Constitution. It was as though the nation was proclaiming to

67

the world once again "that all men are created equal, that they are endowed by their Creator with certain unalienable Rights, that among these are Life, Liberty and the pursuit of Happiness. That to secure these rights, Governments are instituted among Men, deriving their just powers from the consent of the governed, . . ."

But something has happened to the vitality, the cogency, the impact of this heritage for present-day Americans. The Declaration of Independence is quoted in speeches from time to time; the fact that it is a summary of doctrines which were placed as the "Ground and Foundation" of our government is almost never mentioned. The other magnificent documents bequeathed to us by the Founding Fathers are seldom quoted. What is more unnerving is the fact that the doctrines are not being taught in our schools. This writer undertook a random sampling of American History textbooks used in junior and senior high schools throughout the country. Seven out of eight standard texts gave inadequate (I am tempted to use much stronger terms) treatment of the meaning of the Declaration; the great philosophical principles behind it seem not to be understood, or, considering the historical importance of the principles and that these are history texts, the most important segment of our history is given most meager and inept treatment.[1] Only one text gave an excellent but short analysis of the preamble to the Declaration. The Constitution in general fares better, but the Bill of Rights is often misinterpreted as a listing of civil rights instead of the legal implementation of natural rights as intended by the Founders. This is false history. Our children have a right to their true heritage, whether later generations are as conscious of their human dignity vs. civil dignity as were the Founding Fathers or not.

## Sincerity Of The Fathers: Slavery

One other facet of this heritage from the Founders should be mentioned. Sometimes inconsistency, if not insincerity, is implied by a false picture given of the slavery problem as it existed among the Fathers. One high-school text among the above exemplifies this. It includes a quotation from a modern author who misinterprets the institution of slavery as it existed at the time the Declaration was written: "The new state (i.e., the United States) began its history with a declaration that all men are born equal, and have an inalienable right to liberty. This was, indeed, only a general statement, with no practical effects. It did not make any difference to the rights or to the laws of the American people, which remained in all essentials the rights and the laws which they derived from Britain; nor did those among the signatories of this pronouncement who were slave owners, as many of them were, even think of applying their principle by giving their slaves the 'inalienable' right of liberty. . . . But it was a new thing in human history that a great state should thus choose as the motto of the first chapter in its history a proclamation of universal human rights as the ideal to be aimed at."[2]

The violation of the right to liberty raises a doubt for some that the principle of inalienable rights was truly placed as the foundation principle of the American government.

This oversimplified condemnation of the Founding Fathers is not justified by the facts of the situation which confronted them. The Fathers were fully committed to the principle that the first obligation of government is to protect inalienable rights and they were sincerely against slavery; but in the case of this institution they had a wolf by the tail and did not know how to release it.

Slavery had been introduced a century and a half before their time. It had become such a part of the social fabric that to root it out suddenly would cause hardship to many who did not create the situation, even to the slaves themselves; for they were illiterate and had not proven their ability to maintain themselves in freedom. To free one's slaves on an individual basis was not necessarily happy for the black in the context of the times. The freed black was a pariah, with all the customs and laws conspiring to keep him below the white man. It would not have been kind to free children or aged with no visible means of support. There were individual difficulties, too. Washington's slaves were intermarried with those of his wife's. Legal complications were a barrier to the manumission of dower slaves; to free his own, while relatives belonging to his wife remained in servitude, would cause family suffering among the Negroes. Then, too, while the institution itself could be held as an evil, the slave owner might know that he was personally treating his slaves well.

The slave society faced grave problems if it attempted a general abolition. Some were in terror of a possible slave insurrection; if maltreated slaves ever became free, worse than insurrection might follow. The whole economy of the plantation rested on slave labor; how could it be replaced? While they attributed financial troubles to the inefficiency of the system — Washington, Jefferson, Madison and many other planters faced failure when, as Washington said, the farms of Pennsylvania with no more fertile land than Maryland or Virginia were worth much more than the plantations of these states — yet it seemed impossible to change the situation without immediate ruin.

There were attempts even in colonial days to lessen the evil. In 1710 and again in 1772 Virginia, then Pennsylvania (in 1712), and subsequently South Carolina (in 1760), made attempts to interfere with the slave trade, but to no avail because of the opposition of the British government (but, of course, southern slave owners did buy slaves, and Yankee slave traders got their share of the profit). When independence came, successful measures against this inhuman servitude were accomplished. Slavery had been legal also in the North; one northern state after another moved to ban all slavery by law. Congress under the Articles of Confederation made the Northwest Territory forever free soil by the famous Northwest Ordinance. It is a fact, too, that wherever action was not successful in this direction it was blocked by small minorities, when the larger group needed the smaller. Jefferson's castigation of the slave trade was left out of the Declaration of Independence so as not to offend a small group of New England slave traders and the two most southerly colonies which needed slaves for the rice fields. It is with this background in mind that we should read the denunciations of slavery voiced by Jefferson, Otis, Mason, Washington, Madison, Franklin, Charles Carroll, Gouverneur Morris, John Adams, James Wilson and others.

There is also another aspect to these facts which reconciles the Founders' principles with the seeming ineptitude of their practice. One could judge that slavery was destined to a natural death in the not distant future, and no prudent man would apply violent remedies if time was already working on his side. It is the nation as a whole which subscribed to the Declaration of Independence. Slavery existed originally in the northern colonies as well as the southern, but never to such a great extent as it was never profitable there, and one northern state after another banned it. It was proving basically unprofitable in most of the South. When Roger Sherman and Oliver Ellsworth voiced the expectation that slavery was a temporary condition they had some basis for their hope.

What changed all this was the invention of the cotton gin in 1795. One machine had the seed-cleaning capacity of 300 men; cotton became king where tobacco had reigned. An evil and unjust institution took new roots. By 1825-1830 there were people in the South who began to rationalize; the Founding Fathers never dreamed of the new natural law Calhoun used to justify slavery. The Founders were utterly sincere in their principles, and the nation paid dearly when in a difficult situation they compromised one of these principles. It is totally unfair to think of the Declaration of Independence as window dressing; it expressed a creed for which the Fathers were shedding blood; it proclaimed deeply held convictions upon which a nation was to be built.

Millions of Americans will make a pilgrimage to the National Archives Building in Washington to view the parchment text of the Declaration during this Bicentennial celebration. Millions have been inspired by the document in the past and have been intrigued by the efforts made to preserve it for posterity. It is enshrined in a glass-covered case — air-conditioned and filled with an inert gas to prevent deterioration — part of an apparatus which will lower it automatically into a bombproof shelter in time of crisis. We have done all in our power to preserve the physical text; it is quite as much an example of American ingenuity as Apollo XIV. But if we preserve the document without the doctrine, we have a mummy, a lifeless example of American materialism which has lost its soul. Unless the doctrine lives in American hearts, it becomes an epitaph of a dead civilization.

This must not happen; the principles of the Founding Fathers are the priceless heritage which belongs to our children. They have

71

a right to receive it intact and alive. To ignore the doctrines of the Declaration; to reduce the Constitution to merely a clever legal document rather than the product of sincere and gifted men who were conditioned by thousands of years of Western and Judeo-Christian tradition; to interpret the Bill of Rights as the source of civil rights rather than the implementation of natural rights; to do all these things is to cheat our children of their heritage. We have no right to do this.

Our children also have a right to this heritage as a standard for judging the working of our present-day government. The nation needs this yardstick to measure the principles and achievements, the immoralities and failures of present-day leaders. Without such a yardstick the people drift, sometimes sensing wrong but with no criterion to measure the wrong.

Our children, furthermore, have a right to this heritage because it is the only adequate American answer to the great external threat to the American way of life: the ideology of Communism. It is an answer based on truths perceived and held by the bulk of the American people. America established herself on moral truths which come from God, and she endeavored to conform her legal system to these truths. If examined point by point the principles of the Founders will be seen as the certain rebuttal to atheistic Communism. Compare, for example, the Declaration of Independence with the teaching of Lenin: "We say that our morality is wholly subordinated to the interests of the class struggle of the proletariat. We deduce our morality from the facts and needs of the class struggle of the proletariat. . . . That is why we say that a morality taken from outside of human society does not exist for us; it is a fraud. For us morality is subordinated to the interests of the proletarian class struggle."

The first project to make the 1976 Bicentennial meaningful should be to give back to our children their heritage: return an adequate teaching of the Declaration and Constitution to our schools.

# part two:
# an examination
# of conscience

# chapter 8

# AN EXAMINATION OF CONSCIENCE?

The foregoing chapters were an attempt to analyze the American ideology as understood by the founding generation of our country and to point out the condition of this heritage as we approach our 200th birthday. As objective history it belongs in our schools; our children have a right to their heritage.

This adult generation has a personal interest in it also, and we have the obligation to pass it on to posterity. The philosophy of the Founding Fathers requires a forum today for still another reason. The nation has passed through the trauma of Watergate. We saw an orderly transfer of power at the summit of government when the elected President and his aides failed dangerously in their responsibilities. In editorial and news commentary, from politician and private citizen, in official Washington and from foreign capitals, we heard a universal comment: the American system works!

The constitutional wheels placed in our government to insure morality (not merely legality) by men long dead, set in motion by public opinion after being alerted by the communications media, ground on to a sad but necessary conclusion. This is the reality: the Founding Fathers established a government based on principles of morality; they set up a system in which the moral rights of the citizens would be protected because government officials would be forced to fulfill their sworn obligations. The Founders knew that no law could make a truthful man out of a liar, but for the public welfare they made laws that lies under oath would be punished. They knew that no law could make an honest man out of a thief, but to protect the public they passed laws that public officials who took bribes would pay the penalty. The whole constitutional system and the laws which flow from it presupposed a people whose rights it was meant to protect, and it was drafted to establish a government the mechanics of which would almost automatically insure that government officials would fulfill their obligations to the people.

To those who drafted the Constitution there was a philosophical foundation upon which they built, the one expressed by the Declaration of Independence. The constitutional system helped us to solve Watergate but it is not too much to say that if the principles of the Declaration were more vitally lived today Watergate would never have happened. Basically, the Declaration outlines a philosophy which teaches men to fulfill their obligations to God and fellowmen. This philosophy does live in the hearts of the American people; unfortunately, this does not mean it is observed by all the people or by all government officials. Even more curiously, the Constitution is today interpreted as if the philosophy had never existed.

To understand the present position of the country relative to the principles and ideals of the Founding Fathers the five major points developed in the preceding chapters can be used as an outline for an examination of the national conscience: where does the country stand today in reference to God, to acceptance of a natural moral law which binds all men, to the observance of inalienable rights for all, to the fact that our Constitution was written as a compact between the people themselves and between people and government, and to the Fathers' principle that a democracy will not work if the people are not virtuous?

Traditionally an examination of conscience has more to do with vices rather than virtues, with sins rather than good deeds. The object is to see what must be improved rather than complacency in achievement. Therefore in this examination concentration is directed toward how we have fallen away from the Founders' ideals.

The people have indeed kept these ideals deep in their hearts, have returned expressly to them in times of crisis. The leadership groups in the country (especially the most visible ones: churches, schools, communications media, government) have to a great extent failed the people in holding to and expressing the foundation principles. The good points and achievements of these groups are, of course, present, and sometimes mentioned in passing. The good may outweigh the bad in each group, but the cumulative effect of the failings of these groups together appears as an overall failure in leadership that has produced confusion among the people and a tendency to drift without direction. The people deeply feel and cling to the principles of the Founding Fathers; the leadership groups have not done their share to keep the ideals and principles alive, and have sometimes implicitly denied them.

Instead of voicing the ideals, formulating the principles which the people feel but cannot easily express, leaders who should know better have often produced confusion rather than clarity. To be pointed, the principles of the Declaration of Independence mean a great deal to the majority of our people; there is little evidence of adherence and meager expression of these ideals from our leadership groups. It is these failures that this examination of conscience points out. It does not deny other achievements; there is no need to examine them in an examination of conscience and no place to really investigate them in a short essay.

The preceding chapters were concerned with objective history; this examination of conscience of its nature must be subjective, one man's judgment. It has as much value as the reasonableness of the judgment and the data brought forward to substantiate the opinions expressed. It shall have been worthwhile if it spurs others to make their examination of conscience concerning the state of our country as we approach the Bicentennial.

# chapter 9

# THE FOUNDING PHILOSOPHY LIVES IN THE HEARTS OF THE PEOPLE

The distinguished historian Clinton Rossiter once wrote: "Perhaps Americans could achieve a larger measure of liberty and prosperity and build a more successful government if they were to abandon the language and assumptions of men who lived almost two centuries ago. Yet the feeling cannot be downed that rude rejection of the past, rather than level-headed respect for it, would be a huge mistake. Americans may take the advice of their advanced philosophers and adopt a political theory that pays more attention to groups, classes, public opinion, power-elites, positive law, public administration, and other realities of twentieth-century America. Yet it seems safe to predict that the people, who occasionally prove themselves wiser than their philosophers, will go on thinking about the political community in terms of unalienable rights, popular sovereignty, consent, constitutionalism, separation of powers, morality, and limited government. The political theory of the American Revolution — a theory of ethical, ordered liberty — remains the political tradition of the American people."[1]

There is much evidence to justify this statement. Rossiter distinguishes between the people, who instinctively adhere to the founding philosophy, and philosophers who reject it. In this examination of conscience it is helpful to distinguish the people, who hold the philosophy in their hearts, from those members of the American leadership which to a greater or lesser extent have failed the people

78

by not consciously helping the people to comprehend clearly their heritage, and which in some cases have deliberately abandoned it.

It all begins with God. Our people overwhelmingly build on this foundation. "We are a religious people whose institutions presuppose a Supreme Being" was four times repeated by the Supreme Court in the space of some 150 years.[2] From 1941 to 1968 seven investigations indicated 94%-99% of Americans believe in God; the *World Almanac* (1973) shows approximately 62% with definite church membership.[3] The most recent statistics, from the *Yearbook of the American and Canadian Churches* issued May 13, 1974, register church affiliation by 62.4% of the total population. We are neither an atheist nor secularist people.

President Ford, after taking his oath of office at his inauguration, spoke from his heart to the hearts of the American people when he said: "My fellow Americans, our long national nightmare is over. Our Constitution works. Our great republic is a government of laws and not of men. Here the people rule. But there is a higher power, by whatever name we honor him, who ordains not only righteousness but love, not only justice but mercy. As we bind up the internal wounds of Watergate, more painful and more poisonous than those of foreign wars, let us restore the Golden Rule to our political process. And let brotherly love purge our hearts of suspicion and of hate. . . . With all the strength and all the good sense I have gained from life, with all confidence my family, my friends and dedicated staff impart to me and with the goodwill of countless Americans I have encountered in recent visits to forty states, I now solemnly reaffirm my promise I made to you last December 6 to uphold the Constitution, to do what is right as God gives me to see the right and to do the very best I can do for America. God helping me, I will not let you down."

The people of 1776 recognized a law which governed all men because they are men, and they knew how to formulate this law precisely as natural law; the Declaration of Independence was a succinct and beautiful expression of American convictions. It was not an exhaustive enumeration of what the laws of nature and nature's God required but it was a clear statement of the function of that law in governing man's relation to his fellowman. All men and all governments are the subjects of rights and obligations because the divine Legislator placed a law within men's hearts which could be perceived by men of goodwill.

Americans today have absolute and universal standards which they apply to all human beings in all nations. This is not so precisely stated as part of the Founders' natural law which governs human nature everywhere, yet the same natural law is implied by these absolutes. Thus whether a rape is reported as happening on Park Avenue in New York or to a missionary in Africa it makes news because it violates one universal standard just as an attack on a Philadelphia housewife is no more heinous to us than one in a Latin-American slum. We have the same aversion for incest whether it happens in rural America or rural China. The torture of a child whether done by Communists or Nazis or a sadistic American is just as revolting to American people. We read with disgust the account of police tortures in Latin America and Communist countries and we fight against its possibility here. The My Lai murders by our soldiers upset us more than accounts of Viet Cong massacres. We resent a lie in our private relationships; we resented the perjury connected with Watergate; we abhorred the lie of the Russian Ambassador to President Kennedy during the Cuban missile crisis.

The concentration camp/murder system of the Nazis awakened revulsion as did the same tactics under Stalin. It did not matter to us whether these things were legal under the dictatorship of Hitler or a legalized Communist arrangement. We always recognize man's inhumanity to man whenever or wherever committed; we adhere to a law for human nature itself. To judge the Nazis at Nuremburg we used a term nowhere existing in previous civil law: crimes against humanity, crimes forbidden not because they were contrary to civil law but because they were against human nature itself. In our thinking we cannot get away from the principle that there can only be one norm to govern man's relations with his fellowman, and that norm is based on the humanity of each man, woman or child involved. We recognize it as a law that requires all men be treated with justice, equity and, yes, mercy.

Our history for the past two centuries indicates the same. Slavery was the great underlying cause of the Civil War; we could not reconcile our national conscience with an inhuman institution which denied the basic equality of all men. All the succeeding crises with other nations indicated the same American principle. In the first world war the rape of Belgium by the Imperial German government revolted the American people. Stories of German atrocities (after the war we found out that much was mere propaganda) incensed us further. The sinking of the *Lusitania,* a passenger liner, met a passionate reaction in the United States.

Hitler was the legal head of state in the Germany of the '30s. He had the backing of Nazi laws but his treatment of the Jews and other victims made him answerable to a higher law in the eyes of the American people. We were a united people in World War II, struggling for the proposition that all men everywhere have a right to be treated with humanity, with objective justice. It mattered not to Americans that the Nuremburg criminals could point out that they were carrying out the legal orders of their government in the atrocities they committed. In Korea we were satisfied that our government was acting for humanity in containing the inhumanity of Communism. In Vietnam those who supported our intervention were convinced for the same reasons which justified Korea. Those Americans opposed to the American Vietnam policy kept pointing out that our very methods were dehumanizing, cruel to innocent victims, not worth the cause. Only history will give the final answer, but the paradox is that both American camps were on the side of humanity, both implicitly on the side of natural justice, of natural law.

Natural rights are the consequence of natural law. American people have through the generations adhered to the doctrine that all men have certain inalienable rights. Lincoln summed up the problem of America's attitude toward the right to liberty in his first inaugural address: "One section of the country believes slavery is right and ought to be extended, while the other believes it is wrong and ought not be extended. This is the only substantial dispute." The Civil War settled the question of which was the American philosophy. In World Wars I and II our people were convinced and willing to fight for the rights to life, liberty, justice and human treatment for the victims of unjust and totalitarian government. Our consistent opposition to Communism is based on the same beliefs. Detente with Communist governments does not signify agreement with their principles, and our deepest hope is that past inhumanitarian practices by these governments are truly passing away. Americans have always believed in inalienable human rights.

The American people still believe in government by compact. We still think government should be of the people, by the people, for the people. Our people have never relinquished the claim that only they can change the Constitution, that this compact belongs to them. The surest way for any politician to be destroyed is for the people to be convinced that he has tried to place himself above the law; we expect government officials to fulfill their side of the contract with the people, made when they took their oath of office to uphold national or state constitutions. Watergate is the great witness to this.

Finally our people still believe that it is "substantially true that virtue or morality is a necessary spring of popular government" as Washington expressed it in his farewell address. Again Watergate. Every politician has to give the image of honesty and morality or he does not get votes. Gerald Ford was nominated to be Vice-President, and became President, because after an exhaustive search he was found to be "Mr. Clean." And that there is a deep-seated respect for virtue in the American people comes out in paradoxical ways. One could sell books, fill movie houses by a story that flaunts morality; it invites publicity just because it is contrary to accepted standards. Pornography is (mistakenly) defended as freedom of the press; one does not defend it as pornography. We are dismayed by the rise in crime statistics, by the increased use of dope or alcohol among our youth, by increased premarital sex, not just because it harms individuals but because it indicates a decay of morality in society and the nation is afraid of this. . . . What is good in human actions, human relations, is still idealized; evil is still despised by most of our people. That there is not always agreement as to what is good or evil is also true, and there is confusion beyond what is permissible even in a pluralistic society; as the following chapters imply, this confusion can be attributed to the leadership of our people rather than the people themselves.

82

# chapter 10

# THE FOUNDING PHILOSOPHY VS. AMERICAN LEADERSHIP: THE CHURCHES

"The political theory of the American Revolution — a theory of ethical, ordered liberty — remains the political tradition of the American people";[1] thus Rossiter claimed. But this theory is felt, sensed, rather than formulated or well expressed, and as Rossiter indicated, there are some who have abandoned it. Yet often it is not expressed, formulated or answered even by those who have left it. John Courtney Murray, a truly respected analyst of the American scene, writes: "Not that they (the 'advanced philosophers') have made a 'rude rejection of the past.' They are never rude. And they can hardly be said to have rejected what they never knew or understood, because it was never taught them and they never learned it. The tradition of natural law is not taught or learned in the American university, it has not been rejected, much less refuted. 'We do not refute our adversaries,' said Santayana; 'we quietly bid them good-bye.' I think, as I shall later say, that the American university long since bade a quiet good-bye to the whole notion of an American consensus, as implying that there are truths that we hold in common, and a natural law that makes known to all of us the structure of the moral universe in such wise that all are bound by it in a common obedience."[2]

If what Rossiter says is true, the common people have a wisdom not always apparent in intellectual circles; this seems close to what Jefferson and Lincoln held. If John Courtney Murray is right, we have one portion of our university leadership not willing to search for truth wherever it might lead. The people are the losers for this. What they sense and feel has been held by the greatest minds through the ages in addition to our greatest political philosophers, the Founding Fathers. The people deserve to have their principles formulated, expressed as the great moral truths upon which mankind has rested human dignity. They deserve to know their heritage for what it meant in American history, and they have a right to know the implications of the political philosophies (or even the absence of any philosophy) which are taught in university and law school. If we examine the national conscience relative to the various leadership groups of our society, using the same founding philosophy headings that we did for our people as a whole, we may find the causes of a good number of current problems, and implicitly a suggestion for their solution.

## Churches

The leadership groups which have the most influence with our people would include the churches, schools, the communications media and government. We can examine them relative to adherence to the founding principles that a sound society is built on God, on natural moral law, on inalienable rights, on a compact of one form or another and the virtue of the people. It is quite obvious that some groups have a special reference to certain points of examination; God and the churches go together.

## God

The starting point of the Founders' philosophy was God, the Creator who established natural law and gave man his inalienable rights. Our institutions presuppose belief in God. To the Founding Fathers belief in the same God was a point of contact with each other. To insure freedom of conscience the Founders achieved the American principle of separation of church and state under the leadership of Thomas Jefferson and James Madison. Yet they never intended a secular state where in practice God would be separated from society. To insure political unity the Declaration of Independence was worded in philosophical rather than theological terms; but all knew they were appealing to the same God.

Of course, churches bear the main burden of keeping the principle of a God-centered society in the hearts of the people. Yet today pivotal areas have become secularized, are treated as though belief in God has no relationship with practical life. Public education has been separated from religion, and the relationship lost between morality and legality. In the minds of the Fathers sound education required religious training (it was given even in the public schools of the day) and legality presupposed morality. We clergymen can ask ourselves if this present condition has not come about because of petty rivalry and bigoted prejudices between churches, that an interpretation has been given to the separation of church and state which is foreign to the Fathers because churchmen are not willing to fight together the common adversaries of atheism and secularism. Has this separation of religion from education, helped sometimes by the churches, been the cause of widespread perjury (Watergate is perhaps the tip of an iceberg) that Washington predicted in his farewell address? Let us ponder Washington's words:

". . . Where is the security for property, for reputation, for life, if the sense of religious obligation *desert* the oaths, which are the instruments of investigation in the courts of justice? And let us with caution indulge the supposition, that morality can be maintained without religion. Whatever may be conceded to the influence of refined education on minds of peculiar structure, reason and experience both forbid us to expect that national morality can prevail in exclusion of religious principle."[3]

In context Washington says that national morality will never be produced by education separated from religion. Perhaps it is time that churchmen take a second look at the dissenting opinions of Supreme Court Justices in the decisions which have secularized the tax-supported schools of the country. The McCollum decision[4] in 1948 forbade civilian clergy the right to use public-school facilities to teach their own parishioners; in parallel circumstances military chaplains always use public facilities. Having seen the harm of the McCollum decision, why should not the churches now seek to have it reversed and return to the educational practice of the Founding Fathers?

## Natural Law

The Founders were achieving tolerance of each other's religious convictions and in both theory and practice they were establishing freedom of conscience as the best political doctrine. The practical means to achieve this freedom became separation of church and state: in the wording of the First Amendment, "Congress shall make no laws respecting an establishment of religion, or prohibiting the free exercise thereof." (Later, by Supreme Court decision, this was applied also to the states.)

However, from the context in which the Founders worked, we know that freedom of conscience did not mean that anything held as a personal religious belief became automatically legitimate. They fought the Revolutionary War because they believed in a natural law which gave the inalienable rights to life and property; they would not accept as a proper exercise of religious freedom the proposition that murder or stealing became good if some individual thought murder allowable in some contexts or stealing moral by *his* religious belief. All legitimate freedoms had proper limitations; they believed in liberty, not license.

The Founding Fathers held that the objective morality which underlay the laws of the nation they were establishing was best proclaimed by the traditional Judeo-Christian morality. It is the function of the churches to uphold this moral concept. Any church or group of churchmen within a church teaching today that freedom of conscience gives the right to contravene this traditional

86

moral doctrine should clearly state to its people and to the public that a change has been made, and endeavor to show the basis for their shift from traditional Christian morality. Any other practice would violate the principle that there is an objective religion called Christianity and contravene the Founding Fathers' conviction that there are certain moral standards common to Christian churches which can be a basis for American civilization.

The most common current example of a change in moral judgment by churches (or better yet, by groups of churchmen within churches, since it is doubtful that any whole church has changed) is to be found where official religious groups endorse abortion on request, as now permitted by the Supreme Court. The shift on abortion morality speaks of such a fundamental change in the ethics of our civilization that churches and churchmen as moral leaders should face the issue openly and fearlessly. Any attitude other than this would imply a lack of honesty or courage. The issue is so decisive it should be opposed or defended.

Abortion as a problem of morality is to our generation what slavery was to the country 125 years ago. Many men of goodwill supported the institution of slavery. Churches split over the issue. From this safe distance of more than a century all Americans of all religious backgrounds now realize that the final solution was right: slavery was destroyed. The cost of the solution in terms of Civil War blood is one of the tragedies of our history. Yet if abortion is a moral evil we are paying now an almost hidden but much higher cost in human blood: over a million human lives deliberately destroyed each year in hospitals, doctors' offices and clinics — with the blessing of civil law. And this in the nation built on the moral foundation that "we hold these truths . . . that all men . . . are endowed by their Creator with certain unalienable rights, that among these are Life, . . ."

This is a moral issue which is determining the future of the nation, its devotion to moral principle, its concept of government which at present gives to private citizens the power not given hitherto to government itself: the power of life or death over helpless and innocent human beings. Because of the lack of scientific knowledge the Founding Fathers did not know the evidence for the full humanity of unborn human offspring, but their principle of the inalienability of all human life as a gift from the Creator leads only to one conclusion: legalized abortion on demand implies an attack on the right to life and is a moral evil dangerous for the country.

An editorial in *California Medicine,* the "Official Journal of the California Medical Association," in September of 1970, states the problem in terms which churchmen cannot in conscience ignore:

"The traditional Western ethic has always placed great emphasis on the intrinsic worth and equal value of every human life regardless of its stage or condition. This ethic has had the blessing of the Judeo-Christian heritage and has been the basis for most of our laws and much of our social policy. The reverence for each and every human life has also been a keystone of Western medicine and is the ethic which has caused physicians to try to preserve, protect, repair, prolong and enhance every human life which comes under their surveillance. This traditional ethic is still clearly dominant, but there is much to suggest that it is being eroded at its core and may eventually even be abandoned. This, of course, will produce profound changes in Western medicine and Western society.

"There are certain new facts and social realities which are becoming recognized, are widely discussed in Western society and seem certain to undermine and transform this traditional ethic. They have come into being and into focus as the social byproducts of unprecedented technological progress and achievement. Of particular importance are, first, the demographic data of human population expansion, which tends to proceed uncontrolled and at a geometric rate of progression; second, an ever-growing ecological disparity between the numbers of people and the resources available to support these numbers in the manner to which they are or would like to become accustomed; and third, and perhaps most important, a quite new social emphasis on something which is beginning to be called the quality of life, a something which becomes possible for the first time in human history because of scientific and technologic development. . . .

"What is not yet so clearly perceived is that in order to bring

88

this about choices will have to be made with respect to what is to be preserved and strengthened and what is not, and that this will of necessity violate and ultimately destroy the traditional Western ethic with all that this portends. It will become necessary and acceptable to place relative rather than absolute values on such things as human lives, the use of scarce resources and the various elements which are to make up the quality of life or of living which is to be sought. This is quite distinctly at variance with the Judeo-Christian ethic and carries serious philosophical, social, economic and political implications for Western society and perhaps for world society.

"The process of eroding the old ethic and substituting the new has already begun. It may be seen most clearly in changing attitudes toward human abortion. In defiance of the long-held Western ethic of intrinsic and equal value for every human life regardless of its stage, condition or status, abortion is becoming accepted as moral, right and even necessary. It is worth noting that this shift in public attitude has affected the churches, the laws and public policy rather than the reverse. Since the old ethic has not yet been fully displaced it has been necessary to separate the idea of abortion from the idea of killing, which continues to be socially abhorrent. The result has been a curious avoidance of scientific fact, which everyone really knows, that human life begins at conception and is continuous whether intra- or extra-uterine until death. The very considerable semantic gymnastics which are required to rationalize abortion would be ludicrous if they were not often put forth under socially impeccable auspices. It is suggested that this schizophrenic sort of subterfuge is necessary because while a new ethic is being accepted the old one has not yet been rejected. . . ."[5]

The context of this editorial indicates the writer both understands the fundamental nature of the abortion controversy and is willing to go along with a changing ethic; in analyzing he has the intellectual honesty to face all the implications of the problem. The editorial brings out that the pro-abortion movement by attacking the most fundamental right held sacred in Western civilization and the Judeo-Christian heritage constitutes an attack on this civilization and heritage. The writer of the editorial states that "abortion is becoming accepted by society as moral, right and even necessary. It is worth noting that this shift in public attitude has affected the churches, the laws and public policy rather than the reverse."

There is a deep implication of the failure of the churches to perform their function in society in what this editorial writer says, although perhaps he did not mean it as such: the churches are being led by the lower moral standards of contemporary society instead of guiding it to higher things. The most fundamental social obligation of religious leaders is to guide and uplift the ethics of society; instead some are adjusting to the (apparently) popular demand. In this case the adjustment constitutes an attack on the moral foundation of the Judeo-Christian tradition of Western civilization. Could there be a greater failure for churchmen? Does not this failure to defend the ethic that all human beings have the right to life parallel the failure of so many church groups to defend the right to liberty of black men in the nineteenth century?

The Founding Fathers represent a high point in the ascent of Western civilization toward a firm legal and social establishment of human dignity and the rights of each individual, no matter how weak or defenseless. They placed this dignity and these rights as the foundation of the American nation. Is it possible that churchmen of the Judeo-Christian tradition are satisfied now to drift with the (apparent) tide and to deny what is most sacred in American, Western and Judeo-Christian civilization?

This does not mean that the problem of world overpopulation and the improvement of living standards for the underprivileged of the world can be ignored; it does mean churchmen must struggle that the means taken to solve population problems be moral, humane, civilizing. According to the Judeo-Christian tradition, abortion is not an ethical or humanizing means. Churchmen, especially, should point out that no legitimate ethical system can be built on the principle that the end justifies the means; unfortunately, this seems to be the principle that satisfies the writer of the above editorial. But by implication he is a medical man — his specialty is medicine; it is easy for nonspecialists in ethics to be overwhelmed by the immediate good they hope to accomplish and with little reflection accept the ethic that the end justifies the means. But this is an ethic

90

which makes Communism an ever-present danger; it is the ethic which guided the Nazis in their inhuman cruelties.

The churchmen of the Judeo-Christian tradition can find within their heritage the moral principles which, when followed, will guide mankind toward humane solutions for the most serious problems, including that of potential overpopulation. The Founding Fathers built the American nation upon these principles. Modern-day churchmen, if true to their calling, will sustain these principles. The "quality of life" as now offered to be the product of the new ethic will not be American, Judeo-Christian, humane, civilizing. It will place material comfort and selfishness as the guide and goal for the new American way of life to replace the greatness of American civilization built upon the principles of the Founding Fathers. There are moral means to solve population problems, standard of living problems; abortion is not one of them.

## Natural Rights

The natural right to life as the primordial right flowing to each human being from natural law was considered above. Churchmen who do not sustain this right, always mentioned first in the list of inalienable rights by the Founding Fathers, implicitly accept an attack on the law from which it flows. There are no inalienable rights which belong to each human being if the right to life does not first exist; all presuppose life. And there really can be no law if the most basic right which it gives does not exist; to say there is a law under such a condition would be meaningless.

The Ninth Amendment to the Constitution states: "The enumeration in the Constitution of certain rights shall not be construed to deny or disparage others retained by the people." This amendment was accepted by the First United States Congress under the leadership of James Madison and ratified quickly by the states. It implies natural rights "retained by the people." Today many churchmen are struggling to implement these rights both as civil rights before the law and social rights in practice. The struggle for desegregation in public facilities and schools falls into this section.

91

Such activity on the part of churchmen has not always been so and it is a heartening sign of the vitality of the churches today. The right of convicts to humane treatment, the right of the poverty-stricken in cities and deprived rural areas such as Appalachia, to at least the minimum standard of living which befits human dignity, follow as natural developments of the principles of the Founding Fathers and are part of the "rights retained by the people."

Where many churchmen fall into dangerous error here is the current psychology to treat such rights as these merely as civil rights rather than natural "rights retained by the people." Churchmen loyal to the Judeo-Christian tradition do not see fundamental rights as grants of government; the Founding Fathers certainly did not so conceive them.

If one perceives rights merely as civil, courts or legislatures can arbitrarily determine what rights in practice belong to the people, and can determine priorities among these rights; there really would be none "retained by the people." The term "constitutional" is often today used in place of the word "civil," and in practice the Constitution means what the Supreme Court says it means. According to the philosophy of the Founding Fathers the ordering of rights, the priority among them, was determined by God-given human nature; the right to life was always listed first. It would seem impossible for the Fathers to have fallen into the trap that the right to privacy is more important than the right to life, as did the seven Supreme Court Justices who in the Blackmun decision of January 22, 1973, struck down the state laws which protected the lives of human unborn babies in favor of the "privacy" of the mothers. The Founding Fathers' thought is consonant with the whole Judeo-Christian tradition; the thinking of the Justices is not. It is important that churchmen in defending the rights of oppressed groups not only realize that basic human rights according to the Judeo-Christian tradition are more than civil rights, but that in this tradition there must always be a proper ordering of these rights. As examples, the right to life is more important than the right to property, and freedom of conscience is more basic than freedom of assembly, though all such rights are worthy of the churchmen's loyalty.

# Virtue

The churches have always had the mission to foster the virtue of the people, the virtue deemed so necessary in a democracy by the Founders. The efforts of the churches in this area have been a constant gift to the general welfare of the nation. But there have been selective preaching and teaching. The abuses of alcohol and sex have had their share of attention. Yet one capital vice condemned in the Judeo-Christian tradition has been generally ignored by the churches: that vice is avarice. The Founders were very strong on the principle that the right to property is an inalienable right. The profit motive is necessary to American capitalism; but the lust for unlimited profits was an American vice at the time of the Founding Fathers and so remains. That this lust for profit can destroy other human rights has not been faced by the churches.

Churchmen have been part of the American public which has allowed the profit motive to be glorified at the expense of the workingman, the consumers, the environment. What churches have condemned the rape of Appalachia as the result of the avarice of coal producers? But businessmen, we are told, are not the only culprits in the search for unlimited gain. How often have churchmen pointed out that the demand for ever-increasing wages by unions powerful enough to enforce their demands can be an injustice to owners unable to meet the demands? More than one newspaper, to cite an example, has been destroyed by such union tactics. The public also is injured when wage demands force prices beyond the value of the commodity. The theory that the "bargaining table" in labor-management relations automatically achieves justice (especially when the rights of the public are not represented at the table) is simply not true: both sides are often motivated by avarice. One wonders whether the Fathers, if they were living now and could see the results of the lust for profit, would have thought these by-products of the right to private property and the natural freedom to bargain, are products proper to a virtuous people. Any areas which affect justice and morality should be areas of interest and activity for churchmen.

# chapter 11

## THE SCHOOLS

Just as churches and clergymen are natural leaders in society and therefore must take responsibility for the direction in which the people go, so schools and educators bear a proportionate share of responsibility. Church, school and home develop the young; the young of today are the adults of tomorrow, adults who will be moral or immoral, clear-sighted or confused, people known for character and stability, or decaying people. This is an examination of conscience; we are bypassing evidences of achievement and concentrating on what is wrong in the schools to see if there is some indication that to the extent we are not following the Founding Fathers' philosophy we have one cause of present school problems, with a consequent spillover to a troubled society.

### God (And The Teaching Of Religion)

"We are a religious people whose institutions presuppose a Supreme Being." The Supreme Court has repeatedly stated this but has created an anomaly of history by being the major cause that God is not presupposed by one of the greatest American institutions, the public-school system. Due to an unhistorical interpretation of the meaning of the First Amendment, positive teaching on the existence and nature of God, as well as on religion and religious beliefs as they have been historically used to form good character,

94

has been virtually eliminated from our tax-supported school system. Many educators believe this to be good but such was not considered a principle of sound education by the Founding Fathers. As one example, Washington's statement to posterity is utterly clear: "Of all the dispositions and habits which lead to political prosperity, Religion and morality are indispensible supports. — In vain would that man claim the tribute of Patriotism, who should labour to subvert these great pillars of human happiness, these firmest props of the duties of men & citizens. . . . And let us with caution indulge the supposition, that morality can be maintained without religion. Whatever may be conceded to the influence of refined education on minds of peculiar structure — reason & experience both forbid us to expect that national morality can prevail in exclusion of religious principle. . . . Promote, then, as an object of primary importance, institutions for the general diffusion of knowledge. In proportion as the structure of government gives force to public opinion, it is essential that public opinion should be enlightened."

Tax-supported education as implemented today is contrary to our founding principles. All the schools, whether private or public, in the Founders' day were religious schools; this was considered as the only sound way to educate.[1] Sometimes it was the local minister who was also the school teacher, but lay or clerical the teacher gave fundamentals about God, the Bible, morality. Freedom of religion would be protected easily enough when the minister was also teaching his own church members, or when the teacher was under the surveillance of local people. The drift toward secularizing the schools started after the first third of the nineteenth century.

There are ways to promote the teaching of morality and religion by cooperation between church and public school within the American tradition of separation of church and state. Illinois made a great effort in this direction when it legislated that ministers of all religions would be permitted to teach their own church members in public schools during regular school hours. The Champaign Board of Education worked out a practical system whereby public-school and religious-group authorities set up a program to teach religion for thirty minutes each week to children of parents who so desired it. In 1948 this was challenged by one Vashti McCollum to be against the First Amendment.[2] The case went to the Supreme Court and the Illinois statute was declared unconstitutional. Justice Reed's dissenting opinion deserves now to be reread; he was clearly in line with the thinking of the Founding Fathers, while the majority were not. The Supreme Court has many times reversed itself when previous decisions were proven harmful to the country. It is time for educators and churchmen to get together to press for a reversal of McCollum vs. Board of Education. It does not seem possible that the oft-repeated dictum of the Supreme Court, "We are a religious people whose institutions presuppose a Supreme Being," should not be reflected in that great American institution, the public-school system.

## Natural Moral Law Vs. Subjectivism

It has already been pointed out that the principles and ideals of the Founding Fathers are not taught in our schools; typical high-school texts are gravely deficient even in teaching the historical fact that the Fathers believed all men were governed by the same moral code, a code written in human nature itself. In the public schools, — inhibited by the wall of separation between church and state as it is presently interpreted by the Supreme Court — there can be little positive teaching of moral principles, since morality is intertwined with religion. But what is the reason for omitting the historical fact that our country was founded on a clear-cut philosophy or morality, that this philosophy proclaimed a natural moral law which taught respect for human rights and human dignity, respect for property, for authority, that happiness and virtue go hand in hand?

A sample of what is substituted for the positive teaching of a moral code in our public schools is given in a book issued in the Fall of 1969 by the University of the State of New York, the State Education Department, Division of Higher Education, Albany, New York. It is entitled: *Special Issue on Psychological Humanistic Education.* There is a statement on page IV of the introduction to the effect that the opinions expressed do not necessarily reflect those of the New York State Education Department, but the book

96

surely indicates what can happen when educators violate the principles of the Founding Fathers that religion, morality and sound education are inseparable.

The title, *Psychological Humanistic Education,* would imply a secularist approach — that this book on education will not rely on God as a starting point, or religion as part of the matrix of education.

The sixth section, "Promoting the Search for Values," was written by Dr. Sidney B. Simon of Temple University. Dr. Simon begins: "It is value, ultimately, which gives a man the stars by which he steers his life; yet the schools are doing almost nothing to help young people make any sense out of the clamoring and bewildering appeals running rampant in these baffling times. The old 'shalt nots' simply refuse to retain relevance in 1969."

To Dr. Simon the Ten Commandments lack relevance today; to the Founding Fathers they had eternal relevance; our civilization was built upon them as absolutes. "Thou shalt not kill" is another way of saying each man has an inalienable right to his life. "Thou shalt not steal" gives a man the right to his honestly owned property; he may not steal from another, but by the same token the thousands with whom he comes into contact cannot steal from him. "Thou shalt not commit adultery" protects family life. "Thou shalt not bear false witness" requires truth in our social contacts. Upon these and other moral obligations American civilization is built. If such basic values disappear our civilization itself will collapse; when respect for life, honesty, family life and truth cease to be guiding stars there is no compass that can point away from the shoals of social chaos.

"Everyone is for values," Simon continues. "Every set of objectives has a platitude or two about them. The problem has been what to do about them in the classroom. Telling students which are the right and good values has been the most common approach to the values problem. At a higher level, there have been attempts to demonstrate with exemplary lives something about values, but still something has been missing. Values need to be more than verbal responses if they are to be truly significant and beautiful in real

97

lives. One mouths 'shoulds,' but values must penetrate to the far corners of one's waking days. *Consequently, teachers cannot afford to waste time on the transmission of values. Values just don't transmit, but they can be learned.*"[3] (Emphasis author's.)

From this point on, Dr. Simon — who is unwilling (and perhaps unable because of Supreme Court decisions?) to transmit the moral standards of the Founding Fathers by positive teaching (that is, telling a pupil murder is wrong, stealing is a vice, lying and adultery are morally evil) — advocates a method which leads to the morass of subjectivism. He encourages students to establish their own values; the guiding stars common to American civilization are lost. He calls this a process of value-clarification. "Value-clarification involves a series of strategies which are not guilty of forcing one set of right values down the throats of all students. Instead, it tends to raise issues to confront the student with inconsistencies, and to get him to sort out his own values, in his own way, at his own pace."

Among the "strategies for value-clarification" Dr. Simon suggests: Weekly Reaction Sheets, Weekly Values Cards, An Autobiographical Questionnaire, a Time Diary and Confrontation Questioning. Typical questions to be answered by the students on the reaction sheets, biographical questionnaires, etc., are: What was the high point of your week? With whom were you in emphatic disagreement or agreement this week? What are the things you like to do best in your free time? What magazine do you subscribe to with your own money? "Confrontation questions are asked about areas which will ultimately show up in a student's life. . . . The tone is 'what is your position, where do you stand? How did you arrive at that value?' . . ."

In his summary Dr. Simon says: "I have tried to explain seven different value-clarifying strategies. They are methods for helping students to learn values without the teacher getting caught in the bind of moralizing, inculcating, or teaching values."

It is evident that Dr. Simon advocates subjectivism, that each student sets his own standards, creates his own values. It matters not whether a student values honesty, truthfulness, develops a respect for the rights of others, even for the inalienability of another's life. There are no self-evident truths, truths worth fighting for, which must be maintained if American civilization is to endure. The wisdom of Judeo-Christian and Western civilization, the 3,500 years of experience it took to build this civilization, need not be passed to the new generation if today's high-school boys and girls decide they prefer other values. Dr. Simon would have us believe he has done us a favor by devising a method of education which pinpoints the problem created by the elimination of positive religion and moral teaching from the curriculum.

Dr. Simon has pinpointed the problem, and to the extent that tax-supported education does not protect the values upon which the nation was built, it destroys the nation. There was a limit to the pluralism adhered to by the Founding Fathers; all values are not equal, certain ones are "self-evident" and the nation is built upon them. "Of all the dispositions and habits which lead to political prosperity, religion and morality are indispensable supports. In vain would that man claim the tribute of patriotism who should labor to subvert these great pillars of human happiness — these firmest props of the duties of men and citizens. . . . Let it simply be asked," Washington said in his farewell address, "Where is the security for property, for reputation, for life, if the sense of religious obligation desert the oaths which are the instruments of investigation in courts of justice? . . ." Dr. Simon shows the extreme of the absence of moral teaching; he takes its absence for granted. But any curriculum which leaves out religion and morality is to that extent defective by the principles of the Founding Fathers. The situation calls for a reexamination of Justice Reed's position on the method used by the schools in Illinois until overruled by the Supreme Court majority in the McCollum case.

## Virtue Vs. Actual Conditions In Schools And Colleges

The omission of the positive teaching of religion and the natural moral code as such (not just as history), which was desired by the Founding Fathers, is at least a partial cause of the breakdown of discipline and morality in the schools. In this examination of conscience the question implicitly asked is: To what extent are the school conditions due to the lack of religious and moral teaching?

One authority, Charles E. Silberman, in his book *American Education: Success Or Failure?* itemizes conditions in our schools which indicate that the virtue thought especially necessary in a democracy by the Fathers is not being produced by our system of education:

"In a four-month period, for example (November and December of 1968, January and February of 1969), Professor Alan Westin, director of the Center for Research and Education in American Liberties at Columbia University's Teachers College, has reported, some 348 high schools in thirty-eight states and the District of Columbia experienced serious disruption as a result of student protests. The disruptions occurred in every kind of school in every kind of community in every part of the country — in Tucson, Arizona; Edcouch, Texas; Middletown, Connecticut; Billings, Montana; Minneapolis, Minnesota; and Brooklyn, New York, to name only a few. Some 60% of a sample of high school principals surveyed at their annual convention in March, 1969, in fact, reported that they had experienced significant student protests in their schools during the school year.

"Colleges and universities would seem to face equally serious, if somewhat different, problems. As the 1960s were ending, hardly a major institution of higher education had escaped student demonstrations and disturbances, some on a scale amounting almost to insurrection, with acts of violence and sabotage becoming more frequent. The base of this dissent is much broader than had been generally assumed; the relative handful of activists draws support from a surprisingly large minority of students — perhaps as many as 40%. Threats, demands and defections from faculty members were also increasing, sometimes involving faculty grievances unrelated to, or in opposition to, student demands."[4]

Later on Silberman says:

"In the United States, however, unlike such countries as Russia, Germany, China and Japan, young people rarely challenged the legitimacy of their parents', or their universities', or their government's authority. They claim that authority had been abused or that the wrong people were exercising it; at times they simply defied authority. They rarely questioned the legitimacy of authority itself.

"They are questioning it now! Indeed, they are questioning not only the legitimacy but the very concept of authority. 'The most dangerous intellectual aspect of the contemporary scene,' the sociologist Robert A. Nisbet states, is the refusal of the young, and of the would-be young, 'to distinguish between authority and power. They see the one as being as much a threat to liberty as the other. But this way lies madness,' for 'there can be no possible freedom in society apart from authority.' Authority, after all is built into the very fabric of human association."[5]

Again, the Founding Fathers would ask: To what extent is this lack of discipline due to an absence of positive teaching of morality, of religious teaching, of teaching about God?

The *U.S. News & World Report* of June 3, 1974 reports an interesting survey conducted by Daniel Yankelovich, Inc., on the changing attitudes of youth. Results were based on in-depth interviews of 3,522 young people between the ages of sixteen and twenty-five. The change in attitudes over a five-year span implies decaying values among our youth, with decay increasing in proportion to education.

In 1969 45% of college youth thought living a clean, moral life was important; in 1973 it had dropped to 34%. To the same question in 1969, 77% of non-college young people thought a moral life was important and in 1973 the number had gone down to 57%. Patriotism was a very important value to 35% of college youth in 1969; only 19% thought it important in 1973. The same question indicated 60% of non-college youth thought patriotism important in 1969; 40% believed in flag and country in 1973. Religion was an important value for 38% of college students in 1969, as compared to only 28% in 1973; religion on the other hand was imporant to 64% of non-college youth in 1969, and was of vital concern to only 42% in

1973. More sexual freedom would have been advocated by 43% of the college youth of 1969, while such freedom was desired by 61% in 1973; for non-college young people in 1969, 22% wanted more sexual freedom; by 1973, the number had more than doubled, up to 47%. Having an abortion was morally wrong to 36% of the college students in 1969, as compared to 32% in 1973; while 64% of non-college young people thought abortion wrong in 1969, only 48% judged it wrong in 1973.[6]

Clear-cut religious and moral values are being lost, but not all idealism; according to this poll an overwhelming majority of our young people believe political parties are in need of major reforms; they also believe business is too concerned with profits, not enough with public responsibility. But it all apparently indicates that high schools are failing to teach fundamental moral values and colleges are destructive of them.

The changes going on do not imply an increase of happiness among our youth. An article in the August 27, 1973 *U.S. News & World Report* reported that "Between 1965 and 1971, the number of children under 18 getting psychiatric treatment at established mental-health facilities rose by nearly two-thirds — a growth attributed by experts in the field to increasing stress in families, uncertainty about values, and according to one psychiatrist, 'a more automated, less personal society.' "[7]

There is one other statistic which indicated something drastically wrong with the training of our youth. One education magazine estimated that damage and destruction done to U.S. schools by vandals in the school year 1972-73 cost the U.S. taxpayer one-half billion dollars: 260 million dollars for vandalism damage, arson losses and similar property damage, and 240 million to pay for security personnel and equipment. It works out that the cost per pupil for vandalism is about the same spent for textbooks that year. And vandalism is not confined to any particular area. It is a stirring concern in big-city ghettos, affluent suburbs and small country towns.[8]

We ought to ask ourselves also whether the breakdown in education (and in this context, especially in our public schools, since it is in them that positive principles of morality are not allowed to be taught) is part of the reason for the breakdown in society outlined by Attorney General Saxbe to the public safety directors and police chiefs from most of the large cities on August 27, 1974:

"He also noted that in the final quarter of 1973 crime had risen 16 per cent above the rate of that quarter in 1972 and in the first quarter of 1974 15 per cent above the first quarter of 1973. . . .

"He lashed out at the social climate of America, charging that permissiveness was rampant, that parents 'often' failed to teach or poorly disciplined their children, that alcoholism was 'our major health problem,' and that pornography had 'become as widespread as baseball.' "[9]

This is a moment of truth. It does no good to defend the secularism in our tax-supported schools because many sincere educators thought that education could be separated from religion, that home and church would be sufficient to teach morality, that teachers by good example and indirect methods could develop sound characters. This is not to condemn the sincerity or personal integrity of educators. Experience has now taught us something is wrong. The Founding Fathers deserve a hearing on their insistence that education cannot be separated from religion and positive criteria of morality if good men and women, and therefore good citizens, are to be formed. They saw with remarkable clarity that the freer a society is, the more democratic the nation, the higher must be the grade of private and public morality. It is not difficult to have law and order in an authoritarian society. When, however, liberty and license are confused, when physical freedom is confused with moral freedom, a free society carries within itself its self-destruct mechanism. This is the destiny of a society guided by secularist education in the thinking of the Founding Fathers.

# chapter 12

# THE COMMUNICATIONS MEDIA

The schools are not the only channels of education today; there is another segment of American leadership which guides the American people along the paths they follow. Charles Silberman in his book, referred to in the foregoing chapter, quotes a distinguished authority to indicate the extraordinary influence of the communications media:

" 'When we look realistically at the world in which we are living today and become aware of what the actual problems of learning are,' the anthropologist Margaret Mead wrote in 1958, 'our conception of education changes radically. . . . We are no longer dealing primarily with the *vertical* transmission of the tried and true by the old, mature, and experienced teachers to the young, immature, and inexperienced pupil. This was the system of education developed in a stable, slowly changing culture. In a world of rapid change, vertical transmission of knowledge alone is not enough. What is needed, . . . and what we are already moving toward is the inclusion of another whole dimension of learning: the *lateral* transmission, to every sentient member of society, of what has just been discovered, invented, created, manufactured, or marketed.' The need is acute: 'the whole teaching-and-learning continuum, which was once tied in an orderly and productive way to the passing of generations and the growth of the child into a man — this whole process has exploded in our faces.' "[1]

# Television And Radio

What Dr. Mead foresaw in 1958 has happened drastically. Formerly education could be passed down quietly from one generation to the next; the child could be given civilizing principles and values acquired through the ages and his character could be developed before he met the problems of life. Now with TV the child meets the problems, sees and hears the violence, the lack of honesty, the vices and sins of the human race all over the world, along with the achievements of mankind, before he has the maturity to put everything in proper perspective. He takes part vicariously in the landing on the moon; he sees and hears the viciousness and cries of hoodlums and mobs along with police heroism or brutality; he hears the promises of politicians and sees their lack of fulfillment. Before he has been able to appreciate the dignity of human life he is told that the world is overpopulated and that killing the unborn is a reasonable solution.

Every day it is dinned into the child's ear that health is the most important thing in life, and that one infallible product will guarantee it: the wonderful truth that a bad-smelling mouthwash will win friends, that teeth free from cavities, sufficiently white, will attract the opposite sex, that happiness is around the corner if one has the right automobile; all these are pounded home with much more persistence than the multiplication tables were to the last generation. Living TV and, when old enough to read, followed by longer and almost instant press reports is a source of education and character development — or defilement — at least as important as the schools. It is estimated that ninety-seven percent of American homes have television sets, that they are turned on six and one-half hours per day. Students graduating from high school today will have spent more time in front of the video than in the classroom.

This education by TV is a mixture of good and bad. In Silberman's words:

"Television has taken over the mythic role status in our culture; soap operas, situation comedies, Westerns, melodramas, are folk stories or myths that convey and reinforce the values of the society. These programs and, equally important, the commercials that accompany them transmit a large amount of information relative to these values or world view: what people are wearing, how the system works, which occupations have status or promote mobility, how to outsmart authority, what products to consume, and how, and so on. They convey a great deal of information relevant to — perhaps necessary for — socialization of the adult as well as of the child."[2]

Thus we have a factual situation that TV is one of our great educators today, and must share the responsibility for where the people are going. TV (radio in proportion is meant to be included in this critique) requires its examination of conscience according to the standards of the Founding Fathers, in reference especially to three points of their doctrine: the universal moral law which governs all mankind, the basic rights which belong to all men, and the principle that if a democracy is to thrive the people must be virtuous.

## Natural Law And Inalienable Rights

The Founders held there is a moral law which binds right-thinking human beings. To apply it today means that the distinction between liberty and license must be clear in the TV and radio producer's mind, that there are bounds within which, as a human being, he must keep himself. He has no right to break down the morals of society, to glorify crime or criminals, to make vice attractive, to produce plays that advocate even subtly the violent overthrow of society in the Communist sense that out of violence comes progress. The producer has no right to subvert patriotism. He has no right to paint adultery as the road to happiness, or to weaken the family as the unit of society. The best short summary of absolute don'ts in the mind of the Founders would be the Ten Commandments; they are valid guideposts of the boundaries of human liberty today. The Commandments express theologically the same doctrine the Declaration of Independence proclaimed as a philosophy of inalienable rights. Beyond the Commandments lies license, not liberty.

Inalienable rights are derived from the natural moral law. If TV had existed before 1860 and advocated the retention and expansion of slavery, as many newspapers did, it would have violated our founding philosophy; time or circumstances did not change the laws of morality. The Founding Fathers were honest in their opposition to slavery; they did not know how to get rid of it, and the Founders held the right to life more precious than the right to liberty. Part of the confusion in the people's minds today (the portion especially which confuses legality with morality) can be blamed directly on television. As an example, this happens whenever a TV program gives a favorable impression of abortion without pointing out the grave ethical problems involved or the fact that for the first time in our history the right to life itself has been destroyed with the acquiescence of law. The TV producer who fosters the spread of abortion today ought to ask himself whether the Blackmun decision gives him any more right to propagandize abortion than the Dred Scott decision gave the pre-Civil War editor the moral right to advocate the extension of slavery.

It is evident that the rapid growth of world population is a problem which should concern thinking people. It should also be evident that much written about the "population explosion" is scare propaganda; but the problem is real. It is axiomatic that any means taken to lower the rate of increase of population should be humane and moral. We do not want wars or famine, but we must not undermine the base of civilization by using inhuman or immoral means. Any method such as abortion which destroys the principle that each innocent human being has an inalienable right to his life destroys the foundation upon which American civilization is built.

The most blatant use of TV to propagandize the destruction of the unborn as a useful means to diminish population occurred on CBS's situation comedy *Maude*. Middle-aged Maude is not at the time of life when babies are ordinarily welcomed. This prime-time situation comedy tackled her problem and solved it by having the heroine opt for abortion. That a life-and-death situation should be treated as comedy insulted human decency to begin with, but the use of TV to lead the public in a direction contrary to our most sacred principles, without the public knowing what was being done and with no opportunity for the other side to be aired to the same viewers, is insidious.

The magazine *America* gives pertinent information concerning *Maude*. There is a group calling itself the Population Institute, with some tenuous connection to the United Methodist Church. A former national staff member of the United Methodist Church is the Institute's president and its headquarters are in the United Methodist Building in Washington, although one can be sure it does not speak for all Methodists. According to *America:*

"The Population Institute was established in 1969, in order, according to a descriptive brochure it publishes, to 'perform a unique catalytic function in halting population growth.' The Institute lists three general goals of its various activities: 1) 'change population attitudes of . . . adults'; 2) 'guide tomorrow's society toward reduced childbearing by increasing the population information content of the news, entertainment and advertising media'; 3) 'motivate the leaders of the coming generation to further effort, by reaching them both in and out of the classroom.' . . .

"Subsequently, according to the Institute, the Communication Center (of the Institute, based in New York) hosted a 'series of luncheons for other key TV executives with a notable population person speaking at each.' It also enlisted the National Academy of Television Arts and Sciences as a 'sponsor of TV population education.' In the winter of 1971-72, it conducted two-day conferences in Los Angeles and New York at which 'leading creative people in the TV industry discussed with population experts means whereby population education might be advanced and attitudes changed.'

"The Institute's interest in the television industry has, however, extended beyond sponsoring luncheons and conferences. It has also conducted contests, with substantial cash prizes, for writers and producers of TV shows dealing with population matters. A leaflet describing the current competition lists cash awards for script writers of $10,000 for 'the best prime-time entertainment of

60 minutes or longer,' $5,000 for 'the best half-hour prime-time entertainment program' and $5,000 for the best day-time serial episode or series of episodes.' A separate competition offers a $10,000 prize to producers of 'evening entertainment television programming.'

"In the estimate of the Population Institute its efforts have paid off. Its brochure states: 'Results from the (Communication) Center's conferences and contests cannot, of course, be traced in full detail, nor until more time has elapsed can their impact be felt. But a substantial reduction of pregnancies on "soap opera" TV has already been noted. And the producer of *Maude,* a highly rated program, has made it clear that the attention his scripts have given to abortion and vasectomy originated in his attendance at the first of the conferences.'

"Other sources tend to confirm the Population Institute's view that its efforts had an impact on *Maude.* The Dec. 10, 1972 entertainment section of the Sunday *New York Times* carried an interview with Norman Lear, producer of *Maude.* Quoting him as saying that in 1972 'half a dozen writers came in with late-life pregnancy ideas,' reporter Aljean Harmetz adds: 'Writers were probably prodded to look into the areas of vasectomy and abortion by a $5,000 prize offered by Population Institute for the best 30-minute script on population control produced on prime-time television between September, 1972 and June, 1973.' However, she emphasizes, it was Mr. Lear's own decision to have Maude herself, rather than some other character in the series, become pregnant and have an abortion.

"A further comment on the subject comes from the Pathfinder Fund, a Boston-based foundation active in the population field. Its January, 1973 *Family Plans* newsletter carries an item reporting the *Maude* episodes on abortion and vasectomy. 'The inclusion of these unusual topics,' it states, 'was the direct result of a program of the Population Institute to make the TV industry aware of the ways in which its programming may affect people's attitudes toward the population problem, and the factors which may alleviate it. . . . What better way to dramatize and gain acceptance for vasectomy and abortion than to have them used on a TV show which goes at prime time into nearly 20 million homes across the nation? The Population Institute is to be congratulated.' "[3]

With such an insidious approach to creating attitudes in an unsuspecting public it is not surprising that a pregnant high-school girl will solve her problem by the easy but character-destroying method of abortion. TV is a biased educator at its worst here; the unsuspecting public is victimized by one-sided propaganda, neither being told that it is propaganda nor that the solution violates the Judeo-Christian ethics upon which our civilization is built.

According to our founding philosophy, TV producers have no right to substitute their private opinions for the absolutes of the natural moral law, to confuse legitimate liberty with license. They have no right to advocate the violation of any inalienable human right such as those to life or liberty. The Fathers shed their blood rather than agree to this; and they built the nation on the principle that the first obligation of government is to protect these rights.

## Virtue

The third principle held by the Founders which particularly apply to TV producers is the thesis that a democracy can only be built on a virtuous, moral people. A corollary to this thesis was the working principle that moral training must always be part of education. But it also follows that educators as such are not the only ones responsible for the health of democratic society in the sense that they alone educate toward morality, or immorality. In proportion that a group influences public opinion, to that extent must it be responsible for what it does to the thinking which motivates and guides our people. The television industry is always an educator, always a maker of public opinion, and so always must be responsible for its acts.

The whole *Maude* incident illustrates a technique for changing the moral principles of society drastically and quickly. It is almost terrifying to think that ten years ago an abortionist doctor was despised in his profession, and was an outcast in society; now he is a

110

hero to some segments of the people. What changed public opinion so rapidly, when the ethics of abortion were never really analyzed, when the fact that abortion is an attack on American civilization was almost never mentioned? The mass media accomplished this; it is an example of the terrifying power of the lateral transfer of knowledge indicated by Margaret Mead. Yet when this power is broken through there is evidence that the people do see the depths of the problem, do see the evil involved. Michigan and North Dakota had grass-roots debates concerning abortion in 1972 because referenda to legalize it were put on the election ballots of those states. When the people got an in-depth view they voted overwhelmingly against its legalization: 80% vs. 20% in North Dakota, 61% vs. 39% in Michigan. The mass media are always an educator but not always a responsible educator; when given an opportunity the people think more deeply. With almost no analysis the media tend to spread the current popular interest, the current novel idea; the implications of the idea do not always make for entertaining programs.

The clergy as a group feel responsible for public morality; so do the police. Doctors as a group accept their responsibility for public health. Yet the responsibility for public morality and public health ought to be a concern of all. TV as a powerful educator should help people to be moral citizens. The constant diet of crime drama, violence on prime time, or family triangles on soap operas are not contributions to morality. . . . The Fathers were convinced that democracy could survive only if the people keep high moral standards; the people deserve inspiration for high ideals, not desecration of the standards on which the country was founded.

Perhaps one example of news handling (in contrast to entertainment) without a sense of responsibility for the long-range effect will also indicate the impact of TV on public morality. Howard K. Smith, national anchor man for ABC, in late July, 1974, commented on a report that nudity was spreading (to the dismay of local police) on one of the California beaches. He said it with half a smile, and it was accompanied by living pictures, taken at a discreet distance, of course. The situation was not without humor: why in heaven's name would people want to run around like their primate ancestors? Mr. Smith is one of the best commentators, ordinarily balanced, incisive; and here was an item which perhaps only illustrates the foibles of humanity. But a little in-depth thinking: through long centuries of history all civilizations have somehow come to the realization that men and women relate better to one another when clothed. In the Judeo-Christian tradition this modesty in clothing has been recognized as a protection for the virtue of chastity, for morality. There is always something relative about modesty; what is modest in mid-Africa might be immodest in New York; and surely there is no need to keep prudish Victorian styles. But nudity is something else. There is nothing relative here; the common sense of all civilizations, the Judeo-Christian tradition to which we belong, has rejected it as dangerous.

But there were some thirty million people watching and hearing Howard K. Smith that night. If only two out of each thousand would be inspired to follow the liberated Californians, it means that 60,000 viewers from all parts of the country will be trying nudity out on beaches from Florida to New York, or on lakeshores from Maine to Oregon. (The first Broadway play to get away with nudity was performed in New York only about ten years ago; the stage and movie screen show such scenes with great abandon now all over the country.) The police will have problems nationwide, as the police in California have now. California neighbors were demoralized; one resident close to the California beach where it was occurring put it to a reporter of a newsmagazine that characters came equipped with binoculars, and the neighbors had to contend with "perverts watching perverts watching perverts."

This is where the lack of responsibility of Mr. Smith and his news team shows up. The reduction of speed on our highways to 55 miles per hour due to the energy crisis has resulted in a decrease in the death rate from auto accidents amounting to about twenty-five percent. Just as surely as traffic accidents went down with the speed limit, just that surely can we expect that the incidence of rape will go up with the upsurge of nudity on beaches. How much does it take to trigger a pervert with binoculars? Rape is no laughing matter. Where was the sense of responsibility of the ABC news team on this occasion?

It is unfortunate to have to criticize TV newscasters who ordinarily are responsible. They are a better part of an industry which has failed the country badly. Thomas Griffith, an editor of *Life* magazine for four years and previously one of *Time's* top editors, summarizes the situation caustically:

"The most immediate medium ever invented is now largely a conduit for canned films, canned commercials, reruns, old movies and live sports. Networks have built their fortunes around government-granted exclusivity to the public air which they did not have to pay the government for; they relentlessly compete at the lowest common denominator in programming; they play the Washington lobby game for all its worth; they are arrogant in their disdain for those who question how they fulfill their public obligations.

"Television has left its mark on a generation raised in front of this seductive monster, this shifting parade of images and emotions, all separated by a demanding succession of commercial impulses that trivialize what precedes and what follows it — is it any wonder that a generation that has spent more hours before the television set than in school should be different, should be such amalgams of knowledge and cynicism, and have such little integrity of belief? Should seem united in only in what it rejects and uplifted only by a succession of sensations? Television has raised a generation inexperienced and vicariously knowledgeable — the perfect audience."[4]

The impact of TV on the people is measureless. In principle the airwaves belong to the people, not to the networks. No private person or corporation should or could own the airwaves any more than the air can be owned. And as the air can be polluted physically, the airwaves can be polluted morally. In theory the British system is better; the people own the airwaves, therefore the people's government should keep broadcasting as a public monopoly. The direct power of the people can be brought to bear on TV and radio programs. But the Founding Fathers were rightfully afraid of government censorship of the press, and we should be afraid of government control of broadcasting. Yet if the broadcasting industry does not measure up to its responsibilities, if our people and represent-

113

atives come to the conclusion that lack of responsibility in the broadcasting industry is lowering the moral tone of the nation, not positively contributing to public morality, such a step should be considered, with built-in checks to prevent Big Brother from brainwashing us. TV and radio are as much a public trust as are the schools. The only mentality legitimate for the industry is to remember that this public trust is more important than profits.

## *The Press*

If the impact of the broadcasting industry on the moral tone of the people requires that its leadership foster morality, the same is equally true of its companion in communications, the press. TV and radio have a strong impact through repeated brief encounters with the people; the press, newspapers and magazines, oftentimes create a deeper impression because what it says can be read and reread. The same three criteria which were used to judge TV and radio can be applied to the press. According to the principles of the Founders the editors and publishers are subject to the same natural moral law which obliges all men and required TV and radio producers to make a clear distinction between their legitimate liberty and illegitimate license in what they give to the public. No editor has more of a right to advocate the violation of the absolutes of the Ten Commandments than does the TV producer. Likewise no writer has the privilege of pressing for the destruction of inalienable rights. And because democracy relies more on a virtuous people than do other forms of government, newsmen who influence the public must try to do it in the direction of virtue. With the proper changes understood most of what was said above concerning TV applies also to the press.

The press has its own unique place in American history. We had a tradition of freedom of the press inherited from Britain when the Contitution was framed: "Liberty of the press consists in laying no *previous* restraints upon publications, and not in freedom from censure for criminal matter when published"[5] was Blackstone's definition; thus censorship was the thing to be avoided — with the risk of

114

a libel suit to guarantee what was written. But the Sedition Act of 1798 retained the common-law feature of "seditious libel" which operated to put persons in authority beyond the reach of public criticism. This did not restrain the obstreperous editors of the time from writing in vivid language by any man's terms.

President Adams was able to put some critics in jail; this backfired and helped Jefferson win the election of 1800. But Jefferson in office wanted the protection of the same legal principle, and wrote: "The federalists having failed in destroying freedom of the press by their gag-law, seem to have attacked it in an opposite direction; that is, by pushing its licentiousness and its lying to such a degree of prostitution as to deprive it of all credit. . . . This is a dangerous state of things, and the press ought to be restored to its credibility if possible. The restraints provided by the laws of the States are sufficient for this, if applied. . . ."[6] Jefferson suggested a few prosecutions of prominent offenders "would have a wholesome effect in restoring the integrity of the presses." It does seem as if the problem was, whose ox is gored? To Hamilton is given credit for phrasing freedom of the press as it has come down in American history: "The liberty of the press is the right to publish with impunity, truth, with good motives, for justifiable ends, though reflecting on government, magistracy, or individuals."[7]

It is interesting to note that Blackstone's common-law principle, Jefferson's idea of what a free press should be, and Hamilton's wording which became the basic American principle, all imply liberty, not license. According to Blackstone there was to be no previous censorship, but not freedom from court prosecution when criminal matter was published. To Jefferson it was possible for the press "by pushing its licentiousness and its lying to such a degree of prostitution as to deprive it of all credit." And for Hamilton the press could only "publish with impunity, truth, with good motives, for justifiable ends."

In Edward S. Corwin's *The Constitution and What It Means Today,* the most authoritative brief commentary on the Constitution, Hamilton's dictum is called a brocard which is today repeated in twenty-four state constitutions. Thus Hamilton coined what amounts to a "brief maxim, rule, or proverb in philosophy, ethics or

115

law." In this case we have a rule of law based on philosophy, ethics. "The liberty of the press is the right to publish with impunity, *truth, with good motives, for justifiable ends,* though reflecting on government, magistracy, or individuals." (Emphasis author's.)

The key word is *truth.* The most obvious application of the principle is that no lie can knowingly be published, no fact maliciously tampered with. But there is another application of Hamilton's maxim for freedom of the press. According to the Declaration of Independence, "We hold these *truths* to be self-evident, that all men are created equal, that they are endowed by their Creator with certain unalienable Rights, that among these are Life, Liberty and the pursuit of Happiness. . . ." (Emphasis author's.) It is not only that lies or distorted facts must be avoided; according to the Founding Fathers there are certain basic truths which must guide men, including editors and reporters and publishers, and at all times. Our civilization is built upon certain truths. Of its nature it would be a greater crime to attack these truths than to publish lies. Freedom of the press lies upon a foundation of truths that all men are equal, that each has rights which belong to men as men.

If our civilization is built upon certain self-evident truths for which the Founders fought and died, in other aspects of human experience life is a search for truth. In this search each man has a right to his own opinion, to learn from the opinions of others, to express his opinion without heed from government. In back of the founding philosophy is the conviction that such a search for truth is legitimate. Madison's *Remonstrance* and Jefferson's *Bill to Establish Religious Liberty* are eloquent in their implicit defense of the search for religious truth.

## Natural Law

The Fathers were also convinced that they had reached some moral truths, some moral absolutes. No man had a right to deprive his innocent neighbor of life, of honestly owned property, of liberty. Nor could an editor advocate that these things be done. Basically an editor would be held to stay within the Ten Commandments in

116

his causes. The basic opposition of the Founders to the morality of today's secular society would be to the proposition that all morality is relative, that each individual or group can set its own standards, that there are none common to human nature in general. Implicitly, too, the Fathers condemn ideologies and actions based on such relativity, v.g., the Nazi murder of the Jews, the Communist habit of distortion of truth and language in presenting national policies to the world. An act does not become moral because some individual or group says it is moral. Somewhere along the line one must ask himself, "What is fitting to humanity as such?" The writing which undermines morality by claiming there are no universal moral laws is much more dangerous than pornography when judged by the Founding Fathers' standards.

We are back to the foundation principle that there is a natural moral law which governs all men and which must govern journalists also. It is not difficult to find violations of this principle in the press. In the Sunday, August 18, 1974, edition of the *New York Times* there was a long article by Urjo Kareda, drama critic of the *Toronto Star,* entitled "Is There Any Future for Bad Taste?" The writer says the bad-taste movement seems to be waning for commercial movies. What is pernicious about the article is its projection of what constitutes bad taste: the most serious violations of the moral law are merely bad taste, violations of the "taboos" of society, put on the same level as mere vulgarities.

"Every society has its unspoken taboos," Kareda says. "They linger in the twilight of public consciousness until something called bad taste brings them into the open. Bad taste triggers a kind of shock by the very fact that the unspeakable has been spoken, the unpresentable presented." . . . "In American above-ground films, the pioneers (of 'bad taste') have been comedian-directors like Woody Allen, with his skits about bestiality, transvestism and rabbis with pork-fixations in 'Everything You Always Wanted to Know About Sex,' and Mel Brooks, with his 'Springtime for Hitler' musical numbers in 'The Producers.' " . . . "Roman Polanski's 'Chinatown,' for instance, seems almost desperate in its eagerness to discover a taboo which might still startle us. The view of 1930's

117

California is so overgrown with corruption and decay that the film's structure needs that final de luxe frisson. What screen writer Robert Towne finally comes up with is incest, presumably thinking it one of the few remaining sexual taboos with the power to alarm us." "However," Kareda continues, "since incest in drama is usually recollected rather than enacted, it usually has no shock effect; even if it were enacted in 'Chinatown,' it probably wouldn't rock us, unless the actors playing the secret lovers happen to be related in real life. (The melodramatic revelation of the incestuous relationship between John Huston and Faye Dunaway [Kareda goes on] strikes us as an affectation, but what if Henry Fonda and Jane Fonda had played the father and daughter roles?)

"On its limpest level, this new approach (to bad taste) is exemplified by the black cleaning woman in 'For Pete's Sake,'" Kareda pursues his thought. "The character sarcastically announces her arrival with the statement, 'It's the colored woman,' works through the cliches of shiftlessness by demonstrating an unwillingness to do anything much besides eating lunch, and then informs Barbra Streisand that she herself couldn't afford a white cleaning lady but has hired a Puerto Rican." . . . "In 'Blazing Saddles,' however, director Mel Brooks seems to be striving for complete, rather than partial, offensiveness. The film studiously insults every special-interest group; it hits out at black men, white women, Indians, Jews, and it even takes a few extra minutes at the end to ridicule homosexuals and — if I am not mistaken — Esther Williams. It invites us to laugh at the unspoken social taboos — as in the 'Hallelujah' chorus scene, where a band of men break wind after a bean dinner around the campfire — and at people who have the misfortune of being aged or unattractive or physically handicapped."[8]

Of course, all the examples given by Kareda are in bad taste (as is his article and the *New York Times* for printing it); but what are we to believe about the thought patterns of a writer who levels bestiality with a black who caricatures her race to teach whites a lesson, who equalizes incest with cowboys who let nature work around a campfire? Are these equally silly taboos of society from which

118

these movie directors are liberating society? Is incest merely a taboo of society on a level with vulgarity?

To the Founding Fathers the natural moral law was a unity imposed by God on the human race to make social living possible. Whether expressed as the Ten Commandments or a list of inalienable rights (and inherent obligations) all parts obliged all men. The Commandment may say, "Thou shalt not kill," and murder was punishable with death; but its corollaries for lesser crimes were eye for eye, tooth for tooth, limb for limb. The Old Testament morality, while not followed in the severity of its punishments, which decreed death for adultery, for incest, for bestiality, taught the Founding Fathers the evil of sin and the nature of morality. Later Jewish or Christian teaching did not require an eye for an eye, nor decree death for adultery; but it never changed the evil nature of the acts committed against the law.

It is this same unchanged nature of morality which judged the Nazi gas-chamber murders as evil though legal to the Nazi mentality; it is this unchanged nature of morality which condemns Communist lies (or any lies!) though such could be justified by Lenin's teaching on the nature of Communist morality. It is this whole system of moral truths of the Founding Fathers which is under attack when incest, bestiality and adultery are listed as merely taboos for *Times'* readers. Insofar as the *New York Times* is one among other papers and magazines which deny there are universal moral principles binding all men, it as the leader symbolizes a moral relativity condemned by the philosophy of the Founding Fathers.

thou shalt not is an
absolute

## Natural Rights Vs. Advocacy Journalism

The Founders held that all men, as individuals, had inalienable rights; and the primordial right belonging to each was the right to life itself. This right is being attacked today in the press by the newspapers and magazines which advocate abortion. There is a type of journalism today which is called, not without reason, advocacy journalism; liberalized abortion, the denial of the protection of civil law to unborn humans is one of the major "causes" of advocacy

119

journalism. According to Thomas Griffith, former editor of *Life* magazine, "Advocacy journalists, the other branch of the new journalism, are not fictionalists, but polemicists. They believe all journalism bloodless that isn't pushing a thesis, are never content to describe or explain a situation but get in front of the reader pointing out who are the black hats and who are the white hats, tediously moralizing and making their own virtues and bravery perfectly evident."[9]

A newsletter put out by the Mindszenty Foundation of St. Louis, Missouri, has this to say: " 'Advocacy journalism' — the creation and propagation of what is news — has backfired. Although editors attending the important 1974 Pennsylvania Society of Newspaper Editors seminar voiced objections to 'advocacy journalism' the practice continues to grow and thrive. Private citizens — including former journalists — are now counterattacking distorted and manufactured 'news' through organizations such as 'Accuracy in Media' (AIM) and winning important battles."[10]

Advocacy journalism in one sense is not new; the abolitionist journals before the Civil War were certainly advocating a cause, the right to liberty. What seems to be new is that advocacy journalism now often amounts to "slanted" news; it is given as news, and the public is not informed that it is promoting a cause. Thomas Griffith in his book, *How True (A Skeptic's Guide to Believing the News)*, writes that when he was the editor in charge of national affairs for *Time* magazine, Henry Luce, *Time's* publisher, wanted his Republicanism more explicit in the magazine. This was not Griffith's way, and "... I early learned not to write defensively against Luce's known prejudices, for the result always failed in its wishy-washiness. Best to write as forcefully as you could what you thought was right, counting on your facts to carry the day."[11] He mentioned that some writers tried sly tricks to counteract Luce: "A writer on *Life* was much admired by some when he diminished the effect of a laudatory article on Dewey (Thomas E., presidential candidate in 1948) by noting deadpan in a picture caption that Dewey, at his governor's desk, was sitting on a telephone book to increase his height."[12]

Again abortion as an example. This major "cause" propagated

by advocacy journalism today is an attack on the right to life held by the Founding Fathers as the primordial right of American society. There was a national protest a year after the Supreme Court decision of January 22, 1973 took the protection of state laws from the unborn. In Washington a crowd estimated between 15,000-20,000 formed a gigantic "ring of life" around the Capitol building, holding hands and standing ten abreast. *Time* and *Newsweek* downplayed this demonstration by concentrating on a counter-demonstration of a handful of radical feminists gathered on the steps of St. Patrick's Cathedral in New York, with one of their members who declared herself "Pope Patricia I." Pictures of Patricia I appeared in both magazines; but there was not one single picture of the Washington demonstrators. And in the *New York Times'* account of Washington happenings, the pro-life group was reported as 5,000 strong.

Perhaps a perfect example of abortion advocacy reporting occurred in an article by Richard E. Behrman, M.D., in the *New York Times* of June 9, 1974:

"Current efforts to prohibit or significantly limit research involving fetuses and infants seriously jeopardize the health and welfare of our children and of our children's children. Senate and House conferees have agreed on legislation banning for four months research on the living human fetus, either in the uterus or after abortion, unless the research is to save the fetus's life. . . . Instead of providing appropriate safeguards from real, though infrequent, abuses by a few investigators," Behrman continues, "these initiatives and recent court actions to prohibit fetal research are likely to severely limit our ability not only to protect children from serious illness but also to promote their optimum growth and development. It may not have been sufficiently communicated to the public and people in positions of political responsibility that the prevention and treatment of diseases that threaten children's health and survival depend especially on fetal and infant research."

Behrman's article states further:

"Those who oppose legal abortions have been some of the

major supporters of prohibitions against fetal research. However, the *goal of fetal research is to preserve the right to life in its fullest sense* by preventing and curing disease. In some instances, research may even eliminate the need for therapeutic abortion. Ethical safeguards are essential in medical investigation. The preservation of life and the treatment of injury are the only ethical and legal bases for physician-scientists to carry out research on a human baby, premature infant or fetus who is developed enough to survive outside the uterus."[13] (Emphasis author's.)

Dr. Behrman is more frank than most of the people who favor abortion since he implies willingness to "carry out research on a human baby, premature infant or fetus who is developed enough to survive outside the uterus." Very often the word "fetus" is used as if it were not a human being; Dr. Behrman makes no distinction in the use of baby, premature infant and fetus, treating them synonymously. But "to carry out research on" is a euphemism for "to experiment with."

The doctor implies that the oldest of ethical fallacies is good ethics: the end justifies the means. This is the ethical principle the Nazis followed in their medical experimentation on human beings. The parallel is complete if one thinks of Nazi victims already destined for destruction rendered unconscious first so that, like a fetus or baby, they would not know what was happening, and provided medicine would learn something the doctor considered useful. The American founding principle is that all human beings are equal in their rights; the unborn or born baby has as much right to its life, health and limbs as the future child (hopefully) to be saved by knowledge gathered by sacrificing the helpless subject of the experiment. We must not forget the progression followed by the medical profession in Germany during Hitler's 1930s: life lost its sanctity when the doctors cooperated in gassing 300,000 mental patients to destroy "life devoid of value";[14] later these same gas ovens were used to kill an uncounted number of Jewish victims in "the final solution."

Of course, neither Dr. Behrman nor the *New York Times* adhere even remotely to the Nazi philosophy. Yet the whole situation cries for a paraphrasing of Hamilton when at the time of the Revolution he tried to demonstrate to a Tory clergyman that there must be a universal moral law which preexists civil law. Hamilton argued that the cleric Seabury adhered to doctrines which could only be justified by the atheism of Thomas Hobbes: "As you, sometimes, swear by HIM THAT MADE YOU I conclude, your sentiment does not correspond with his; in that which is the basis of his doctrine you both agree in; and this makes it impossible to imagine whence this congruity between you arises." It is logically impossible to imagine whence the congruity among the *New York Times,* Behrman and Nazism arises — all see the principle that the end justifies the means is sound ethics.

In review, the first criterion of conscience to judge the press is the recognition by editors and publishers that they are bound by the natural moral law if they are to stay within the boundaries of liberty, not transgress into license. The second standard of the Fathers is the adherence of the press to the equality of men, to the inalienable rights that belong to each member of the human race, with the right to life understood as the primordial right; propagating any other doctrine violates the Founders' philosophy.

## Virtue

The third principle for this examination is the Fathers' conviction that a democratic people must be virtuous. Therefore, if the press contributes to public morality it is aiding the nation; if its effect is the opposite, to that extent it stands condemned. With the exception of religious publications, many newspapers and magazines seem not to have any sense of obligation toward lifting the moral tone of society. This does not mean there is a conscious intention to lower morality; but today most editors would probably be amazed at such an old-fashioned idea that one of their functions is to strengthen morality. There is little evidence to suggest any positive effort toward decency; there is much evidence that the press is willing to make a profit on items which lower community standards.

One can think of the widespread publicity given to the huge number of movies and plays which offend morality. The losing fight of the Legion of Decency some years ago, the saturation of R-rated and X-rated films at the present illustrate this. The readiness of editors to defend pornography as freedom of the press, the uphill fight of police officials and concerned citizens to stem the tide of obscenity, the refusal to separate liberty from license in articles on the subject, point in the same direction. The juicier scandals make the headlines on the front page, cover the inside of the Sunday supplement. Many newspapers and magazines cater to the lowest instincts as a matter of course.

Thomas Griffith, as former editor for *Life* and *Time,* sees the problems of journalism from the vantage point of a professional. He writes while viewing a different facet of the craft than that of the obligation of editors and publishers to strengthen public morality; but his statements which follow point to the same failure:

"Journalism professes to tell you what the world is like, but in fact the real message of each day's newspaper is: this is what has *changed* in the world that you know about since last we reported to you. A journalist is in this respect something like a jazz soloist who assumes you already know the tune that he is playing variations upon. And if the newspaper describes a holdup last night on Beacon Street you are to assume, though the paper feels it unnecessary to say, that there were not similar holdups in hundreds of other peaceful streets.

"The result of such omissions, however, is this picture of the world taken from one Sunday *New York Times:*

" 'A bank closed because of embezzlement; a judge killed by criminals; grand jury indictments against prominent officials; reports on shoddy goods, unhonored warranties, cutthroat credit practices, more water, noise and solid-waste pollution; a hi-jacked plane; rising crime, public housing turned into a concentration camp for crime; senseless violence; muggings, a hospital spreading infections.

" 'Speeches, interviews and complaints about drug traffic, corrupt police, discrimination, uncollected garbage, crowded courts, noxious air, traffic jams, protected monopolies, unworkable laws, official indifference, destruction of the countryside.'

124

"The distorting omission is of the ongoing and satisfactory. Page one is not a mirror of the world; it is the world with all the banality, the ordinary, the uncontroversial and the unchanging left out — that is, with most of the world's experience unnoticed. 'This is the way the world is,' the editor will argue in defense of his page one. But is it? Or is this what is to be found by too absorbed a watch on the rat holes of trouble? You can't blame the editor for manning the danger spots; he is not culpable if he fails to anticipate the unexpected, but should be blamed if he has not prepared his readers for trends and events that might have been foreseen.

"Disaster sells papers, it used to be said, but too much of it fatigues the spirit, so that reading the daily front page can become an unpleasant duty. . . . Good news has first to be *news*, which is not apt to be found in an uncritical search for the reassuring. The real good news, if the mind is open to it, is in stories of people courageous against odds, standing up to pressure, asserting their humanity or cussedness, doing selfless acts, scoring quirky victories over circumstances. Such good news does not have to be labeled, merely recognized."[15]

If the *New York Times,* symbol of the most respected journalism in America, is open to so much legitimate criticism, what could be said of other newspapers and magazines? The *Times* does not sensationalize scandals and crimes. The *Times* performs a service for its readers in the completeness of its reports and its custom of printing complete documents, both of which help the reader make personal judgments. But it cannot be said that the *Times* builds up public morality in the manner called for by the philosophy of the Founding Fathers just as this cannot be said for the publishing industry as a whole.

The press and TV take credit for lancing the boil of Watergate. This understates the work: it was not a simple surgical operation; it required months of persistent reporting and publicity. But have the communications media ever considered that Watergate would never have happened had the moral tone of society been higher, and that press and broadcasting have been most responsible for creating this low tone of public morals? The entertainment industry and some book publishers have dug deeper sewers to wallow in, but they could not survive without the publicity given by newspapers and TV, without reviews which praise license as liberty, without the paid advertising which is valued more than the injury done to community morals. In honesty we know that Watergate could have happened in the other political party and with a completely different set of actors playing the same parts with the same ambition, the same love of power, the same desire for money, the same obtuseness of conscience.

While this is being written political analysts state that incumbents of both parties will be in trouble in the coming elections because Watergate was only the summit scandal; the country has had a constant flow of news of local and national scandals. The press and news broadcasts perform a service in reporting them; will the communications media own up to their share of responsibility for creating the scandals? How much of the situation is due to broadcasting media and press which are cooperative tools in building the (false) image a politician needs to be elected? How much is due to the advocacy type of journalism which teaches that there are no absolute standards of right and wrong, only taboos of society? Cover-ups and perjury are not so bad if merely taboos; why get indignant about them?

The reporters who broke Watergate, Bernstein and Woodward, confess to difficult ethical decisions in seeking to get to the bottom of the cover-up. It meant asking friends in the phone company and a credit card company for records of a confidential nature; it meant tampering with grand jury members, asking jurors to give information to the reporters and so break the law. And this but illustrates the doubtful ethics of the press and the broadcasting that depends on it. The public knows that news is made by leaks given to favored reporters, that politicians can be built up by a good press, destroyed by a bad. The word "leak" is so common in Washington that one suspects a flood: how does the press justify the ethics of asking employees and officials to violate *their* personal responsibilities so constantly that the public can judge it has become a system? How much is the public being cheated by favorable publicity planted as ordinary news?

126

The public has its own reaction. Thomas Griffith sums up the situation for us:

"The pollster Louis Harris, who regularly measures how public opinion ranks various occupations, finds journalists scoring considerably below doctors, bankers, congressmen, the military, teachers, preachers, and business executives in public confidence. What is more disquieting about Harris's figures is that, until Watergate at least temporarily halted the decline, the esteem in which journalists are held had dropped 11 percent since 1966 — during a time when, by the old craft standards by which the press measures how well it does its job, it was probably performing better than ever before in circumstances considerably more difficult."[16]

What the public sees are reporters digging up dirt by dirty means, the press accusing others of wrongdoing while itself guilty of enormous crimes, the press destroying politicians who were falsely made by "good publicity." One wonders if editors ever analyze the meaning of the Eighth Commandment, "Thou shalt not bear false witness," as it applies to the press in all its implications. This is one part of the natural moral law which according to the philosophy of the Founding Fathers should be an absolute for editors. If the publisher's conscience says there are no absolutes, only taboos, and his newspaper reflects this, the public is first confused by what it reads, then in its common sense mistrustful of the source of confusion. What the press needs today is a rededication to absolute standards of right and wrong, and an honest confession that it has contributed to the ills of society.

The Founding Fathers keyed the importance of freedom of the press by placing it in the First Amendment to the Constitution. Americans want no government censorship; because of this they have a right to self-censorship on the part of the press. The press has been expert in revealing the sins of politicians, business leaders, doctors, lawyers, clergy; somehow the people sense that editors and publishers are also made of flesh and blood, that they also sin. . . . Editors are professionals; they know false reporting, advocacy writing, planted stories. Perhaps when the *New York Daily News* is

127

willing to blast the *New York Times* openly, when the *Times* is willing to criticize the *New York Post* by name for biased reporting, when the *Philadelphia Bulletin* puts a candid pen on the doings of the *Philadelphia Inquirer* and vice versa — perhaps then will the public trust of newsmen take an upward turn. But as long as the press is shady in its own craft while being the Jeremiah of all other segments of society the public exercises common sense in mistrusting it.

The overall principle of the Founding Fathers — that a democracy is sound as long as the people are virtuous, with the corollary that all (and especially those who influence public opinion) must contribute to this virtue — goes a long way to give editors, reporters, publishers and commentators their guideline. The spirit of America calls for self-censorship by the communications media — according to the principles and ideals upon which the nation was founded. This suggests guidelines for all that is published: articles, pictures, cartoons, advertisements, stories, plays. For news as such, the *New York Times* still retains on its masthead: "All the News That's Fit to Print." What an apt motto this would be in practice for all newsmen and news commentators! "All the News That's Fit to Print"; and let there be no news that's printed to fit.

# chapter 13

# GOVERNMENT AND THE LEGAL PROFESSION

The final center of leadership which has a direct influence on the molding of public opinion, the educating of the people for better or worse, is the government itself. Associated with the government as the leadership group most intimately concerned with either conserving the principles of the Founding Fathers, or changing them by slow evolution or quantum leap, is the legal profession. Within the government, lawyers dominate legislatures, substantially administer executive branches and totally run the judiciaries of state and federal jurisdictions. Outside of government the legal profession contacts the people whenever inalienable rights or the quest for justice become active problems. No other leadership group is so directly involved with founding principles as living realities or dead issues.

The immediate concern here is the political side of government, not the huge bureaucracy as such. Politicians, including many who are not lawyers, have the ultimate responsibility for the direction in which our government goes, and a dominant influence in the way our society goes. Politicians come from the people and reflect the state of society from which they come. But they are leaders, too, and it is reasonable to expect that their vision of what is happening, where they are leading the country, should be clearer than that of the people being led. This was true of the Founding Fathers, but does not seem to be so for most leaders, with the great exception of Abraham Lincoln, since that time. By the standards of the Founders the leaders rather than the people fail. The people through the years have kept a sense of right and wrong, of the ideals of justice and equality among men, of the rights which belong to human nature, though these have not always been formulated in clear terms.

The injustice of slavery was never reconciled with the national conscience. The injustice to working men and women, the abuse of child labor in the nineteenth and early twentieth centuries agitated enough people for a sufficiently long time that legislation was produced and the courts finally had to uphold laws to correct the inequities. The strength of the movement came from the ranks to the politicians, not vice-versa. The evils of segregation finally brought a national response from the people. But too often the politician up to the present day first senses what the people want and then works to correct the abuse; he follows rather than leads. Worse, often in campaign speeches he formulates what the people think only to fail his constituents in practice. The people sense and hold basic moral truths even when leaders are inadequate.

Much of the failure of the political leader must be attributed to the failure of church, school and media leadership. The politician is a product of his environment. The lack of a sense of morality was all-pervasive in the Watergate scandal. Yet it would be foolish to think this could have happened only to the Republican party; different faces, different names could have perpetrated the same acts had the Democrats been in charge. Perhaps two examples related to Watergate illustrate the moral weakness produced by an amoral education and environment. Their names could be changed; they merely represent the tens of thousands of other educated Americans who could have been found to do the same deeds in the same situation. They happen to be appointed officials; they could have been elected officeholders.

Jeb Magruder, White House aide, college graduate, was convicted of perjury spoken at the trial of the Watergate burglars. In a statement before Judge John J. Sirica he said: "I know what I have done, and your honor knows what I have done. . . . Somewhere between my ambitions and my ideals, I lost my ethical compass. I

130

found myself on a path that had not been intended for me by my parents or my principles, or by my own ethical instincts. It has led me to this courtroom." In a report on Magruder's book in *Time* magazine, June 3, 1974, the reviewer says, "Magruder's book suggests that he was, and still is, oblivious of the moral ramifications of many acts he confesses to so candidly. He recounts working on an automobile assembly line the summer after his freshman year (of college). The foreman taught him how to cheat systematically on the job: 'I did as the foreman suggested and even then it was hard to keep up.' "[1]

Egil Krogh, who supervised the White House plumbers in the Ellsberg burglary, "declined to discuss the Watergate case, saying he was under a court order not to talk about it. But he said he felt the scandal had a good effect on the nation. 'The trials, the convictions, the sentences, all are just a small part of coming to grips with what this country means,' he said. 'I'm not sure if you asked everyone what is right that you would come up with the same answer. But at least the question now will be asked.' Asked if he would repeat the actions that led to his conviction, Krogh said, 'I would do it differently. I would certainly not engage in anything that was stupid, unlawful or illegal.' " Krogh thinks the scandal is teaching this generation "what their country means"; but "not everyone would come up with the same answer" as to "what is right." This is in sad contrast to the fact that the Founding Fathers knew clearly what their country meant, what it stood for, what moral foundation they were placing under the nation. With substantial unanimity they would have agreed to what is right and wrong in private and political life.

Dr. Richard B. Morris, Professor of History at Columbia University, is chairman of the American Historical Association's Committee on the Commemoration of the Bicentennial. When asked by *U.S. News & World Report,* "Did the men of the Revolution have a greater sense of morality than politicans generally have today?" he responded:

"They had a greater sense of morality — there's no doubt about that. They also had a greater sense of personal honor. This

131

was very, very important to some of the leaders, notably Alexander Hamilton, who was prepared to confess openly that he had committed adultery with Mrs. Maria Reynolds in order to clear himself of suspicion of having speculated in Government securities on inside information. That was a very astonishing event. Some people believe that Hamilton may have concocted this episode. In any event, he went to extreme lengths — personally embarrassing his family — to disclose a private peccadillo rather than to have his honor besmirched as Secretary of the Treasury. That indicates how sacred these men held their public office, regarding it as a public trust.

"Generally speaking, I would say that the Revolutionary leaders viewed their public offices with great seriousness and dignity and operated with great integrity, although some conflict-of-interest situations were not known then as now."[2]

This is the considered view of a scholar. One reason already suggested for present political amorality is the low moral tone of education and environment. The education of the Founding Fathers was superior to present methods in placing positive moral principles in the minds and hearts of students. The simpler and dominantly agrarian, sometimes frontier, life was a morally healthier climate than modern materialistic and urban society.

## Influence Of The Advertising Industry

As long ago as 1950 a new and disturbing element appeared in the methods of electing candidates for public office which can be added to education and environment to account for low moral standards among politicians. To understand the new technique the term "selling candidates" is more accurate than electing candidates. Vance Packard in his best seller, *The Hidden Persuaders*, analyzes the psychological techniques of the advertising industry which has been adapted to political campaigns:

"As the decade of the fifties was beginning, a portent of things to come appeared in the *New York World-Telegram*, a normally Republican newspaper, in describing preparations for the 1950

Congressional campaign. The headline read: *The Hucksters Take Over GOP Campaign.* And the lead explained that 'the politicians are beginning to apply all the smart advertising techniques used by mass production America to merchandise autos, bath salts, and lawn mowers.' . . .

"By the 1952 Presidential campaign the professional persuaders had been welcomed into the inner councils by at least one party. Stanley Kelley, Jr., of Brookings Institution, made a study of the 1952 campaign, which he reported in his book *Professional Public Relations and Political Power* (1956). He said: 'The campaign . . . reveals some interesting differences in the place occupied by professional publicists in the councils of the opposing parties. The strategy, treatment of issues, use of media, budgeting, and pacing of the Eisenhower campaign showed the pervasive influence of professional propagandists. The Democrats used fewer professionals, were less apt to draw upon commercial and industrial public-relations experience in their thinking, and their publicity men apparently had less of a voice in the policy decisions of the campaign.' The Democrats, of course, took a shellacking and, Kelley suggested, had learned their lesson and would make greater use of public relations and advertising men in 1956. . . .

"By the mid-fifties most enterprising politicians were checking themselves in the mirrors to see if their images were on straight. *Printer's Ink,* the merchandisers' trade journal, quoted a ranking Democrat as saying in 1955: 'Any candidate is aware, of course, that . . . the sooner he begins to build a favorable image of himself in relation to the issues of the day the more likely he is to come through.' . . ."[3]

The art of selling politicians by image has become a staple in political campaigns. It also accounts for some of the corruption in government: it is mighty expensive to get elected, and donors are not quite altruistic in their donations to political campaign chests. After a quarter century we have a somewhat routine entry in the *New York Times* of September 29, 1974:

"THE CAMPAIGNS: GOING PUBLIC MEANS TV"

"The election campaigns in New York and Connecticut have

reached the end of the beginning: The quiet preliminary work of raising funds, developing strategy and repairing intra-party wounds is all but finished, and a full force of stumping candidates is about to go to work in public.

"... It is by now well settled that in New York, at least, the most effective way to reach the most voters is with the television commercial. Last week, in the campaign for Governor, the managers of both candidates were making extensive and expensive plans for television campaigning.

"Governor Wilson has budgeted $1.2 million for such commercials, some of which began to appear last week. The initial group of three concentrates on the Republican Governor and his experience as a state official; a second set will focus on his opponent, Representative Hugh L. Carey, and will reflect unfavorably on the Congressman's record.

"Wilson strategists believe their candidate is behind, in part because he is simply not well known despite (or, perhaps, because of) his 15 years as Lieutenant Governor to Nelson Rockefeller's Governor. In a recent tour of Brooklyn, many failed to recognize him. Mr. Wilson and his camp expect television to correct that problem.

"Mr. Carey, who used television advertising heavily in the primary, plans another extensive TV campaign, though his may cost only half Mr. Wilson's simply because, at this point at least, his resources are more limited. Carey strategists profess concern about the extent of the Wilson TV budget. 'A campaign of the size they're planning can do a hell of a lot,' said David Garth, TV consultant for Mr. Carey. Mr. Garth may have been deliberately picturing Mr. Carey as the unmonied underdog; he also may have meant it, since he knows whereof he speaks — many believe his primary TV ads were the major component in Mr. Carey's victory."[4]

One can conclude from these items a perversion of democracy. An image is elected, not a man. The people have not made a judgment; they have bought a product.

Contrast the emphasis on image in present-day politicians with the sense of personal honor mentioned above by Dr. Morris as "very, very important" to some of the Founding Fathers and exemplified by Hamilton. "In 1950 the politicians (were) beginning to apply all the smart advertising techniques used by mass production America to merchandise autos, bath salts, and lawn mowers." And in 1974 when Congressman Hugh L. Carey was running for governor of New York State: "Carey strategists profess concern about the extent of the Wilson TV budget. [Wilson was the incumbent governor.] 'A campaign of the size they're planning can do a hell of a lot,' says David Garth, TV consultant for Mr. Carey. Mr. Garth may have been deliberately picturing Mr. Carey as the unmonied underdog: he also may have meant it, since he knows whereof he speaks — many believe his primary TV ads were the major component in Mr. Carey's victory."

The image of the unmonied underdog is better than that of the sleek but well-fed greyhound. Compare 1974 campaigns with the debates between Lincoln and Douglas in 1858 to clarify the issue of slavery for the people. We have another reason why the politicians of today are not in the same league as Washington, Jefferson, Hamilton, Adams and Lincoln.

The concentration on the image to be sold in the election, the image to be kept bright through PR men during the politician's term of office, can result in a perversion of democracy. Will the image and the man coincide under stress, in crisis? What guarantee do the people who have bought the image have that the man will produce? The higher the office, the more danger to our democracy.

Is there anything to be learned from the principles of the Founding Fathers which would help the present generation cope with a problem possible only because of most recent advances in psychiatry, psychology and sociology? Very much so. Washington's epigram in his farewell address fits: "In proportion as the structure of government gives force to public opinion, it is essential that public opinion be enlightened." Public opinion, the soul of democracy, must be enlightened. Public opinion must be enlightened, not deceived by PR men. The practical knowledge of human nature, the attitude of distrust for the weakness and selfishness in human nature, led the Founding Fathers to set up the efficient system of checks and balances within our governmental structure, checks which were meant to prevent any man or group of men from becoming too powerful. This attitude can help the present generation to understand and healthily distrust PR techniques and to seek the truth hidden under the image.

The problem can be attacked more directly. One good result of Watergate was the passage by Congress of an election reform bill which will limit campaign expenditures. It is complicated and applies mainly to presidential elections but is an improvement on the preceding inadequate legislation. One of the greatest campaign expenses comes from TV commercials, the slick one- or two-minute jobs which amount to brainwashing the people to create the *image*. Why not by law ban them entirely? They have no legitimate place in the debate over issues by recognizable personalities which should characterize an election and give the people an opportunity to vote intelligently. The airwaves belong to the people; why should any private citizen or group make money on a process which is at the heart of democracy, necessary for our whole way of life? TV and radio broadcasting are basically public trusts. The broadcasting industry as a form of self-discipline, self-censorship, should allot enough prime time to candidates to debate election issues so that an intelligent vote can be the end result. If the industry is not willing to place public responsibility ahead of profit, the British system of publicly owned broadcasting should be considered. Unless the common good is placed before private profit, our democracy is surely doomed.

It is ironic to look to Britain for example here. The last sentence the signers of the Declaration of Independence affirmed in the document, immediately above their signatures, proclaimed: "And for the support of this Declaration, with a firm reliance on the protection of divine Providence, we mutually pledge to each other our Lives, our Fortunes and our sacred Honor." They knew what they risked for the common good. They actually signed the parchment on August 2, 1776. A biographer of Benjamin Franklin records this conversation between John Hancock and Franklin as they prepared to take the pen: "We must be unanimous," said Hancock; "there must be no pulling separate ways; we must all hang together." "Yes," was Franklin's reply, "we must, indeed, all hang together, or most assuredly we shall all hang separately." They were conscious that they risked their lives and their fortunes. It might be educational for broadcasters today to investigate how many were actually destroyed financially by the war which gave us nationhood.

It is not without significance that H. R. Haldeman, Mr. Nixon's chief of staff, was an executive first with the J. Walter Thompson Advertising Agency. Mr. Haldeman had in a sense two careers, alternating between advertising and Richard M. Nixon's political life. He pursued advertising as such on off years but was Mr. Nixon's advance man in the 1956 and 1960 campaigns and managed his 1962 contest for governor of California. One caustic writer sums up the 1968 campaign: "With the help of (John) Ehrlichman, Seattle lawyer and college room mate, Haldeman helped to fashion the new Nixon, the Nixon who squeaked past Hubert H. Humphrey and the divided Democrats to win."[5]

The fact that admen use their techniques to sell a politician does not necessarily mean deliberate fraud; H. R. Haldeman apparently believed strongly in Richard Nixon's ability and presidential qualifications. What is dangerous to democracy is the subtle deception of the people in the whole process: their votes are cast not on issues and the character of the candidates but on the ability of the admen to put across an image the public will buy. The image, once elected, must be kept brightly glittering by public-relations men. In the report on Jeb Magruder's book, *An American Life,* the term "public relations" is used again and again; the very words, "public relations," appeared in capital letters on presidential memos.

## Lawyers In Government

Admen help get politicians elected and keep their images bright. There is one profession which has contributed so many of its members to political ranks that it must take major responsibility for the moral tone of political life. Almost 300 lawyers are in Congress today (the 94th Congress), and tens of thousands more are scattered throughout other branches of government. The tradition of mem-

137

bers of the legal profession as political leaders started at the beginning. The Constitutional Convention of 1787 included thirteen lawyers (twelve active and one retired); but more than half of the fifty-five delegates had studied law at one time or other. There were six really great thinkers, political philosophers who shaped our political structures most in the formative stage of the nation, and all six were lawyers: John Adams, Thomas Jefferson, James Madison, Alexander Hamilton, James Wilson and John Marshall. Madison, Wilson and Hamilton were drafters of the Constitution. When examined fully, the influence of the legal profession on the origin and continual shaping of national ideals cannot be overestimated.

## *Ethics Of The Legal Profession*

It is in this context of power for good or evil that the title of a recent thoughtful article in the *U.S. News & World Report*, "America's Lawyers: A Sick Profession?"[6] should be placed. In an address to the American College of Trial Lawyers, Chief Justice Burger had used this phrase describing the legal profession as far back as 1967. The article starts with the plight of the eleven lawyers tainted by the Watergate scandals, a group which includes a former attorney general and chief presidential counselors — not to mention that Mr. Nixon himself is a lawyer.

It is not just the plight of the Watergate-smeared lawyers that arouses concern; other disturbing conditions exist. Huge legal fees mean, in the words of Judge Shirley M. Hufstedler of the U.S. Court of Appeals, that: "A regular civil trial today, with or without a jury, is beyond the reach of all except the rich, the nearly rich or the person seriously injured by a well-insured defendant."[7] In this context, "Today, many Government lawyers are finding that their 'inside' expertise can reap rich rewards when they return to civilian life — in board rooms of corporations, inner councils of labor unions, and as heads of the nation's biggest tax-consultant firms."

There are lawyers, especially young ones, trying to balance this by giving free services to the poor or helping in "class action" litigation to alleviate social problems or race discrimination. And "some

138

lawyers themselves are taking a hard look at the traditional obligation to represent [their] client to the fullest and asking whether it
requires total disregard of the question of guilt or innocence. Milton Shadur, a well known Chicago attorney, made this comment
about legal ethics: 'Long before Watergate, the flaw of the profession was the "mechanic attitude" — the tendency of lawyers not to
make moral judgements on what they are called upon to do. . . .
Time after time I run into well respected firms which exercise no
moral judgement about what they are doing.' "[8]

The legal profession is in trouble because its code of ethics is
not clearly moral. Chief Justice Burger used the term "a sick profession." Justice Blackmun speaking at the Prayer Breakfast of the
American Bar Association annual meeting in August of 1973 said,
"And the pall of Watergate, with all its revelations of misplaced
loyalties, of strange measures of the ethical, of unusual doings in
high places, and by lawyer after lawyer, is upon us."

Clearly every lawyer is not immoral; there are more than
375,000 lawyers in the country. "Defenders of legal ethics point out
this: since 1965, according to ABA records, the organized bar has
taken disciplinary action against more than 2,000 lawyers. A total
of 694 have been disbarred and 319 have resigned from law practice
while charges were pending against them. Many attorneys echo the
assertion of Earl B. Hadlow, president of the Florida Bar Association, that at least 95% of the nation's lawyers are honest men and
women."[9]

Two observations can be made: A man may be personally
honest but follow a subjective moral code which does not meet high
objective standards. The Ten Commandments, the basic standard
of the Founding Fathers, are not the code of many who today seem
convinced that their personal standards are sufficiently high. It is
the reacceptance of this code which would lift the ethics of the legal
profession. Again, if the legal profession is sick, it reflects a sickness
of society which is apparent in other leadership groups. Lawyers are
the product of the same school systems, are bombarded by the same
communications media, come from the same environment as the
other leadership groups.

The American Bar Association has decreed that every law

school must now teach courses in ethics or lose its ABA accreditation. But if the ethics courses to be taught in the law schools are merely the temporary agreement among each generation of lawyers, to be changed with varying business practices or in accordance with the idea that morals are merely changing social taboos, there can be no permanent upgrading of the law profession. We are back at the heart of the problem: is there such a thing as a moral code intrinsic to human nature so that society itself and all, rich or poor, helpless or powerful, black or white, old or young, can demand and achieve equal justice under law as well as honest treatment from the lawyer who serves them? Does this code, rightly understood, which grants the cherished principle that a man is innocent before the law until proven guilty, give lawyers the right to act as if there is no moral code; or does it give lawyers *carte blanche* to seek loopholes, use technicalities to free the rich from social responsibilities or loose hardened criminals upon society?

"Reflecting on changes taking place in the legal profession, Prof. Paul Freund of Harvard . . . commented:

" 'Now there's a trend toward policy formation and legal philosophy. There's a great interest on the part of students in the philosophy and ethics of law, and they see being trained in law as having a great impact on society.

" 'In New Deal days, they had the same desire, but they found their outlet in government. Now with government somewhat passive, young lawyers find their outlet in private practice and more especially in local and grass-roots government and politics.

" 'In a way, we might be going back to the early days that produced lawyers at the beginning of the American republic. There were no law schools then — law teachers inspired students. They got technical knowledge from Blackstone, along with the philosophy of law; natural law, natural rights — that's what made them great lawyers. . . .

" 'We can't give up specialized training in the highly complex structure of law today, but we do have to return to a feeling of what the whole legal system stands for — how it relates to our own conception of the person as a human being.' "[10]

140

To the Founders, Christians who live by the Ten Commandments could be trusted to administer civil law made according to natural justice, to natural law, to natural rights. If a man obeyed the commandment, "Thou shalt not kill," he would respect my inalienable right to life. If a government official believed and practiced the precept, "Thou shalt not steal," he could be trusted with government taxes and property which was not his own. If a man lived his life by the commandment, "Thou shalt not bear false witness," he would be a man of honor, truthful in private and in public life; his oath would be trustworthy in a court of justice.

There was, of course, the personal element in interpretations of moral obligations. Sam Adams was a Congregationalist with a Puritan background. Rev. John Witherspoon was head of Princeton College, the purpose of which was to train Presbyterian ministers. Thomas Jefferson was a deist who believed in Christian moral principles; Charles Carroll was a Roman Catholic. Yet all signed the Declaration of Independence. There would be quite some latitude in such a group in the application of what each believed the detailed points of Christian morality required in various situations. But on the basics, the obligations of government officials from natural law or its theological expression, the Ten Commandments, they were in complete agreement. Upon the basics they were sure sound character had to be built, and that such ethics would produce ethical lawyers, ethical government officials.

President Ford's pardon of former President Nixon highlights in practice a return to the relationship of ethics to law and the lawyer. He states his main purpose:

"After years of bitter controversy and divisive national debate, I have been advised, and I am compelled to conclude, that many months and perhaps more years will have to pass before Richard Nixon could obtain a fair trial by jury in any jurisdiction of the United States under governing decisions by the Supreme Court. . . . But it is not the ultimate fate of Richard Nixon that most concerns me, though surely it troubles every decent and every compassionate person. My concern is the immediate future of this great country. . . ."[11]

141

In other words, he intended to act for the common good of the country. But he explains how his conscience, his personal ethics, entered into the decision:

"As we are a nation under God, so I am sworn to uphold our laws with the help of God. And I have sought such guidance and searched my own conscience with special diligence to determine the right thing for me to do with respect to my predecessor in this place, Richard Nixon, and his loyal wife and family. . . .

"I deeply believe in equal justice for all Americans, whatever their station or former station. The law, whether human or divine, is no respecter of persons, but the law is a respecter of reality. . . .

"My conscience tells me clearly and certainly that I cannot prolong the bad dreams that continue to reopen a chapter that is closed. My conscience tells me that only I, as President, have the constitutional power to firmly shut and seal this book. My conscience tells me it is my duty, not merely to proclaim domestic tranquility, but to use every means that I have to insure it. . . ."[12]

Without defending or condemning President Ford's action in the pardon it can be pointed out that he used a process to come to his decision which was based on sound ethics and in total agreement with the Founding Fathers. He had the full constitutional authority to grant the pardon. The next problem was: What would a good, an honorable public servant, do in the case? He decided it by his personal conscience. He prayed; he thought it over seriously; he came to the conclusion he ought to pardon. According to background and experience, other men might come to different conclusions. But the method was right, and it is surely what Americans would like to think all lawyers and politicians do: Am I acting in accordance with the Constitution? Am I doing what an honorable man should do in this case?

## Ethical Law

There is always present another element. If the public is to be served, if the common good is to be achieved, laws must be just as lawyers must be ethical. For justice to be established under law, laws themselves must be in accord with natural justice. If the Constitution, or the way it is interpreted, results in an unjust decision, the victim is a victim even if the administrator of the law is personally upright. According to the Founding Fathers the laws would be just when they upheld inalienable rights, when they forced all to respect natural obligations toward other men. The Fathers never fell into the trap that a law was unjust or that they were imposing personal morality on others when they insisted laws be consistent with natural morality, just as they were convinced men in office would be trustworthy only when the Christian moral code was the personal code of the officeholder.

"... We hold these truths to be self-evident, that all men are created equal, that they are endowed by their Creator with certain unalienable Rights, that among these are Life, Liberty and the pursuit of Happiness. That to secure these rights, Governments are instituted among Men, deriving their just powers from the consent of the governed, — That whenever any Form of Government becomes destructive of these ends, it is the Right of the People to alter or to abolish it, . . ." Nature gave equality and inalienable rights to human beings, not civil law; nature imposed upon men and government the obligation of respecting and defending this equality and these rights. Nature imposed this code of morality — not private opinion, not arbitrary government. The code in its basics was self-proving, self-evident. If some odd person were to say it was not his code, and civil law is just only when in accordance with *his personal code,* there was no occasion to argue; instead, there might be occasion to fight. This was the Revolution, the argument with Britain.


### Laws Must Be Moral: Morality Cannot Be Legislated

The Founders adhered to natural law, to the principle that there were rules written in human nature which had to be followed if civil law were to be just, produce a moral people and a healthy society. This is very different from the principle that by law government can make men good, that government can and should legislate morality into people. Americans from the beginning too often fell into this trap. The Puritans were notorious for it; they imposed their private interpretation of Christianity upon their constituents.

The most recent, inevitably unsuccessful, attempt was the Eighteenth Amendment to the Constitution, ratified in 1919 and repealed in 1933 after a decade of disastrous effects. The ethics of one group concerning the use of intoxicating liquor was imposed on the country by the attempt to constitutionally prohibit its manufacture, sale and transportation. But to most people the temperate use of alcohol is not a moral evil, its denial to them not a legitimate object of civil law. Experience soon proved that one cannot sober drunks by unenforceable legislation which deprived others of private rights; one cannot sober drunks by law any more than laws against robbery can make an honest man out of a thief.

But there is a point where ethics and law must meet; there are areas where laws must correspond with basic, natural morality. All the laws on the books will not make an honest man out of a thief, but each citizen has a right to the protection of law for his honestly owned property: hence, there must be laws against stealing. No law can turn the heart of a murderer into a benign human being, but each citizen has a right to the protection of his life by laws which will protect him and deter murderers.

No law will make a liar into a respecter of truth, but for the protection of society there must be laws against perjury. From time immemorial men have fallen into adultery. No civil law will correct an adulterer, but civil law has an obligation to protect the family life of the innocent spouse and children. If American civilization is to remain civilized, laws must accord with sound morality; more positively, our laws should create a climate in which it is easy to be good, difficult to do evil. This is not to impose a private code of morality on those who believe in free love, on terrorists who bomb to attain their end, on racketeers to whom any gain is honest, on liars who would libel honorable men. The code is imposed by the Creator on human nature itself.

No civilization will ever survive except on the true code of morality. America was fortunate enough to have Founders who could read that code in the history of Western civilization, who saw its correspondence with the Judeo-Christian code, and who were willing to shed their blood to attain it as the foundation for our civil society. The thinking of some educated men and women of today who maintain all morality to be merely personal, that any law contrary to their personal code imposes on them, who talk about civil rights and defend constitutional rights as sufficient for society, would be unintelligible to the Founding Fathers.

## Civil Law Must Correspond To Higher Law

The Founders held that there is a higher law to which civil law must correspond. They appealed to it in the Declaration of Independence, in their state constitutions, in the preamble to the Constitution which said that its purpose was "to establish justice," and in the Bill of Rights which reminded posterity that "the enumeration in the Constitution of certain rights shall not be construed to deny or disparage others retained by the people."

After pardoning Nixon, President Ford was challenged on his appeal to the principle that we are a nation under God, that there is a divine as well as human law, that the two must somehow go together. In the context of the Fathers' doctrine and Mr. Ford's application of it the following is quoted. It is a statement by Stephen P. Presser, Associate Professor of Law at Rutgers University, Camden, New Jersey. The statement is in opposition to Prof. Freund's suggestion concerning the need to teach the ethics of natural law in our law schools, and in opposition to the very clear principles of the Founding Fathers. The headline which introduced it in the *Philadelphia Inquirer* of September 12, 1974 reads:

"FORD IS ON SHAKY LEGAL GROUND IN CALLING ON A 'HIGHER LAW' "

"One of the first problems with which a first-year law student must grapple is whether the law is something other than the statutes

145

written in the books and the decisions of the courts which have interpreted them. Sooner or later the young lawyer may be seduced by a concept that has been with us at least since Moses climbed down from Mt. Sinai.

"This notion has been passed on through Plato, the early 17th century English jurists, the New England Puritans, and more recently through the actions of Chief Justice Earl Warren, who habitually disarmed advocates at the bar of the Supreme Court with the insistent query, 'Is it fair?'

"The idea is that tenet of jurisprudence which holds that there is an ultimate law, which exists apart from the men who legislate or adjudicate. It is that there exists, somewhere, a 'brooding omnipresence,' a body of natural law that is God-given and made up of certain immutable principles of right or reason.

"The latest proponent of this view is our lawyer President, Gerald R. Ford. In the statement which explained his recent full pardon of former President Nixon, President Ford said, 'The Constitution is the supreme law of our land and it governs our actions as citizens. *Only the laws of God, which govern our conscience, are superior to it.*' (Emphasis author's.)

"In other words, the law of our consciences, the dictates of religion, or natural law, takes precedence over the Constitution. This may come as a bit of a surprise to those members of the Supreme Court who, interpreting the Constitution decided to ban prayer from our schools.

"It would probably have disturbed Thomas Jefferson, who, in the latter part of the 18th century, wrote an elaborate proof that Christianity was not a part of the Anglo-American Common Law. Finally, the tenor of President Ford's explanation seems strangely at odds with the First Amendment to our Constitution, which prohibits the legislative branch of our government from making any law 'respecting an establishment of religion, or prohibiting the free exercise thereof. . . .'

"With the President's statement he appears to be, in some small way, imposing the dictates of his religious conscience on us, in declaring them, at least in this instance, to be our supreme law. Is this the modest beginning of an American Theocracy? It seems unlikely, but giving the laws of God as a rationale for the carrying out of a Constitutional duty gives a rather ominous meaning to the phrase that ours is a government of laws, not men.

"More immediate, however, is the fact that the tragedy of Watergate came about when a coterie of small men in high positions decided that they were above the law of the land.

"Appealing to a law 'superior' to the Constitution to pardon one of them suggests that he was right. Rather than writing 'the end' to the American tragedy as the President suggested, he may have further written the prologue to the next act.

"Like Watergate itself, one of the ironies of Mr. Ford's appeal to a religious natural law is that it was unnecessary. Article II, Section 2, of the Constitution, to which he referred, clearly authorizes him 'to grant Reprieves and Pardons for Offenses against the United States, except in Cases of Impeachment.'

"This requires no reference to a higher law, and presumably calls for nothing more or less than the exercise of his discretion. Such a discretion is apparently unfettered, but if he needed reasons to bolster his decision he supplied them with that part of his statement that said it would now be impossible for Mr. Nixon to get a speedy fair trial, and the resultant uncertainty would polarize opinion and challenge 'the credibility of our free institutions of government.'

"This is the purest language of the practical lawyer, of course, but a lot less potentially dangerous than a vague, natural law, because it is at least straightforward and transparent.

"The wise freshman law student soon learns that the conception of natural law will not be very useful in practice, and he (or she) is soon content to accept the seemingly pedestrian, but terribly astute, epigram of Oliver Wendell Holmes, Jr., to the effect that our law is nothing more nor less than predictions of what our courts will do in certain instances.

"Further, if the legal trainee studies much in the field of American Legal History — a discipline now finally coming into its own — he sees that resort to 'natural law' among the Puritans justified many acts of religious oppression, and an occasional witch incineration.

"The legal historian notes with no small respect that ideas of natural law such as those of 'certain inalienable rights' to life, liberty, and the pursuit of happiness were important in the writing of our Declaration of Independence, and the Constitution itself, but he knows the danger of justifying expedient moves through resort to a higher law. Does President Ford perceive that danger?"[13]

Prof. Presser's major fallacy is his denial of the place of natural law as part of our legal structure in the thinking of the Founding Fathers. From the Declaration of Independence and the previously quoted documents of the Fathers it is evident beyond discussion that they always presupposed a natural moral law, that civil and constitutional law's first purpose is to protect the just rights which come from this natural law, that one of the main purposes of our Constitution was to implement in our own fashion the way in which the American people wanted these rights to be observed. This *is* the Bill of Rights. Christianity as such was not established as a national religion. Prof. Presser's reference to Jefferson's thesis that Christianity was not part of Anglo-American common law is not here disputed. What is historically evident is that the Fathers' interpretation of the natural moral obligations which produce justice was guided by the Judeo-Christian tradition. It is this natural law as interpreted by this tradition which was considered the foundation of American constitutional and civil law. This is the way it was put by Jefferson in his first inaugural address:

"Let us, then, with courage and confidence pursue our own federal and republican principles, our attachment to our union and representative government. Kindly separated by nature and a wide ocean from the exterminating havoc of one quarter of the globe; . . . *enlightened by a benign religion,* professed, indeed, and practiced in various forms, yet *all of them including honesty, truth, temperance, gratitude, and the love of man*; acknowledging and adoring an over-ruling Providence, which by all its dispensations proves that it delights in the happiness of man here and his greater happiness hereafter; with all these blessings, what more is necessary to make us a happy and prosperous people?"[14] (Emphasis author's.)

148

The sickness of the law profession starts with law-school indoctrination of false principles. There is no ideal for a young lawyer who merely studies to be able to make an intelligent guess as to what succeeding generations of judges will do. And what is the ideal of the lawyer who becomes a judge? Is his standard that anything he decides and his colleagues enforce is law?

Mr. Presser is defending all the attitudes and false principles which have brought the legal profession to its present debacle. The epigram of Justice Holmes, "to the effect that our law is nothing more nor less than predictions of what our courts will do in certain instances," means that the essence of law is force: anything that the courts decree which the executive enforces is law. There is no such thing as the justice which the preamble to the Constitution indicates is the purpose of the Constitution: there is merely naked obedience to what courts or legislatures decree the people should do.

"The legal historian," says Prof. Presser, "notes with no small respect that ideas of natural law such as those of 'certain inalienable rights' to life, liberty, and the pursuit of happiness were important in the writing of our Declaration of Independence, and the Constitution itself, but he knows the danger of justifying expedient moves through resort to higher law." The dozens of documents of the Founding Fathers quoted above indicate that the ideas of natural law and inalienable rights were not just "important in the writing of the Declaration of Independence, and of the Constitution itself" as though they were merely an author's outline for a play or book. The Fathers knew they were dealing with objective rights and obligations which they were implementing by the specific provisions of the Constitution, that these rights and obligations were rooted in nature and were not created as civil rights and civil obligations by the Constitution. The Fathers fought a war and established a nation on the reality of this "higher law" which Prof. Presser says is a seduction for young lawyers!

## Dilemma Of The Legal Profession: What Is Law?

"President (A. Whitney) Griswold of Yale recently said, 'The

American People do not sufficiently understand the rule of law because it has never been properly explained to them.' If this is true certainly an attempt should be made. The logical starting point is a definition of law, but the winds of controversy howl so strongly around that subject that it seems unwise to take it on in a discussion of what law *does*. Therefore the term will not be defined; if this be chaos make the most of it. Though the subject is left uncrystallized the concept is yet sufficiently definite for a broad look at its place in society. Let us say merely that the law embodies all the general rules of civilization, represented by constitutions, statutes, court decisions, and legislative regulations, which channel the daily lives of the citizens and control their relations with the state and with each other."[15]

This is the law in action: we do not often advert to it, yet its manifold effects on our daily lives determine much of the way we live; and the ways in which the laws originate, are interpreted and executed, control the life functions of society as the nerves do the body. One can doubt that the legal profession itself understands its own importance; but if the legal profession is sick, society will be sick.

Yet Mr. Aspell, a representative lawyer, cannot define law itself. Surely it is a sign and cause of deep trouble when a profession cannot agree on the definition of its own work. The Founding Fathers (remember, law was the paramount profession among them) would have no difficulty in defining law. "Law is an ordinance of reason promulgated for the common good by one who has authority over the community" was the classic definition of law given by Aquinas 500 years before the Founders' time; their writings indicate this was their conception of law. It was an *ordinance of reason,* not the arbitrary act of a tyrant's will (thus they described George III) but an order reasonable in its agreement with human nature and with human possibilities. *Promulgated:* publicly and legitimately proclaimed so as to be binding on the whole community. *For the common good:* society was natural to man, men were equal in their nature, laws must be for the welfare of all, neither benefiting a few outrageously nor burdening another group inequitably. *From one who has authority over the community:* not the act of a private citizen, not a military coup, but a sanctioned act of legitimate government.

This definition of law is implicit in the Declaration of Independence. "We hold these truths . . . that all men are created equal, that they are endowed . . . with certain unalienable Rights, that among these are Life, Liberty and the pursuit of Happiness. That to secure these rights, Governments are instituted among Men, deriving their just powers from the consent of the governed, — That whenever any Form of Government becomes destructive of these ends, it is the Right of the People to alter or to abolish it, and to institute new Government, laying its foundation on such principles and organizing its powers in such form, as to them shall seem most likely to effect their Safety and Happiness. . . ." The Declaration indicates Aquinas' definition of law. *Law is an ordinance of reason:* it had to conform to the equality of men and protect their rights. *For the common good:* the purpose of government itself was to achieve the safety and happiness of its citizens. *Promulgated by one having authority over the community:* governments are instituted among men, and by the consent of the people are given adequate power to make laws which will insure their happiness.

James Otis witnesses the same definition:

"Let no man think I am about to commence advocate for DESPOTISM, because I affirm that government is founded on the necessity of our natures; and that an original supreme SOVEREIGN, absolute and uncontroulable, EARTHLY power MUST exist and preside over every society; from whose final decisions there can be no appeal but directly to Heaven. It is therefore ORIGINALLY and ULTIMATELY in the people, . . . and they never did in fact FREELY, nor can they RIGHTFULLY make an absolute, unlimited renunciation of this divine right. It is ever in the nature of a thing given in TRUST, and on a condition, the performance of which no mortal can dispense with; namely, that the person or persons on whom the sovereignty is conferred by the people shall INCESSANTLY consult THEIR good. Tyranny of all kinds is to be abhored, whether it be in the hands of one, or of the few, or of the many. . . ."[16]

151

Compare the inability of present-day lawyers to define law with the clear-cut legal principles of Thomas Jefferson. In a letter to F. W. Gilmer, in 1816, Jefferson declared:

"Our legislators are not sufficiently apprized of the rightful limits of their power; that their true office is to declare and enforce only our natural rights and duties, and to take none of them from us. No man has a natural right to commit aggression on the equal rights of another; and this is all from which the laws ought to restrain him; every man is under the natural duty of contributing to the necessities of the society; and this is all the laws should enforce on him; and, no man having a natural right to be the judge between himself and another, it is his natural duty to submit to the umpirage of an impartial third. When the laws have declared and enforced all this, they have fulfilled their functions, and the idea is quite unfounded, that on entering into society we give up any natural right."[17]

And from Jefferson's first inaugural address:

"All, too, will bear in mind this sacred principle, that though the will of the majority is in all cases to prevail, that will, to be rightful, must be reasonable; that the minority possess their equal rights, which equal laws must protect, and to violate which would be oppression. Let us, then, fellow citizens, unite with one heart and one mind. Let us restore to social intercourse that harmony and affection without which liberty and even life itself are but dreary things. And let us reflect that having banished from our land that religious intolerance under which mankind so long bled and suffered, we have yet gained little if we countenance a political intolerance as despotic, as wicked, and capable of as bitter and bloody persecutions."[18]

Jefferson's description of the function and limits of civil law is clear enough to define law. His analysis satisfies the terse definition of law given by Aquinas: law is an ordinance of reason promulgated for the common good by one having authority over the community.

Jefferson's emphasis, the fewer the laws the better, is still a good rule. However, the problems of society have so multiplied since his day that the amplitude of Aquinas' definition is more satisfying. The main principle is that laws be for the common good, whether few or great.

## Abraham Lincoln:
### Law Is Justice, A Lawyer Is Ethical

Abraham Lincoln chronologically was not a Founding Father, yet in a sense he was the last of the Founders and, on Washington's level, a second "Father to his Country." He was born less than a month before James Madison was inaugurated President; he had reached fifteen on July 4, 1826, the day Thomas Jefferson and John Adams died. Lincoln was nourished on the truths of the Declaration of Independence. On February 21, 1861, he was on his way to his first inauguration; he was warned of a plot against his life. The next day he spoke in Independence Hall, Philadelphia:

"I can say that all the political sentiments I entertain have been drawn, so far as I have been able to draw them, from the sentiments which originated and were given to the world from this hall. I have never had a feeling politically that did not spring from the sentiments embodied in the Declaration of Independence. . . . I have often enquired of myself what great principle or idea it was that kept the confederacy so long together. It was not the matter of separation of the colonies from the mother-land, but that sentiment in the Declaration of Independence which gave liberty, not alone to the people of this country, but, I hope, to the world for all future time. It was that which gave promise that in due time the weight would be lifted from the shoulders of all men. This is the sentiment embodied in the Declaration of Independence. . . . But if this country cannot be saved without giving up that principle, I was about to say I would rather be assassinated on this spot than surrender it. . . ."[19]

Two days afterwards, having learned that a plot certainly existed, he changed his travel plans and proceeded in secret to Washington. Four years later he gave his life for these principles.

Lincoln had the ability to put profound thought in words the common person understood. In 1838, the abolitionist Elijah Lovejoy was killed by a mob at Alton, Illinois. In a speech some weeks later, Lincoln spoke to the Young Men's Lyceum in Springfield, the state capital and at that time Southern in sympathy, on the wickedness of mobs and the necessity of law and order:

"There is no grievance that is a fit object for redress by mob law. In any case that arises, as for instance, the promulgation of abolitionism, one of two positions is necessarily true; that is, the thing is right within itself, and therefore deserves the protection of all law and all good citizens; or it is wrong, and therefore proper to be prohibited by legal enactments; and in neither case, is the interposition of mob law, either necessary, justifiable, or excusable."[20]

Lincoln had already gone on record against slavery but deplored the excesses of the abolitionist fanaticism which he thought would increase the evils of slavery. In analyzing the situation he defined a basic ingredient of true law: law must be moral within itself; law should not enact evil or prohibit good.

Mob law was not to achieve the common good; but neither was true law a product of force, merely what the courts would enforce. He stood firmly with the Founding Fathers against what would later be Holmes' doctrine.

Abraham Lincoln believed in good law; he was also the ethical lawyer. He had earned the sobriquet "Honest Abe" as a small-town businessman scrupulous in paying debts. His honesty penetrated the depths of his character. In 1847, as a Representative in the U.S. Congress, Lincoln doubted the justness of the Mexican War. His home state was borne along with the fever for expansion and fervor of patriotism, and another Congressman from Illinois, William A. Richardson, introduced a resolution declaring the war to be just and necessary. Lincoln voted against it and later introduced his own resolution which would have placed the blame on President James K. Polk. The outcry against Lincoln was so loud that he was admonished by his law partner not to beat against the popular sentiment. Lincoln's answer reveals the man:

"I will stake my life that if you had been in my place you would have voted just as I did. Would you have voted what you felt you knew to be a lie? I know you would not. Would you have gone out of the House — skulked the vote? I expect not. If you had skulked one vote you would have to skulk many more, before the end of the session. Richardson's resolutions, introduced before I made any move, or gave any vote upon the subject, make the direct question of the justice of the war; so that no man can be silent if he would. You are compelled to speak; and your only alternative is to tell the *truth* or tell a *lie*. . . ."[21]

Lincoln represents those lawyers and lawmakers of the generations before the Civil War who idealized personal honor and who could not separate law from morality. Even the great Southerners to whom the Declaration of Independence became an embarrassment defended slavery as an institution which was somehow natural, somehow necessary, somehow not immoral. But this did not satisfy the national conscience; Lincoln's first inaugural address, spoken after seven states had declared themselves seceded and the fire of war awaited only the spark to be ignited, stated the basic problem:

"One section of our country believes slavery is right, and ought to be extended, while the other believes it is wrong, and ought not to be extended. This is the only substantial dispute. . . ."[22]

Lincoln was convinced that the compromises over slavery the Founding Fathers had accepted in establishing the Union were also designed to bring about its ultimate extinction, and he believed that ultimately it would disappear: "A house divided against itself cannot stand." He was not an abolitionist willing to precipitate the horror of war to extinguish what he knew to be an evil institution; with the Founders he would not extend it and expected time to solve the problem. But he knew his moral duty if an illegal secession turned into open rebellion:

"In your hands, my dissatisfied fellow countrymen, and not in mine, is the momentous issue of civil war. The government will not assail you. You can have no conflict without being yourselves the aggressors. You have no oath registered in heaven to destroy the government, while I shall have the most solemn one to 'preserve, protect, and defend' it. . . ."[23]

Four bloody years of war followed. Slavery as an institution was dead and the Union was preserved. The compromises which had defaced the Constitution were obliterated before Christmas of 1865: "Neither slavery nor involuntary servitude, except as a punishment for crime whereof the party shall have been duly convicted, shall exist within the United States, or any place subject to their jurisdiction" (Thirteenth Amendment). Lincoln had sacrificed his life on Good Friday of that year; his farewell address to the nation had been given at his second inauguration:

"Each (North and South) looked for an easier triumph, and a result less fundamental and astounding. Both read the same Bible and pray to the same God, and each invokes His aid against the other. It may seem strange that any men should dare to ask a just God's assistance in wringing their bread from the sweat of other men's faces, but let us judge not, that we be not judged. The prayers of both could not be answered. That of neither has been answered fully. The Almighty has His own purposes. 'Woe unto the world because of offenses; for it must needs be that offenses come, but woe to that man by whom the offense cometh.' If we shall suppose that American slavery is one of those offenses which, in the providence of God, must needs come, but which, having continued through His appointed time, He now wills to remove, and that He gives to both North and South this terrible war as the woe due to those by whom the offense came, shall we discern therein any departure from those divine attributes which the believers in a living God always ascribe to Him? Fondly do we hope, fervently do we pray, that this mighty scourge of war may speedily pass away. Yet, if God wills that it continue until all the wealth piled by the bondsman's two hundred and fifty years of unrequited toil shall be sunk, and until every drop of blood drawn with the lash shall be paid by another drawn with the sword, as was said three thousand years ago, so still it must be said, 'The judgments of the Lord are true and righteous altogether.' "[24]

## Post-Civil War:
### Supreme Court Accepts New Theory Of Law

The inalienable right to liberty had been restored to its rightful place in American law. By 1870, two more amendments had been added to the Constitution to implement in American terms the civil rights which should accompany natural liberty. The Fourteenth Amendment guaranteed citizenship to the freed man, along with due process and equal protection of the laws. The Fifteenth Amendment guaranteed the right of all citizens to vote. The United States had written in blood and declared in law that the philosophy of the Declaration of Independence was still its foundation. ... And yet within a few short years the method of interpreting the Constitution took such a turn that it was as if the war had never been fought and the philosophy which is our foundation had never existed!

That this should have been the reward of war is incredible. It can only be explained by the national distractions which followed the Civil War: the agony of reconstruction in the South due to those from the North who wanted revenge; the total unpreparedness for freedom on the part of the ex-slaves; the despair and bitterness of Southern whites; the absence of a Lincoln and the national corruption of politics during Grant's administrations. As a consequence of these, post-Civil War government was not normal.

Then there was the overwhelming expansion of industry; the opening of the West; the exploitation of seemingly boundless resources; the greed and ruthlessness of the Fisks, Goulds, Vanderbilts and Rockefellers — the "robber barons" of business; the apparent undermining of traditional thought by Charles Darwin, Thomas Henry Huxley, John Stuart Mill, Herbert Spencer and William Graham Sumner, among others; all these distracted the post-Civil War generation of Americans away from the nobility of the country, away from its true nature, away from the fact that violation of natural law had caused the Civil War, and undermined the constitutional foundation which should have been cemented forever by the blood spilled in the war. The philosophy of the Declaration of Independence ceased to be the guide to interpret the Constitution; and though it happened 100 years ago, it leads in a straight line to the debacle of today's lawyers: what is law? And this is also the seedbed of the current sickness of the legal profession.

In the turmoil of the times a sufficient number of members of the legal profession, especially Justices of the Supreme Court, exchanged the natural-law philosophy of the Founding Fathers (which held that each human being, rich or poor, white or black, had equal dignity and certain inalienable rights) for a new philosophy of law. This new natural law theory built the welfare of society on "the survival of the fittest," just as Darwin had built his evolutionary theory on the survival of the fittest in biology. (In passing it might be well to remember that Darwin's explanation of the cause of evolution and the theory of evolution are not the same thing.)

The new theory followed by the Justices was called social Darwinism. The principal originator of the theory was Herbert Spencer and can be capsulized into one sentence of his first book, *Social Statics*: "Every man has freedom to do all that he wills, provided he infringes not the equal freedom of any other man."[25] The Founding Fathers held that a man has freedom to do what he will so long as he does not infringe on the right of any other man. To Spencer there are no rights, only freedoms. This is the law of the jungle; might makes right. In economics and political science it means that the government should never interfere to protect the weak from the strong, the poor from the rich, the workingman from the owner. It was the policy of *laissez-faire*: let the government stay out of business.

In theory only the fittest businesses would survive; natural resources would be exploited most efficiently; wealth would grow most rapidly; in the end all would profit. It was a wonderful theory. John D. Rockefeller, notorious for driving the small fry out of the petroleum business as he built up the Standard Oil monopoly, could say to his Sunday School class: "The growth of large business is merely the survival of the fittest. . . . This is not an evil tendency in business. It is merely the working-out of a law of nature and a law of God."[26] And it just happened that many of the Supreme Court Justices of the late nineteenth and early twentieth centuries were ex-corporation lawyers. . . .

William Marnell in his book, *Man-Made Morals: Four Philosophies That Shaped America,* summed it up:

"Such concepts as natural rights and human equality [according to social Darwinism] are part of the outworn folklore of a romantic past; the scientific study of folkways reveals that all rights are man-made products of the mores of society, subject to change as society develops, and the entire tenet of social Darwinism rebuts the romantic fallacy of human equality. Liberty and property are one and inseparable, progress and the acquisitive instinct are Siamese twins. Government exists to protect one's liberty to exercise his acquisitive instinct in the accumulation of property and thus to forward the progress of civilization. All that really is needed is a properly educated and disciplined legislature to write this philosophy into law, and a properly educated and disciplined Supreme Court to read it in. . . .

"The Supreme Court began to show the requisite training and discipline about 1870, as the influence of the most dedicated social Darwinian in Court history, Stephen J. Field (1816-1899), began to make itself felt. . . . There was an instinct for liberty in the bone and marrow of Justice Field, an individualism rooted in his Calvinistic inheritance, . . . buttressed by the philosophy he learned at Williams College from Mark Hopkins, . . . broadened into a comprehensive philosophy of the law partly by his own legal experience and partly by his reading in such social Darwinians as (Herbert) Spencer and (William Graham) Sumner. This was the philosophy of law Stephen Field brought to the Supreme Court. At first it was the philosophy of one man, then the philosophy of a minority of the Court, and then the prevailing philosophy until it was successfully challenged by the philosophy of Justices Brandeis and Holmes. Field preached and practiced what one might term legal Darwinism, an outgrowth of which it was a part, (of) social Darwinism.

159

"The instrument Field chose to make effective his philosophy was the Fourteenth Amendment. . . .

"Field maintained that the passage of the Fourteenth Amendment made one a citizen of the United States and not a citizen of a specific state, and hence that personal rights do not come from state or local legislation and cannot be abridged or destroyed by state or local authority. . . .

"Thereafter the ideological tide turned in Field's favor. In 1886, the Court decided in *Santa Clara County v. Southern Pacific Railroad* that a corporation was a person within the meaning of the Fourteenth Amendment. In 1887, in *Mugler v. Kansas,* it reversed the long-revered *McCulloch v. Maryland* doctrine, enunciated in 1819, that the wisdom of a regulative act is a question for the legislature's judgment.

"In 1905, it sounded what then seemed the death knell of *McCulloch v. Maryland* when it decided in *Lochner v. New York* that a law which limited working hours violated freedom of contract. In all these cases the due-process and equal-protection-of-the-law clauses of the Fourteenth Amendment were applied to corporations in the guise of persons. Charles Warren, in his definitive *The Supreme Court in United States History,* reveals that between 1889 and 1918 there were 790 cases in which statutes were attacked under these two clauses, the great majority concerning the use of police power. There were fifty-three cases, however, in which the Court ruled a statute unconstitutional as a violation of the Fourteenth Amendment, and two-thirds of them involved the rates and regulations of public service corporations.

"Thus, the legal Darwinians found in the Fourteenth Amendment the instrument needed for their purpose. There is a vagueness to its phrasing that admits and even invites divergent interpretations, and as time passed and the spirit exemplified by Justice Field prevailed, a series of ever widening interpretations made of the Fourteenth Amendment a comprehensive Bill of Rights for corporations. Another series of decisions of an ever narrowing sort finally created a legal vortex into which were sucked most of the newly won rights of the former slaves. Their unimpeded right to vote, their rights of peaceable assembly and petition for redress of grievances, their right to the full and equal enjoyment of public accommodations and private accommodations that served the public were nullified by a series of eight Supreme Court decisions between 1876 and 1884 involving the rights of Negroes.

"Warren concludes that of the enforcement laws passed to implement the three liberation amendments only a small fraction remained even nominally in force. Of the forty-seven sections of the three amendments, forty-two were repealed or declared invalid. A corporation was a person, but a Negro was not. There were racist aspects to social Darwinism also — they are soundly treated by Richard Hofstadter in his *Social Darwinism and American Thought* — but they lie outside the scope of this book."[27]

In direct language this means that the majority of the Supreme Court by espousing a philosophy alien to the Constitution practically nullified three amendments to the Constitution insofar as their original purpose was concerned. They had been designed to protect the newly freed slaves: "Another series of decisions of an ever narrowing sort created a legal vortex into which were sucked most of the newly won rights of the former slaves. . . ." The harm done was corrected by the Warren Court of the '50s; but what untold agony was experienced by the blacks for two generations, suffering which could have been alleviated had the Court endeavored to fulfill the purpose of the Thirteenth, Fourteenth and Fifteenth Amendments? And how much race tension exists today because of the Court's actions?

But the Court between 1887-1937 used the Fourteenth Amendment to implement its philosophy of social Darwinism by determining that corporations were "persons" within the meaning of the amendment. Since to the majority of the Court members *laissez-faire* economics were necessary to insure business and consequently national prosperity, these "persons" must have full freedom to make any contracts useful to their business — even if human persons are injured. Human persons, too, must be "free" to make contracts; states could not use police powers to force minimum-wage contracts even when workers were obliged to accept pay below human standards because of inability to bargain collectively. And this was during the period of the seventy-hour work week, of "yellow dog" employment contracts wherein workmen were forced to agree not to join a union as a condition of employment, of children in factories and women used under conditions injurious to health and morals. . . .

## Supreme Court Justices
### Dissent From Social Darwinism

For half a century the Supreme Court was dominated by men who substituted their own philosophy of social Darwinism as the criterion to interpret the Constitution for the philosophy of the Founding Fathers who drafted it. This was done over the protest of other Justices. Samuel Freeman Miller was a Southerner bitterly opposed to slavery; Lincoln appointed him to the Court in 1862; he was on the bench until 1890. He is considered one of the great Justices and in his own time was compared to John Marshall. Miller believed in human rights:

"'Hence, he fought to have the Constitution's Fourteenth Amendment used, as it was originally intended, to defend the political and civil rights of Negroes instead of as an excuse for the judicial veto of state laws which regulated business. It was a losing fight on both levels and it drove him increasingly into dissent as the Court became staffed and stuffed with 'railroad lawyers.' But before he began to be outvoted, Miller had been able to proclaim in the famous Slaughterhouse Cases that the Amendment's 'one pervading purpose' was 'the freedom of the slave race, the security and firm establishment of that freedom, and the protection of the newly-made freeman and citizen' — and, prophetically, that to read the Amendment otherwise 'would constitute this Court a perpetual censor upon all legislation of the states. . . .' "[28]

Another great Justice in the tradition of the Founding Fathers was a member of the Supreme Court during the same grim period when, because of social Darwinism, property was more important than people. Louis D. Brandeis, on the Court from 1916 until 1939, was a brilliant graduate of Harvard Law School and an extremely prosperous lawyer and leader in the profession. But he was also on the side of the little man; at times he represented consumers and workingmen without pay. He was considered too radical by the wealth and power of his day and when appointed to the Court by President Wilson was opposed by formidable personages, including seven former presidents of the American Bar Association, the president of Harvard and a number of important business leaders.

Brandeis was of Jewish origin but was reared outside any formal religion.

"His mother later wrote: 'I do not believe that sins can be expiated by going to divine service and observing this or that formula; I believe that only goodness and truth and conduct that is humane and self-sacrificing towards those who need us can bring God nearer to us, and that our errors can only be atoned for by acting in a more kindly spirit. Love, virtue and truth are the foundation upon which the education of the child must be based. . . . And this is my justification for bringing up my children without any definite religious belief: I wanted to give them something that neither could be argued away nor would have to be given up as untenable, namely, a pure spirit and the highest ideals as to morals and love.' When she added, 'God has blessed my endeavors,' she did so with entire right. Louis Brandeis measured to his mother's ideal about as well as any man can measure to his mother's ideal, and in his case the ideal can do double duty as the description of the man.

"Brandeis, then, was essentially a humanist, but unlike the pragmatist Holmes there are traces here and there in Brandeis of a sort of religion of humanism that suggests a belief in permanent values of the sort enshrined in the religion of the churches. . . . 'Always and everywhere the intellectual, moral and spiritual development of those concerned will remain an essential — and the main factor — in real betterment. This development of the individual is, thus, both a necessary means and the end sought.' And after stressing the thought that the great developer is responsibility and that no pattern of society demands the responsible individual quite as urgently as the democratic, he concludes: 'Democracy in any sphere is a serious undertaking. It substitutes self-restraint for external restraint. It is more difficult to maintain than to achieve. It demands continuous sacrifice by the individual and more exigent obedience to the moral law than any other form of government. Success in any democratic undertaking must proceed from the individual. It is possible only where the process of perfecting the individual is pursued. His development is attained mainly in the processes of common living. Hence the industrial struggle is essentially an affair of the Church and is its imperative task.' The man who believes in the objective reality of evil and immorality, and their opposite, a moral law, and who stresses that reform comes first in the heart of man if it comes at all, is the man with the essentials of a religious faith. . . .

"There were, then, fundamental attitudes present in Brandeis consistent with belief in a permanent and objective moral order. Indeed, the parallel which has occasionally been drawn between the thinking of Thomas Jefferson and Louis Brandeis, a fairly superficial parallel based upon an instinct for a wholesome limitation upon political and economic power, may itself have a more significant parallel of a different sort. Essentially Brandeis was such a deist as Jefferson, one who believed in an objective moral law but one who found himself in an intellectual halfway house between belief in a divinely created order and belief in a man-made order. Perhaps belief in a man-made order constructed in accordance with objective moral principles best defines the belief of Brandeis, with the basis for the objectivity of the moral principles left undefined."[29]

Justice Brandeis was so often joined in dissent with his brilliant colleague on the Court, Oliver Wendell Holmes, both opposing the *laissez-faire* principles of the majority, that they became linked in the public mind. But herein lies a deep paradox. Brandeis and Holmes often reached the same conclusion by different paths.

Holmes opposed the Court majority because he held that no constitution should be interpreted by any economic theory. He went on to state that constitutions were made for people of fundamentally differing views; and when read in the context of his personal philosophy he meant that there are no fundamentals which a people must hold in common when bound by a written constitution. For Holmes there were no absolutes, no inalienable rights, no natural moral law which can be presupposed when a constitution is adopted. This is the exact opposite of what the Founding Fathers meant by the American Constitution; our Constitution was to be an implementation of how the American government and people were to protect and nourish the rights given them through their equal human nature. . . . But Brandeis reasoned in the same channels as the Founding Fathers even if he did not quote them.

Holmes' mind is given in his most famous dissent, in the case of Lochner vs. New York:

"This case is decided upon an economic theory which a large part of the country does not entertain. If it were a question whether I agreed with that theory, I should desire to study it further and long before making up my mind. But I do not conceive that to be my duty, because I strongly believe that my agreement or disagreement has nothing to do with the right of a majority to embody their opinions in law. . . . The Fourteenth Amendment does not enact Mr. Herbert Spencer's Social Statics. . . . But a Constitution is not intended to embody a particular economic theory, whether of paternalism and the organic relation of the citizen to the State or of laissez-faire. It is made for people of fundamentally differing views, and the accident of our finding certain opinions natural and familiar or novel and even shocking ought not to conclude our judgement upon the question whether statutes embodying them conflict with the Constitution of the United States. . . ."[30]

Holmes and Brandeis had different starting points, traveled different routes, paradoxically meeting at the end of the decision road:

". . . The fallacy of combining the philosophies of Oliver Wendell Holmes and Brandeis by the same link that so often bound their judicial decisions has, of course, long been recognized and is expounded in all responsible studies of the Supreme Court, its justices, and their legal attitudes. It is true that Holmes and Brandeis frequently reached the same judicial conclusions, but it is also true that they frequently did so by markedly different routes and always

165

did so from different intellectual starting points. Holmes had precisely the correct pattern of mind for a pragmatist: he was ironic, skeptical, detached, a Yankee who didn't really descend very often from Olympus but stayed mainly on its remote heights, like an Olympian in the tradition of deism. It would be pleasantly simple to say that Brandeis had precisely the wrong frame of mind for a pragmatist, but it would not be true. Brandeis had in some respects an excellent frame of mind for a pragmatist, and yet one utterly incompatible with a philosophy that flourished on irony, skepticism, and detachment. Brandeis was not ironic but direct and sincere, not skeptical but dedicated to belief in the progress of the human order, not detached but body and soul involved. His direct sincerity, dedicated belief, and total involvement in the betterment of the human order almost kept him off the Supreme Court in 1916 when President Wilson's unexpected nomination precipitated a forensic hurricane exceeded in intensity during the twentieth century only by the typhoon that Roosevelt's Court-packing plan whipped up. . . ."[31]

Justice Brandeis' thought is in the tradition of the Founding Fathers. Justice Holmes was an atheist, a skeptic who had lost belief in God, who could see no basic order or meaning to the universe. In one of his letters he wrote:

"I often say over to myself the verse 'O God be merciful to me a fool' the fallacy of which to my mind (you won't agree with me) is in the 'me' that it looks on man as a little God over against the universe, instead of as a cosmic ganglion, a momentary intersection of what humanly speaking we call streams of energy, such as gives white light at one point and the power of making syllogisms at another, but always an inseverable part of the unimaginable, in which we live and move and have our being, no more needing its mercy than my little toe needs mine. It would be well if the intelligent classes could forget the word sin and think less of being good. We learn how to behave as lawyers, soldiers, merchants or what not by being them. Life, not the parson, teaches conduct."[32]

By the philosophy of the Founders it was accidental that

Holmes' dissents brought him to the side of the little man. Justice Brandeis came to the right conclusions for the right reasons; Holmes came to the right decisions for the wrong reasons. And Holmes' philosophy in time was to wreak havoc in American legal thought; it would finally justify constitutional decisions which epitomize the opposite to what the Fathers stood for, v.g., the 1972 Blackmun decision denying the right to life of unborn babies; and it would be a source of today's confusion in the legal profession.

## Justice Oliver Wendell Holmes: Law Is Force

Aspell in the quotation given above says "the winds of controversy howl so strongly around that subject (the definition of law) that it seems unwise to take it on in a discussion of what law *does.* Therefore the term will not be defined; if this be chaos make the most of it." This *has* led to chaos; this is perhaps the main cause of sickness in the legal profession and one of the causes of sickness in society. Helping to cause the confusion is Holmes' definition of law so strongly adhered to by lawyers who agree with Prof. Presser, who disagree with President Ford's approach to his legal obligations or Prof. Freund's remedy for the sickness in the legal profession quoted above. Prof. Presser gives his definition of law as the ". . . terribly astute . . . epigram of Oliver Wendell Holmes, Jr., to the effect that our law is nothing more nor less than predictions of what our courts will do in certain instances." Here is a root of the confusion of the legal profession: law is nothing more than what the courts will enforce, not an ordination of reason which will promote the common good as held by the Founding Fathers.

Prof. Presser truly interpreted Holmes' idea of law. Holmes gave probably the most famous summation of his doctrine when he spoke at the dedication of a new building for the Boston University School of Law in 1897:

"The object of our study (law), then, is prediction, the prediction of the incidence of the public force through the instrumentality of the courts. . . .

"The means of the study are a body of reports, of treatises, and of statutes, in this country and in England, extending back for six hundred years, and now increasing annually by the hundreds. In these sibylline leaves are gathered the scattered prophecies of the past upon the cases in which the axe will fall. These are what properly have been called the oracles of the law. Far the most important and pretty nearly the whole meaning of every new effort of legal thought is to make these prophecies more precise, and to generalize them into a thoroughly connected system. . . . The primary rights and duties with which jurisprudence busies itself again are nothing but prophecies. One of the many evil effects of the confusion between legal and moral ideas, about which I shall have something to say in a moment, is that theory is apt to get the cart before the horse, and to consider the right or the duty as something existing apart from and independent of its breach, to which certain sanctions are added afterward. But, as I shall try to show, a legal duty so called, is nothing but a prediction that if a man does or omits certain things he will be made to suffer in this or that way by judgement of the court; and so of legal right. . . ."[33]

There was a complete divorce between law and morality in the thinking of Justice Holmes, but he explained himself:

"I take it for granted that no hearer of mine will misinterpret what I have to say as the language of cynicism. The law is the witness and external deposit of our moral life. Its history is the history of the moral development of our race. The practice of it, in spite of popular jests, tends to make good citizens and good men. When I emphasize the difference between law and morals I do so with reference to a single end, that of learning and understanding the law. . . ."[34]

But the context shows that Holmes *is* saying there is no intrinsic connection between law and morality; law is merely the witness of the external deposit of our moral life — witness, but not guide. The Founding Fathers insisted that there must be an intrinsic connection between the two. To Holmes the essence of law is force; to the Fathers the essence of law is its reasonableness, its correspondence with human nature properly understood.

Yet Holmes was a great judge, and the author or origin of some of the wisest Supreme Court decisions of our time; sometimes his dissents on the side of the common man became law in the next generation. Part of the reason is that he worked with a long tradition of English and American precedents in law which were reasonable and humane, decisions given by men who believed in the Judeo-Christian tradition and interpretation of justice and law. Holmes did not tear up by the roots, and he was willing to put the power of the government behind social-reform legislation. He did not say that law is naked force in the way the Nazis practiced it, or in the traditional way that tyrants cover their acts with legalisms as they impose upon helpless citizens. Rather he planted a seed idea which insisted that law is force, but in practice is built on past precedents which gradually change in meaning according to what a judge thinks is expedient for a community. Francis Biddle, former secretary and biographer of Justice Holmes, later Attorney General of the United States (1941-1945), said in a lecture:

"The substance of the law, according to Holmes, at any given time pretty nearly corresponds with what is then thought to be 'convenient.' He constantly recurred to this thought. Since law is but one expression of community life, you must look to the community to discover the existing notions of public policy, which are continually changing. He would not speak of justification, for that presupposed an absolute criterion, whereas the problem was: 'Does this decision represent what the lawmaking power must be taken to want?' He would have liked to get a more definite reason than that the decision was in consonance with our sense of justice, and find a more specific policy than that. Law is what the supreme power in the community wills; and all that could be expected from modern improvements is that legislation should easily and quickly, yet not too quickly, modify itself to the will of that *de facto* power, and that the spread of an educated sympathy should reduce the sacrifice of minorities to a minimum."[35]

William H. Marnell sums this up:

"That is pragmatism in the law, succinctly and clearly stated.

No longer do the rights of minorities depend upon the doctrine of the rights of man and its enshrinement in the Constitution of the United States, but upon 'the spread of an educated sympathy' among the majority. Such thinking is quite consistent with the thought of Oliver Wendell Holmes when he said, 'Our system of morality is a body of imperfect generalizations expressed in terms of emotion.' "[36]

Melville M. Bigelow, a friend of Holmes, was one of the men who helped found Boston University School of Law. As if to implement Holmes' theory, which he endorsed, he wrote in 1906:

"The conception of law which the faculty of Boston University Law School stands for is that the law is the expression, more or less deflected by opposition, of the dominant force in society. . . . It follows from the view that law is the resultant of actual, conflicting forces in society, that the notion of abstract, eternal principles as a governing power, with their author the external sovereign, must go."[37]

One of our great legal scholars has this to say:

". . . Holmes' thought had a quite traceable and significant influence on a movement during the 1920s and '30s that came to be known as American Legal Realism. . . . No doubt he did not find to his liking what might be called its style. One can hardly imagine his subscribing to the Realist definition of law as 'the behavior patterns of judges and other state officials,' though this definition merely converted into the clichés of the day his own conception of law as a prophecy of what courts will do in fact."[38]

In some famous dissents Holmes pointed out clearly that the other Justices were violating the compact which is our Constitution: they were making themselves a super-legislature, imposing their own theory of *laissez-faire* economics on a country which they could not prove agreed with them, and going over the heads of the legislative branch to which some decisions were given by the Constitution. But in his philosophy such an action was law; it would be enforced by the courts and by the executive branch. To Holmes law is nothing but force, the prediction of where and how the public force will fall in a particular situation. . . . He was a kindly man; one wonders what he would have done if presiding on a Nazi bench, where the force of German law was falling on millions of helpless victims. . . . It could very well be that he would have the courage to become a victim rather than enforce such "laws". . . . But by the standards of the Founders his theory has wreaked havoc in succeeding generations of American legal thinking, and his theory permitted an illegitimate growth of law; whatever the courts decided became part of the American legal structure.

## Law Is More Than Force; The Founders' Tradition Lives

Holmes did not convince all lawyers that his theory of law was the true one or that the doctrine of the Founding Fathers was dead. Men like Samuel F. Miller and Louis D. Brandeis, rated among the greats of Supreme Court Justices, disagreed strongly, incisively. One can call natural law dead, but one cannot bury human nature. Prof. Charles L. Black, Jr., of Yale University School of Law indicates in his book, *The Two Cities of Law,* why the principles of the Founding Fathers live perennially:

"On the ground of man's public life, two shapes of law may be discerned — sometimes in mutual complement, sometimes in contrast.

"First, there is the law that prevails in society. Courts decide cases and give reasons for their decisions. Statutes are printed and read. Precedents are recorded and used as lawyers' ingenuity may devise. People enjoy legacies, lose cars to the finance company, get married, go to the penitentiary. And as a matter of psychological fact, there exists, in the minds of judges and lawyers, a conceptual framework to guide and explain all this activity. This structure of legal ideas is not exactly the same in any two minds, but there is enough agreement for law to do its work — and even the fact of disagreement is a fact about law as it exists. This law that palpably prevails in each nation may be called 'positive law.'

"Second, as misty as a Chinese painter's mountain, but as insistently there as the Chinese painter makes his mountain seem, is another shape of law — the image of law as men in their time think law ought to be. This ideal law cannot be known, as positive law can be known, from the deeds and words of lawyers and judges at their professional tasks. Those who would persuade us of its requirements cannot point to the readable print of code or reported decision. All we can know from all these sources is the tenor of such law as exists and prevails — and that may be good law or bad law.

"Yet we are compelled to seek the shape of right law. By taking up this quest, we may be transgressing the canons of scientific positivism, but if we do not take it up we strip ourselves of the insignia of humanity. And so from the earliest inscriptions in pyramid tombs down to the latest article in the Yale Law Journal, from the Cheyenne Indian before Custer to the man riding uptown on the Broadway express, we try and always have tried not only to know the law as it is but also to discern, however dimly and uncertainly, what it may be that justice requires of law.

"This search for light in law has taken many forms. Recurrently through Western history, the name 'natural law' has been given to the projected image of law as it ought to be. Aristotle and Cicero wrote of a law of nature, against which human positive law was to be measured. Aquinas brought the concept within his mighty synthesis. Grotius built it into the foundations of modern international law. John Locke made the idea a perdurable part of liberal thought in England, whence it crossed the Atlantic to enter our own Declaration of Independence, in that document's opening appeal to 'the Laws of Nature and of Nature's God. . . .' 'Natural law' thought permeates the epochs of our intellectual tradition.

"Natural law, as conceived by its proponents, bears none of the marks of positive law. It is not set up by the state; no court shapes it; no legislature establishes or changes it. Instead, its expounders have been philosophers and publicists, professors and ecclesiastics. Each proposition in each natural-law system can claim

172

validity solely on the basis of arguments advanced by people who write books on the subject. Their reasoning starts with stated or assumed beliefs about the nature of man; from these beliefs are drawn conclusions as to what law ought to be. The end product, when fully developed, is a system of ideal law, which can be held up as a model for comparison with positive law.

"Hugo Grotius, one of the greatest of the natural lawyers, shortly stated the underlying assumption:

" 'The law of nature is a dictate of a right reason which points out that an act according as it is or is not in conformity with the social and rational nature of man has in it a quality of moral baseness or moral necessity, and that, in consequence, such an act is either forbidden or enjoined by the author of nature, God.'

"In the reach of historic time not one but many systems of natural law have been elaborated in this way. These have differed widely. But the root idea remains surprisingly constant; from it 'natural law' thought takes its name. In age after age it has been maintained or assumed that there is a right law, a just law, inferrible by reason from the nature of man, and of his relations to his society and to the cosmic order.

"It is implausible — though not impossible — that so richly accredited a tradition should turn out after all to be entirely worthless. It is therefore surprising that what may fairly be called the dominant view in British and American jurisprudence today rejects the concept of 'natural law,' and waves away the whole corpus of natural-law speculation. It is not that any single system of purportedly 'natural law' is rejected, but rather that the value of natural-law reasoning as a whole is denied — expressly or by eloquent disregard."[39]

## Judges Make Law

Oliver Wendell Holmes spoke his famous definition of law in 1897; he was at that time a member of the Supreme Judicial Court of Massachusetts. His words were: "The object of our study (law), then, is prediction, the prediction of the incidence of the public force through the instrumentality of the courts." This became the epigram quoted above by Prof. Presser "to the effect that our law is nothing more nor less than predictions of what our courts will do in certain instances."

It is somewhat jolting to the layman to find that court decisions are the final source of law for the lawyer. Do not the legislatures in each state make the laws for their jurisdiction? Does not the Constitution say, "All legislative powers herein granted shall be vested in a Congress of the United States which shall consist of a Senate and House of Representatives"? But in practice law is what the courts say it is, from the Supreme Court down to a local municipal court; in this sense at least Holmes' definition is true. Of course, in enforcing statute law passed by legislatures, judges are presumed to interpret and apply laws according to the intention of the legislatures which passed them. But when doubt exists, it is the court's determination of what the legislature meant that holds. Even of the Constitution, in the expression of Chief Justice Hughes (between his two terms on the Supreme Court), the Constitution means what the Supreme Court says its means.

But in a more hidden way, evident from our history, courts actually make law. Because the people do not realize this, it carries a constant danger to society. Supreme Court Justice Felix Frankfurter, while yet a professor at Harvard Law School, summed up the mysteries of "declared law":

"So the problem is not whether the judges make the law, but when and how and how much. . . . I used to say to my students that legislatures make law wholesale, judges retail. . . . One of the evil features, a very evil one, about all this assumption that judges only find the law and don't make it (is) the lack of candor. By covering up the law-making function of judges, we miseducate the people and fail to bring out into the open the real responsibility of judges for what they do."[40]

The people do not advert to the fact that judge-made law may be more important for the future of society than statutes passed by legislators. Justice Frankfurter describes the process which leads to judicial lawmaking:

"What are the sources of law and what are its sanctions? What is appropriate lawmaking by courts and what should be left to legislation? What are the ingredients, conscious or unconscious, of adjudication? What are the wise demands of precedent and when should the judicial process feel unbound by its past?"[41]

Very early in his career Holmes gave a series of lectures which later became his book *The Common Law*. He gives his version of the ingredients of judicial lawmaking as he takes it from English and American legal history:

". . . In substance the growth of the law is legislative. And this in a deeper sense than what the courts declare to have always been the law is in fact new. It is legislative in its grounds. The very considerations which judges most rarely mention, and always with an apology, are the secret root from which the law draws all the juices of life. I mean, of course, considerations of what is expedient for the community concerned. Every important principle which is developed in litigation is in fact and at bottom the more or less definitely understood views of public policy; most generally, to be sure, under our practice and traditions, the unconscious result of instinctive preferences and inarticulate convictions, but none the less traceable to views of public policy in the last analysis. And as the law is administered by able and experienced men, who know too much to sacrifice good sense to a syllogism, it will be found that, when ancient rules maintain themselves in a way that has been and will be shown in this book, new reasons more fitted to the time have been found for them, and that they gradually receive a new content, and at last a new form, from the grounds to which they had been transplanted."[42]

Again we have Holmes' thesis that law is expediency, law is public policy — law is force. But he makes a more historically true statement: judge-made law is legislative. English common law which the colonists brought with them from England to the New World had its origin in judicial decisions going back 500 years; these were still valid unless superseded by later decisions or specifically changed by Parliamentary statutes of newer times. But the

Founding Fathers never accepted the principle that laws are merely matters of public expediency: common law as they made it the basis of American law has as its foundation natural law, the laws of morality. Thus Hamilton, quoting Sir William Blackstone, pointed out:

"Good and wise men . . . have supposed, that the deity, from the relations we stand in to himself and to each other, has constituted an eternal and immutable law, which is, indispensibly, obligatory upon all mankind, prior to any human institution whatsoever.

"This is what is called the law of nature, 'which being coeval with mankind, and dictated by God himself, is, of course, superior in obligation to any other. It is binding over all the globe, in all countries, at all times. No human laws are of any validity, if contrary to this; and such of them as are valid, derive all their authority, mediately, or immediately, from this original.' "[43]

Hamilton in quoting Blackstone was citing the great law authority for all America; it was his interpretation of common law that Americans accepted. And Edward S. Corwin in *The Constitution and What It Means Today*, the standard basic text in constitutional law since 1920, states:

"The initial source of judicial review, however, is much older than the Constitution and indeed of any American Constitution. It traces back to the common law, certain principles of which were earlier deemed to be 'fundamental' and to comprise 'higher law' which even Parliament could not alter. 'And it appears,' wrote Chief Justice Coke in 1610, in his famous dictum in Bonham's case, 'that when an act of Parliament is against common right and reason . . . the common law will control it and adjudge such an act to be void.' "[44]

In other words, common law included the moral law so clearly that in accordance with its commands judges could void acts of Parliament. This is the law superior to all human law; as Blackstone indicates, no human law, including judge-made law, is valid if against

176

the natural moral law. The Fathers would never concede that law was merely public expediency; for this reason they fought a bloody war.

From the long history of English common law we find a justification of the vital power of judges to legislate, and, contrary to Holmes' oversimplification that law is public expediency in action, that common law was a search for justice.

"Common Law is the body of customary law based upon judicial decisions and embodied in reports of decided cases, which has been administered by the common-law courts of England since the middle ages."[45] Its remote origin is comprised of ancient English customs, but it replaced the more barbarous ones such as trial by ordeal. The customs were the customs not just of a section but common to all England. In the early days most of the judges were clergymen, the educated men of the times who knew Roman law, canon law, moral theology and natural law.[46] Common law was judge-made law; that is, once a judge made decisions which were recognized to coincide with custom and sound moral principles, natural justice, succeeding judges would follow the decision: if it were just the first time it was considered to remain just. As society grew and changed, the law grew with it, so that after several centuries there was a recognized body of principles upon which judges could draw to decide new cases.

"During the 15th century (after common law became rigid and partly inadequate), petitions to the king to 'do justice' went to the lord chancellor, 'keeper of the king's conscience,' "[47] The chancellor was the secretary to the king, almost always a cleric. A court separate from the common-law courts with chancellor as judge thus grew into existence; it was primarily concerned with the moral concept of equity rather than legal rights. Thus it was a court to apply principles of natural justice, natural fairness, natural law. Both common law and equity were presumed to reach solutions which were just.[48]

The history of common-law courts and the court of chancery which came into being when common-law courts became inadequate indicates the continuing search for justice in England. When Parliament passed laws which were unjust, Chief Justice Coke in

1610 would assert "that when an act of Parliament is against common right and reason . . . the common law will control it and adjudge such an act to be void." It is this common law and the custom of judges making law based on moral principles that the United States inherited from England.

American colonies had power from the beginning to make laws; v.g., the Maryland charter granted Lord Baltimore the right to make laws "consonant to reason and . . . not repugnant or contrary to the Laws . . . of England." To enforce laws courts were set up, and these in their use of juries and grand juries, writs and summons show their English heritage. By 1774 the First Continental Congress in its "Declaration and Resolves" declared "that the respective colonies are entitled to the common law of England. . . ." In a common-law system judges make part of the law even if this has been denied in theory.

Thus American judges inherited naturally the power to make law by judicial decision; their colonial background indicated this as a normal process. But the new states also framed new constitutions which defined the powers of the three branches of each government. The process of framing governments with specified written rules and powers was America's unique contribution to modern law; England had no written constitution, and the only Parliamentary statutes which a court could assert to be null were those against natural law. In America the constitutions were ratified by the people at large, were considered to be the fundamental law of the state, and guided the running of the three branches of government. But it was the courts which would interpret the constitutions. It was Hamilton who explained this natural power of the judiciary in Federalist Paper No. 78:

"The interpretation of the laws is the proper and peculiar province of the courts. A constitution is, in fact, and must be regarded by the judges, as a fundamental law. It must therefore belong to them to ascertain its meaning as well as the meaning of any particular act proceeding from the legislative body. . . ."[49]

So American judges inherited the power to make law retail,

piece by piece, as Justice Frankfurter said, and inherited the power to determine the final meaning of statutory and constitutional law. . . . But the judges were to be governed by the written constitutions: honest men it was presumed would interpret each constitution according to the meaning they knew it had when the people accepted it; otherwise there was no value in a written constitution. And above, beyond all else, judges were to be guided by natural, moral law. Bills of rights, in philosophical terms, were appended to these constitutions. These natural rights were part of natural law which no judge, no legislator could change. . . .

## Legitimate Growth Of American Law

The Founding Fathers not only knew what law was, they knew that law must grow as the country grew, and they intended it to grow in an orderly way in accordance with the natural-law principles developed in Western civilization. Prof. Black outlined their principles for living law in the above quotation.[50] The English tradition of law which grew with judges meeting new situations by new precedents went back 500 years in common-law history; it was a natural inheritance for American judges who were heirs of common law. But within common law were the guidelines for its growth; new decisions were not to be the arbitrary will of judges currently on the bench. The guidelines had been first established half a millennium before by the early judges, mostly clerics learned in Roman and canon law, in moral theology and rules of natural justice. When common law became rigid and partly inadequate in the fifteenth century, English kings set up a court of chancery, a court of equity, where the chancellor as judge could bypass common law and by using natural-law principles see that justice was done. It was all this English law which Americans received as colonists; they lumped it under one name as common law, and as accepted by the Americans it included natural law:

"It (American judicial review) traces back to the common law, certain principles of which were earlier deemed to be 'fundamental'

179

and to comprise a 'higher law' which even Parliament could not alter. 'And it appears,' wrote Chief Justice Coke in 1610, in his famous dictum in Bonham's case, 'that when an act of Parliament is against common right and reason . . . the common law will control it and adjudge such an act to be void.' "[51]

America has a written Constitution, but the Constitution included the same principles for orderly growth which were possessed by the common law. The founding generation not only ratified the Constitution, it established legal and moral principles which were to be the guidelines for its interpretation, implicitly for its growth. The principles are summarized in the preamble to the Constitution:

"We the People of the United States, in order to form a more perfect Union, establish Justice, insure domestic Tranquility, provide for the common defence, promote the general Welfare, and secure the Blessings of Liberty to ourselves and our Posterity, do ordain and establish this Constitution for the United States of America."

More specific philosophical words for their intentions are found in the Declaration of Independence; more specific legal terms for the implementation of these purposes are found especially in the Bill of Rights, the first ten amendments.

To ". . . establish Justice, insure domestic Tranquility, provide for the common defence, promote the general Welfare, and secure the Blessings of Liberty to ourselves and our Posterity . . ." are but statements of the function of a just government according to natural law: thus implies the Declaration of Independence. "To establish justice" is the most all-embracing phrase that can be used to indicate adherence to natural law. Justice is something to be sought after, found; it is established, not created. It exists in the nature of things when men respect each other's human rights, when government protects these rights and enforces just obligations. Thus along with the Constitution the Founders enunciated the rules for its interpretation: natural law, natural justice.

According to the Declaration, and intended by the Constitution, the individual human person is central, comes before society. Chief Justice Marshall believed in the rights of each individual; as a young soldier in Washington's army he suffered through the bitter winter at Valley Forge for the inalienable rights. The British by taxation without representation had violated the natural right to property of the Americans. In practice the right to private property became the paramount natural right to some Founding Fathers. To those of the Federalist party (and Marshall became a strong Federalist as he pursued his political career) the protection of property was the keystone of good government and a prosperous society. To the Federalists liberty was linked to property. At the time there were literally millions of acres of land up for grabs in an essentially agrarian society; anybody with gumption could be a property owner. They were afraid of the propertyless thousands of the cities; men who have no stake in society lack incentive to be stable and reliable citizens:

"Freedom for property would result in liberty for men — perhaps not for all men, but at least for all worthy men. Because men have different faculties and abilities they acquire different amounts of property. To protect property is only to protect men in the exercise of their natural faculties. Among the many liberties, therefore, freedom to hold and dispense property is paramount. Democracy, unchecked rule by the masses, is sure to bring arbitrary redistribution of property, destroying the very essence of liberty."[52]

Unfortunately, Marshall was prone to defend property rights to the extent that other human rights suffered. Many dubious land titles of dishonest land speculators were upheld by him. He also permitted the Cherokee Indians to be robbed of their land. Marshall can only be condemned for these decisions. But he worked within a sound philosophy of law, and the only major defeat he suffered as Chief Justice came about in 1827 when, according to natural-law principles, four of the seven Justices on the Supreme Court ruled against his excessive zeal to protect property rights and held that state bankruptcy laws were constitutional. Justice William Johnson wrote for the majority:

"It is among the duties of society to enforce the rights of humanity, and both the debtor and the society have their interest in the administration of justice, and in the general good, interests which must not be swallowed up and lost sight of while yielding attention to the claim of the creditor. The debtor may plead the visitation of Providence, and the society has an interest in preserving every member of the community from despondency — in relieving him from a hopeless state of prostration in which he would be useless to himself, his family and the community. When this state of things has arrived, in which the community has fairly and fully discharged its duties to the creditor, and in which, pursuing the debtor any longer would destroy the one without benefiting the other, must always be a question to be determined by the common guardian of the rights of both; and in this originates the power exercised by governments in favor of insolvents."[53]

As the Founding Fathers understood it, and as the Supreme Court of 1827 interpreted it, a written constitution specifies how the natural law will be implemented in a particular country. Its concrete wording, to which judges can ordinarily go to declare how justice will be accomplished in an individual case, does not eliminate the fact that the natural law is always presupposed as the foundation of the civil constitution and therefore part of it.

Alexander Hamilton gives the Fathers' understanding of the relationship of all law, common law and constitutional law included, to natural law:

"Good and wise men . . . have supposed, that the deity, from the relations we stand in to himself and to each other, has constituted an eternal and immutable law, which is, indispensibly, obligatory upon all mankind, prior to any human institution whatsoever."[54]

And Hamilton quotes Blackstone, the bible from which American lawyers of the founding generation drew their understanding of all law, including the new state and national constitutional law then planting roots:

"This is what is called the law of nature, 'which being coeval

182

with mankind, and dictated by God himself, is, of course, superior in obligation to any other. It is binding over all the globe, in all countries, at all times. No human laws are of any validity, if contrary to this; and such of them as are valid, derive all their authority, mediately, or immediately from this original.' "[55]

Pennsylvania opened its Constitutional Convention on July 15, 1776, adjourning on September 28, 1776. After stating in a preamble the reasons for separation from Great Britain, Chapter I is entitled *A Declaration of the Rights of the Inhabitants of the Commonwealth or State of Pennsylvania.* The members must have had the Virginia Bill of Rights before them, since many of the articles are substantially the same. Then the Pennsylvania Constitution advances to its *Plan or Frame of Government for the Commonwealth or State of Pennsylvania.* The *Declaration of Rights* is couched even more philosophically than Virginia's Bill of Rights, in sound natural-law expressions. But to make it quite clear that the *Declaration* is part of the Constitution, Section 46 under the *Plan or Frame of Government* states:

"The Declaration of Rights is hereby declared to be a part of the Constitution of this Commonwealth, and ought never to be violated on any pretence whatever."[56]

Natural law was not only the foundation for civil law, but part of it.

There is, of course, the basic reason for putting natural law in specific terms, in constitutional or common-law terms. This guarantees that law builds on the wisdom and experience of past generations; that individual judges are not given a license to impose their subjective ideas of justice on the community; that the community knows where it stands. For example, the natural law teaches that all men have a right to justice. In France this is implemented ordinarily by trial before trained judges, but Article VI of our Bill of Rights states:

"In all criminal prosecutions the accused shall enjoy the right to a speedy and public trial, by an impartial jury of the State and district wherein the crime shall have been committed, . . ."[57]

In other words, by natural law always binding in all countries, a man has a right to a just trial; in the United States that right to justice becomes more specific — he has a right to attain justice by means of an impartial jury. The benefit of the written Constitution gives a benefit similar to that given by any sound code of law. Justice achieved by past precedents becomes stabilized as law. A particular judge may not tamper with procedures or introduce his subjective code of justice in reaching decisions. From one point of view the more specific the words are which implement the attaining of natural justice the better the constitution. In our practice it has been found that grants of general powers, rights and duties, plus some which are specific, make for a constitution more able to meet the needs of changing times. But always, constitutional growth was to be made in accordance with the words of the Constitution and the natural law it presupposed.

The Johnson decision referred to above was handed down in 1827, forty years after the Constitution was drafted, more than a generation later in terms of people. Abraham Lincoln was eighteen years old. Had Abraham Lincoln been appointed to the Court in the 1850s instead of heading toward the White House, and had such a case been brought before him, we can be sure he would have used almost the same words in favor of human rights. What this implies is that as new problems would come, as conflicts would arise between the priority of the rights themselves, when the wording of the Constitution even broadly interpreted proved inadequate, the philosophy which was the foundation of constitutional law gave the ultimate guidelines for its growth. Thus believed the Founding Fathers; thus concurred the Supreme Court in 1827; thus were the principles which guided Lincoln all through his career. The Constitution was not to go through gyrations caused by Justices imposing their private philosophies on its interpretation.

Justice Johnson in the context of his decision rebuked Marshall when the Chief Justice had allowed the right to property to dominate the other human rights. Johnson spoke for the Court majority which upheld reasonable state bankruptcy laws; he reasoned in the natural-law tradition of the Fathers. Abraham Lincoln said all his political philosophy was rooted in the Declaration of Independence; as a lawyer Blackstone was his legal bible, the same Blackstone quoted by Hamilton to prove that civil law has its basis in the natural law ordained by the Creator to guide men in their mutual relations. As late as 1874 the Supreme Court used pure natural-law doctrine to void an act of the Kansas legislature which permitted municipalities to issue bonds to private enterprises to encourage manufacturing plants in their towns. In Loan Association vs. Topeka the Court ruled:

"It must be conceded that there are such rights in every free government beyond the control of the State. A government which recognized no such rights, which held the lives, the liberty, and the property of its citizens subject at all times to the absolute disposition and unlimited control of even the most democratic depository of power, is after all but a despotism. It is true it is a despotism of the many, of the majority, if you choose to call it so, but it is none the less a despotism. It may well be doubted if a man is to hold all that he is accustomed to call his own, all in which he has placed his happiness, and the security of which is essential to that happiness, under the unlimited dominion of others, whether it is not wiser that this power should be exercised by one man than by many.

"The theory of our governments, State and National, is opposed to the deposit of unlimited power anywhere. The executive, the legislative, and the judicial branches of these governments are all of limited and defined powers.

"There are limitations on such power which grow out of the essential nature of all free governments: implied reservations of individual rights, without which the social compact could not exist, and which are respected by all governments entitled to the name. No court, for instance, would hesitate to declare void a statute which enacted that A. and B. who are husband and wife to each other should be so no longer, but that A. should thereafter be the husband of C., and B. the wife of D. or which should enact that the homestead now owned by A. should no longer be his, but should henceforth be the property of B."[58]

Justice Clifford made the lone dissent:

185

"Courts cannot nullify an act of the State legislature on the vague ground that they think it opposed to a general latent spirit supposed to pervade or underlie the constitution, where neither the terms nor the implications of the instrument disclose any such restriction. Such a power is denied to the courts, because to concede it would be to make the courts sovereign over both the constitution and the people, and convert the government into a judicial despotism."[59]

But, of course, Justice Clifford obscures the issue. The Founding Fathers thought some truths self-evident, not merely "opposed to a general latent spirit supposed to pervade or underlie the constitution." Such are the evident natural rights to life, liberty, and the legitimate pursuit of happiness. His colleagues on the bench thought it was evident that mere civil law could not transfer one woman's husband to another woman, or one man's property to another. The American nation came into being because men thought these truths evident enough to fight for.

## Responsibility Of The Legal Profession

"It is implausible — though not impossible — that so richly accredited a tradition [of natural law as the basis and ideal of civil law] should turn out after all to be entirely worthless. It is therefore surprising that what may fairly be called the dominant view in British and American jurisprudence today rejects the concept of 'natural law,' and waves away the whole corpus of natural law speculation." (Prof. Charles L. Black, Jr.)[60]

The precepts of natural law were understood by the Founding Fathers and constituted the basis for American law. As late as 1874 the Supreme Court was invoking natural-law guidelines to interpret the Constitution. But within the next decade the Court began to substitute the tenets of social Darwinism, the "survival of the fittest" in economic affairs, by imposing *laissez-faire* criteria to interpret the constitutionality of state and federal legislation, in place of the previously held criteria of natural rights and the right to justice of each human being. About the same time, Justice Holmes' new definition of law as the prediction of the incidence of public force through the courts came into vogue. The confusion within the American legal profession dates in large measure from these happenings.

It is shocking to remember that the nation was built on clear-cut and ennobling principles of law which have fallen into such disuse and are studied with so little understanding that the legal profession is itself in disarray. With such leadership there is danger that the nation may lose the foundation of its civilization, its belief in the inherent dignity of each human being. Yet this belief is too deep in the hearts of the people to be replaced by less noble or less true theories; it coincides too much with common sense and human aspirations to be brushed aside. The struggle of the blacks for equal dignity, the women's liberation movement are but today's phases of the quest for inalienable rights which in past history was exemplified by the abolitionist struggle against slavery, the workingmen's fight for justice through labor unions, the successive waves of immigrants entering the land of freedom and then striving for rights equal to those of native Americans. But if the leadership most responsible for maintaining the foundation of our legal system fails, there must result uneasiness and confusion among the people, and a healthy society becomes impossible.

What does society have a right to expect from the legal profession as a profession in this situation? Most obviously the principle that a nation's legal philosophy be not pushed aside by members of the profession even on the bench. Surely only a people have the right to change the basis of their civilization. It is sad to realize that men like Justices Miller and Brandeis were in the minority among lawyers.

Another reflection can be made which points directly to the cause of sickness within the legal profession and which can justify the thought that society has been cheated by the failure of the profession to keep America's founding principles flourishing. None would disagree that one function of the medical profession as a group in society is to protect and upgrade public health. In the same vein, if the clergy as a profession do not sustain and elevate public morality they are failing in their obligations to society. Teaching, as a profession, must concern itself with the passing on of knowledge, the tools of arts and science and culture. What does society have a right to expect from the legal profession as a profession?

Just as doctors as a group must promote public health, just as the teaching profession must encourage culture among the people, and just as the clergy must sustain public morality, so the function of the legal profession is to promote the establishment of justice in society. . . . Any other conception of its own function by the legal profession indicates it debases itself. The purpose of the Constitution is to "establish justice." Can the profession which is its guardian have a lesser purpose? The sickness of the law profession begins when student lawyers are told "that terribly astute epigram of Oliver Wendell Holmes, Jr., to the effect that our law is nothing more nor less than predictions of what the courts will do in certain instances."[61] In practice, this is what transpires:

"Some lawyers themselves are taking a hard look at the traditional obligation to represent a client to the fullest and asking whether it requires total disregard of the question of guilt or innocence. Milton Shadur, a well known Chicago attorney, made this comment about legal ethics: 'Long before Watergate, the flaw of the profession was the "mechanic attitude" — the tendency of lawyers not to make moral judgements on what they are called to do . . . Time after time I run into well respected firms which exercise no moral judgement about what they are doing.' "[62]

The "total disregard of the question of guilt or innocence of a client" means a total disregard for the existence of justice in society. But James Madison said that the purpose of government is justice, that the end of civil society is justice.[63] The Founding Fathers held that justice is objective, that it can be found; that is what "to establish justice" means. The drafters of the Constitution did not claim they could create justice, but only create a government and a civil society within which a state of justice would exist for the people. The legal profession is the profession which by its natural function ought to help establish justice in society. While it was never achieved perfectly, this justice had been reflected in the British laws which the colonists took with them to the new world; when the British Parliament passed laws which denied their rights, denied them justice, the Americans fought.

Contrasted to this clear reasoning of the Founding Fathers is the consumptive thinking of some of the most respected modern members of the legal profession:

"Another equally perilous way of separating judicial philosophies is to divide them into those who elevate 'justice' and those exalting 'law.' The judge, [Benjamin] Cardozo, said, 'Is not a knight-errant, roaming at will in pursuit of his own ideal of beauty and goodness? He is to draw his inspiration from consecrated principles. He is not to yield to spasmodic sentiment, to vague and unregulated benevolence.' Law in this sense is the written and accepted body of rules that guide the society; justice is whatever is morally right. But justice is then a subjective determination, dependent on the morality of the beholder, whereas law is objective and codified. 'I hate justice,' Holmes said, staking out his own position with characteristic cogency.

"Learned Hand, the greatest judge who [unfortunately] never sat on the Supreme Court, explained what Holmes meant. 'I remember once I was with him,' he recalled. 'It was Saturday when the court was to confer. It was before he had a motorcar, and we jogged along in an old coupé. When we got down to the Capitol, I wanted to provoke a response, so as he walked off I said, "Well Sir, goodbye. Do Justice!" He turned quite sharply and he said, "Come here, come here." I said, "Oh, I know, I know." He replied, "That is not my job. My job is to play the game according to the rules." ' "⁶⁴

Fortunately the rules, the "consecrated principles," for the most part were made by men who believed there is objective justice, who with the Founding Fathers would never admit that "justice is . . . a subjective determination, dependent on the morality of the beholder, whereas law is objective and codified." Justice is written in the equality of nature of each human being who has inalienable rights. The rights are written in the moral law which comes from God. The common man knows when he is being cheated. Good rules of law in their basic meaning are sound morality codified; this is the origin of English and American common law from which sprung the rules that enable Justices Cardozo and Holmes to be brilliant judges.

The judge was not a knight-errant until within the past century, and with the confusion which came in large part from Holmes and his contemporaries, judges (having been torn loose from the traditions of Western civilization and the Judeo-Christian objective concept of morality) began to impose their subjective consciences on American law. Whatever was enforced as laws by courts became law to lawyers. Historically this was especially true of Supreme Court decisions which imposed *laissez-faire* economics on the country; the Court became the knight-errant of big business against the workingman, against the public. To the extent that the legal profession in general failed to conserve the legal tradition of justice handed down from the Founding Fathers it failed the country and itself. To the extent that justice ceased to be the purpose of judicial decisions for each little person the courts failed society.

The common people never lost their sense of the purpose of law; the legal profession by and large did. In doing so it lost its true function in society; it nourished the germs of its own sickness. The profession lost a sense of its mission; it produced generations of judges who would administer courts of (judge-made) law, not courts of justice. It is not without significance, and with total consistency, that Justice Holmes once corrected a lawyer for suggesting the Supreme Court was a court of justice. Holmes reminded him it was a court of law.

# chapter 14

# THE SUPREME COURT

"To consider the judges as the ultimate arbiters of all constitutional questions (is) a very dangerous doctrine indeed, and one which would place us under the despotism of an oligarchy. Our judges are as honest as other men, and not more so. They have, with others, the same passions for party, for power, and the privilege of their corps. Their maxim is 'boni judicis est ampliare jurisdictionem,' and their power the more dangerous as they are in office for life. . . . The Constitution has erected no such single tribunal, knowing that to whatever hands confided, with the corruptions of time and party, its members would become despots." (Thomas Jefferson)[1]

"There is in each of us a stream of tendency, whether you choose to call it philosophy or not, which gives coherence and direction to thought and action. Judges cannot escape that current any more than other mortals. All their lives, forces which they do not recognize and cannot name, have been tugging at them — inherited instincts, traditional beliefs, acquired convictions; and the resultant is an outlook on life, a conception of social needs, a sense in James' phrase of 'the total push and pressure of the cosmos,' which, when reasons are nicely balanced, must determine where the choice shall fall." (Supreme Court Justice Benjamin N. Cardozo)[2]

"As the decisions now stand I see hardly any limit but the sky to the invalidating of those rights ('the constitutional rights of the

191

states') if they happen to strike a majority of this Court as for any reason undesirable. I cannot believe that the (Fourteenth) Amendment was intended to give us carte blanche to embody our economic or moral beliefs in its prohibitions." (Supreme Court Justice Oliver W. Holmes)[3]

According to the principles of the Founding Fathers the examination of conscience proper to the Supreme Court includes the same points by which other leadership groups were judged; these are the essential doctrines upon which the Founders built American society and which they were convinced must be maintained if the nation was to perdure. Included are a belief in God, natural law, natural rights, the compact as the basis for society, and virtue among the people as a civic necessity.

## The Supreme Court Is Human

The coming Bicentennial celebration reminds us that the Founding Fathers won independence for the nation at the risk of their lives and endowed their posterity with a legal heritage which gave succeeding generations an ordered freedom unsurpassed by any other nation. They structured a government "of the people, by the people, for the people" to serve rather than exploit its citizens. In a sense they laid up a capital investment; we have been living on the interest. This becomes apparent when we ask ourselves: What have succeeding generations contributed to the philosophy or structure of government in comparison to what they gave? Or indeed, what have later generations whittled away from the foundation principles which have damaged it?

The Fathers were political philosophers, not merely lawyers. They recognized principles from natural law as undergirding the civil structure; if this foundation were weakened they foresaw the ultimate ruin of the structure. Totally accepted as the foundation, natural law became the "unvoiced axiom underlying American political thought in the earlier nineteenth century."[4] In 1827 Justice Johnson and the Supreme Court majority used it directly in rebuking Chief Justice Marshall's excessive zeal for property rights. As late as 1874, in Loan Association vs. Topeka, the Court relied directly on natural law to prevent the use of tax money for private purposes. The Supreme Court of the past hundred years, against dissenting opinions and many times giving judgments which later had to be reversed, attacked the natural-law principles which the Founding Fathers held as necessary and permanent. *Laissez-faire* majorities ruled the Court and applied theories of social Darwinism to interpret the Constitution in place of the natural-law principles which brought it into being — and this without the people's permission.[5]

Ultimately the people themselves are responsible for the continuance of the Founders' ideals, especially the leadership groups — among them, the churches, schools and communications media. But in a very true way these principles have been built into a governmental and legal structure and therefore the legal profession along with the courts have become the focal point of responsibility. The Supreme Court, at the apex of the legal structure, of necessity, must be uniquely accountable whether the constitutional system remains as given by the Fathers, whether it is different, whether it is stronger or weaker. Unfortunately, according to the criteria given by the Founders, Supreme Court decisions have weakened the foundation of our constitutional system.

The Founding Fathers in establishing the nation followed principles which they used sometimes explicitly, sometimes implicitly. The Declaration of Independence outlines the main tenets: there is a Creator; from Him men get inalienable rights; to protect these rights governments are instituted among men; the powers of the government come from the consent of the governed; the purpose of government is to secure the safety and happiness of the people. These principles of the Founders were discussed in Part One of this book under the headings of *God, Natural Law, Natural Rights, Compact* and *Virtue.* Comparing the Fathers' attitude toward them with that of the Supreme Court as exemplified in its decisions provides an outline for an examination of conscience for the Supreme Court in the light of the Founders' ideals and principles.

The Supreme Court has handed down tens of thousands of decisions in its 185-year history. The Justices were capable lawyers

193

who reached the top of their profession; one cannot doubt that most of their adjudication upheld the law of the land and contributed to peace and justice within American society. But there are some decisions which awakened distrust, resentment, sometimes anger, among large segments of the American people, and were challenged by capable and high-minded men within and without the legal profession. They are the decisions which veered from the ideals of the Founding Fathers. One, the Dred Scott decision, led to civil war. It is this type of decision we are concerned with here.

The Founding Fathers included not only capable lawyers among their number, but profound political philosophers who foresaw the long-range effect of the principles they were enshrining in law: witness Adams, Jefferson, Madison, Wilson, Hamilton and Marshall. Unfortunately, the Justices of the Supreme Court who have interpreted our law since that time were qualified, even brilliant lawyers, but for the most part inferior political philosophers. During the heyday of *laissez-faire* many of the Justices were ex-corporation lawyers, men whose decisions reflected the selfish principles of the wealthy class whom they had represented as lawyers. It was men from this group who stand condemned by the Founders' principles because they tampered with the Constitution by applying principles alien to it and never accepted by the people.

## The Supreme Court And God

According to the Founding Fathers, American civil society begins with an acknowledgment of the existence of God and is built on the foundation that He as Creator endowed His creature, man, with certain rights which government must protect. The Declaration of Independence says this explicitly; the Bill of Rights was designed to implement in specific terms this philosophy. The Supreme Court in 1952 said, "We are a religious people whose institutions presuppose a Supreme Being." Three times previously the Court had enunciated the same principle — in 1815, in 1892 and in 1931.[6] In spite of these words the Supreme Court has repeatedly made decisions which violate their own statement and the God-centered principles of the Fathers.

If one examines the conviction of the Founders that a healthy civil society begins with a respect for God and a spirit of obedience to His laws for man's relations with each other, and compares it with the total lack of God-centered or moral principles in the adjudication of American law today (the total secularization of constitutional law especially), the conclusion is inevitable that the Founding Fathers' vision of American society does not now exist for most Supreme Court Justices. In other words, we must look at the forest, not the trees: it is impossible to reconcile the amoral and a-religious applications of American constitutional law today with the legal structure permeated with God-centered moral principles as it came from the Founders.

This has come about especially because of the secularizing decisions of the Supreme Court, usually by its interpretation of the First Amendment in a way contrary to the intentions the Founders had in drafting and ratifying it. In reaching these decisions that Court has violated the spirit of the great majority of the American people, ninety-five percent of whom believe in God, more than sixty percent of whom are church-affiliated. The Fathers began with God and founded a nation according to His natural moral law. The American people today still believe in God, and in many ways show that they are still convinced that there is a moral law more basic than civil law, for all men; but the Supreme Court ignores God and the possibility that their decisions somehow should correspond with morality.

Repeated Court decisions have secularized the public-school system to the extent that the connection between belief in God and the sanctity of inalienable rights or the religious base for morality cannot be adequately taught our children. The 1948 McCollum decision analyzed in Chapter 10 is a prime example of the Court's secularization of education. In 1963 the Supreme Court in Abington School District vs. Schempp voided Pennsylvania's statute requiring that: "At least ten verses from the Holy Bible shall be read, without comment, at the opening of each public school, on each school day. Any child shall be excused from such Bible reading, or attending such Bible reading, upon the written request of his parent or guardian."[7] The Founding Fathers who drafted the Constitution took for granted such Bible emphasis. In 1962, in Engel vs. Vitale the Court voided the use of an official prayer in the New York schools: "Almighty God, we acknowledge our dependence upon Thee, and we beg Thy blessings upon us, our parents, our teachers, and our country."[8]

These things were done by reading into the First Amendment a meaning which is not substantiated by history but which by repetition the Court has canonized as if certain and evident. The quotation below from Edward S. Corwin's *The Constitution and What It Means Today* analyzes the amendment. We must remember that the Justice Story to whom Corwin refers sat on the Supreme Court bench with Marshall, that he lived when the drafters of the Constitution were still alive, and that he wrote the first authoritative commentary on the Constitution. The First Amendment states: "Congress shall make no law respecting an establishment of religion, or prohibiting the free exercise thereof. . . ." Corwin had this to say:

"An establishment of religion: Two theories regarding the meaning and intention of this clause have confronted each other in decisions of the Court. According to one, what the clause bans is the *preferential* treatment of any particular religion or sect by government in the United States. This theory has the support of [Associate Justice Joseph] Story, except for the fact that he regarded Congress as still free to prefer the Christian religion over other religions. It is also supported by Cooley in his *Principles of Constitutional Law,* where it is said that the clause forbids 'the setting up or recognition of a state church, or at least the conferring upon one church of special favors and advantages which are denied to others.' This conception of the clause is, moreover, foreshadowed in the Northwest Ordinance of 1787, the third article of which reads: 'Religion, morality, and knowledge being necessary to good government and the happiness of mankind, schools and the means of education shall forever be encouraged.' In short, religion as such is not excluded from the legitimate concerns of government, but quite the contrary.

"The other theory was first voiced by Jefferson in a letter

196

which he wrote a group of Baptists in Danbury, Connecticut, in 1802. Here it is asserted that it was the purpose of the First Amendment to build 'a wall of separation between Church and State.' Seventy-seven years later Chief Justice Waite, in speaking for the unanimous Court in the first Mormon Church case, in which the right of Congress to forbid polygamy in the territories was sustained, characterized this statement by Jefferson as 'almost an authoritative declaration of the scope and effect of the amendment.' "[9]

Corwin further states in a note:

"In his second Inaugural Address, Jefferson expressed a very different, and presumably more carefully considered opinion upon the purpose of Amendment I: 'In matters of religion, I have considered that its free exercise is placed by the Constitution independent of the powers of the general government.' This was said three years after the Danbury letter. Richardson, Messages and Papers, I, 379."[10]

The Fathers established the Constitution in an atmosphere in which the necessity of religion and religious moral training was deemed necessary for the well-being of civil society. It is, for instance, impossible to reconcile the advice of Washington given in his farewell address with the Supreme Court's McCollum decision banning the use of public-school buildings by members of all faiths to teach religion and morality to their own children:

"Of all the dispositions and habits which lead to political prosperity, religion and morality are indispensable supports. . . . And let us with caution indulge the supposition that morality can be maintained without religion. Whatever may be conceded to the influence of refined education, reason and experience both forbid us to expect that national morality can prevail in exclusion of religious principle."[11]

For the Supreme Court to say that the purpose of the First

Amendment was to raise a wall of separation so high between church and state that in effect there could be no cooperation between the two in the training of our children is to distort the Fathers' purpose. They wanted no national church, no establishment of religion. Beyond that they were very positive that religion and moral training should be part of the basic education of all children.

Knowledge of the Bible was considered an essential part of education and moral training. All the schools which existed at the time of the Fathers were religiously founded, run, or oriented, including the common or public schools. As late as 1848, after having done his great work of fostering the public-school system of Massachusetts, Horace Mann wrote:

"Now, it is the especial province and function of the statesman and the lawgiver — of all those, indeed, whose influence moulds or modifies public opinion — to study out the eternal principles which conduce to the strength, wisdom, and righteousness of a community; to search for these principles as for hidden riches; to strive for them as one would strive for his life; and then to form public institutions in accordance with them. And he is not worthy to be called a statesman, he is not worthy to be a lawgiver or leader among men, who, either through the weakness of his head or the selfishness of his heart, is incapable of marshalling in his mind the great ideas of knowledge, justice, temperance, and obedience to the laws of God, — on which foundation alone the structure of human welfare can be erected; who is not capable of organizing these ideas into a system, and then of putting that system into operation, as a mechanic does a machine. This only is true statesmanship. . . .

"I hold it, then, to be one of the excellences, one of the moral beauties, of the Massachusetts system, that there is one place in the land where the children of all the different denominations are brought together for instruction, where the Bible is allowed to speak for itself; one place where the children can kneel at a common altar, and feel that they have a common Father, and where the services of religion tend to create brothers, and not Ishmaelites. . . .

"Such, then, in a religious point of view, is the Massachusetts system of common schools. Reverently it recognizes and affirms the sovereign rights of the Creator, sedulously and sacredly it guards the religious rights of the creature; while it seeks to remove all hinderances, and to supply all furtherances, to a filial and paternal communion between man and his Maker."[12]

The consistency with which the Supreme Court of recent years has furthered the secularization of education and American society is evident from other decisions in addition to the three pivotal ones quoted above. What is particularly appalling is the misunderstanding by the Justices of some of the Founding Fathers' writings used to justify their decisions. A brief analysis of Engel vs. Vitale banning New York's official school prayer ("Almighty God, we acknowledge our dependence upon Thee, and we beg Thy blessings upon us, our parents, our teachers, and our country") brings this out.

Justice Black delivered this 1962 opinion of the Court. In part he said:

"There can be no doubt that New York's state prayer program officially establishes the religious beliefs embodied in the Regents' prayer. The respondents' argument to the contrary, which is largely based upon the contention that the Regents' prayer is 'non-denominational' and the fact that the program, as modified and approved by state courts, does not require all pupils to recite the prayer but permits those who wish to do so to remain silent or be excused from the room, ignores the essential nature of the program's constitutional defects. Neither the fact that the prayer may be denominationally neutral, nor the fact that its observance on the part of the students is voluntary can serve to free it from the limitations of the Establishment Clause, as it might from the Free Exercise Clause, of the First Amendment, both of which are operative against the States by virtue of the Fourteenth Amendment. Although these two clauses may in certain instances overlap, they forbid two quite different kinds of governmental encroachment upon religious freedom. The Establishment Clause, unlike the Free Exercise Clause, does not depend upon any showing of direct governmental compulsion and is violated by the enactment of laws which establish an official religion whether those laws operate directly to coerce nonobserving individuals or not. This is not to say, of course, that laws officially prescribing a particular form of religious worship do not involve coercion of such individuals. When the power, prestige and financial support of government is placed behind a particular religious belief, the indirect coercive pressure upon religious minorities to conform to the prevailing officially approved religion is plain. But the purposes underlying the Establishment Clause go much further than that. Its first and most immediate purpose rested on the belief that a union of government and religion tends to destroy government and to degrade religion. . . . The New York laws officially prescribing the Regents' prayer are inconsistent with both the purposes of the Establishment Clause and with the Establishment Clause itself.

"... To those who may subscribe to the view that because the Regents' official prayer is so brief and general there can be no danger to religious freedom in its governmental establishment, however, it may be appropriate to say in the words of James Madison, the author of the First Amendment:

" 'It is proper to take alarm at the first experiment on our liberties. . . . Who does not see that the same authority which can establish Christianity, in exclusion of all other religions, may establish with the same ease any particular sect of Christians, in exclusion of all other Sects? That the same authority which can force a citizen to contribute three pence only of his property for the support of any one establishment, may force him to conform to any other establishment in all cases whatsoever?' "[13]

Justice Rutledge, in his dissent in Everson vs. Board of Education (in which the Court upheld in 1947 by a 5 to 4 decision a New Jersey law permitting the state to pay for transportation of students to and from parochial schools) gives a demonstrably false interpretation of Madison's importance in drafting the First Amendment.[14] To Madison goes the honor of leading the struggle to put the amendment in the Constitution; but the text went through six different versions before adoption by Congress, and reflects not just the ideas of Madison but of Congress as a whole.[15] Justice Black in calling James Madison "the author of the First Amendment" in Engel vs. Vitale thus repeats an inaccuracy made before by Supreme Court Justices who use Madison as the great authority to justify an unhistorical version of what the Founders meant by separation of church and state. But it is even more painful to see Madison pulled out of context in what he actually did say. Justice Black did this to justify the striking down of New York's prayer law. Madison's *Remonstrance* calls for exactly what New York was trying to do: remind our children to pray to the God from whom Madison and all the Fathers believed help must come if civil society were to perdure and be healthy.

Madison's *Remonstrance* (its full title is *Memorial and Remonstrance Against Religious Assessments*) was written in 1784 to oppose a general tax for the support of religious worship in Virginia, a measure which would have in some way replaced the support given the Church of England before the Revolution. The Anglican Church had been disestablished at the beginning of the war. In 1784 it joined with some Presbyterians to get a subsidy for religious worship, and among those who supported it were George Washington, Richard Henry Lee, Patrick Henry and John Marshall. Madison and his followers reflected Jefferson, then in France as ambassador; they wanted no shadow of a new established religion. The *Remonstrance* was written as part of the political battle in Virginia to defeat the subsidy bill. It mirrors Jefferson and Madison but in no way should be used as the authentic interpretation of the First Amendment, which was passed five years later to reflect the mind of the entire nation restricting Congress from ever setting up a nationally established religion. The amendment was accepted by men who believed in government support of religion, but did not want one religion to be preferred to others. It did not set up a wall between government and religion.

The *Remonstrance* reflects the concrete political battle going on in Virginia over church subsidy, but more than that it is a magnificent philosophical document analyzing the freedom of conscience which belongs to every man as an inalienable right. It is for this reason that it is painful to have it quoted out of context in a Supreme Court decision to justify the very opposite of what the

201

document implies. The *Remonstrance* properly quoted is a full defense and justification of the New York Regents' official prayer composed to be said in public schools by all students and teachers who would want to use it.

The pertinent parts of Madison's *Remonstrance* are:

"1. *Because we hold it for a fundamental and undeniable truth, 'that Religion or the duty which we owe to our Creator and the Manner of discharging it, can be directed only by reason and conviction, not by force or violence.'* The Religion then of every man must be left to the conviction and conscience of every man; and it is the right of every man to exercise it as these may dictate. This right is in its nature an unalienable right. It is unalienable; because the opinions of men depending only on the evidence contemplated by their own minds, cannot follow the dictates of other men: It is unalienable also; because what is here a right towards men, is a duty towards the Creator. *It is the duty of every man to render to the Creator such homage, and such only, as he believes to be acceptable to him. This duty is precedent both in order of time and degree of Obligation, to the claims of Civil Society.* Before any man can be considered as a member of the Civil Society, he must be considered as a subject of the Governor of the Universe: And if a member of Civil Society, who enters into any subordinate Association, must always do it with a reservation of his duty to the general authority; much more must every man who becomes a member of any particular Civil Society, do it with a saving of his allegiance to the Universal Sovereign. We maintain therefore that in matters of Religion, no man's right is abridged by the institution of Civil Society, and that Religion is wholly exempt from its cognizance. True it is, that no other rule exists, by which any question which may divide a society, can be ultimately determined, but the will of the majority; but it is also true, that the majority may trespass on the rights of the minority.

"2. *Because if religion be exempt from the authority of the Society at large, still less can it be subject to that of the* *Legislative Body. The latter are but the creatures and vicegerents of the former. Their

*(*Author's note:* In the context of the present discussion we should substitute "Supreme Court" for "Legislative Body.")

202

jurisdiction is both derivative and limited: it is limited with regard to the coordinate departments, more necessarily is it limited with regard to the constituents. The preservation of a free government requires not merely, that the metes and bounds which separate each department of power may be invariably maintained; but more especially, that neither of them be suffered to overleap the great Barrier which defends the rights of the people. The Rulers who are guilty of such an encroachment, exceed the commission from which they derive their authority, and are Tyrants. The People who submit to it are governed by laws made neither by themselves, nor by an authority derived from them, and are slaves. . . .

"15. *Because, finally, 'the equal right of every citizen to the free exercise of his Religion according to the dictates of conscience' is held by the same tenure with all our other rights. If we recur to its origin, it is equally the gift of nature; if we weigh its importance, it cannot be less dear to us; if we consult the Declaration of those rights which pertain to the good people of Virginia, as the 'basis and foundation of Government,' it is enumerated with equal solemnity, or rather studied emphasis.* Either then, we must say, that the will of the Legislature is the only measure of their authority; and that in the plenitude of this authority, they may sweep away all our fundamental rights; or, that they are bound to leave this particular right untouched and sacred: Either we must say, that they may controul the freedom of the press, may abolish the trial by jury, may swallow up the Executive and Judiciary Powers of the State; nay that they may despoil us of our very right of suffrage, and erect themselves into an independent and hereditary assembly: or we must say, that they have no authority to enact into law the Bill under consideration. We the subscribers say, that the General Assembly of this Commonwealth have no such authority: *And that no effort may be ommitted on our part against so dangerous an usurpation, we oppose to it, this remonstrance; earnestly praying, as we are in duty bound, that the Supreme Lawgiver of the Universe, by illuminating those to whom it is addressed, may on the one hand, turn their councils from every act which would affront his holy prerogative, or violate the trust committed to them: and on the other, guide them into every measure which may be worthy of his (blessing, may re)-dound to their own praise, and may establish more firmly the liberties, the prosperity, and the Happiness of the Commonwealth.''*[16] (Emphasis author's.)

This is evident from Madison's principles (especially from underlined statements):

1. Religion is a duty owed the Creator.

2. Freedom of conscience is a right which cannot be interfered with by other men or by any government.

3. This right and this duty is inalienable; it antecedes all civil rights and duties (and to the Fathers "unalienable" meant that a man cannot either cede the right or avoid the duty).

4. Prayer to God is part of the duty of religion: "It is the duty of every man to render to the Creator some homage, and such only, as he believes acceptable to Him." ". . . Earnestly praying, as we are in duty bound, that the Supreme Lawgiver of the Universe, by illuminating those to whom it is addressed . . . ," etc.

Madison was more than a lawyer; he was a deep political philosopher, and it is in the distinctions he makes between the rights and obligations of human beings antecedent to all civil law which justifies the Regents' prayer. There are two areas of thought to be considered in the problem: rights and obligations of men as men, and of men as citizens. Government has no power to interfere with the rights and duties of men as men, such as that of prayer. A civil law establishing or supporting a church in Madison's eyes is also an unjust law. But the obligation of prayer is on a different level; it is one of the obligations which men have as men, not as citizens.

To say (as the Supreme Court through Justice Black said) that a prayer which is not sectarian, which merely puts a natural right, a self-evident obligation, in terms so simple that a child can understand and fulfill his natural obligation to pray, is to establish a religion, is to lose the constant distinction Madison and the Fathers made between man as a human being and man as a citizen. To protect natural rights and to make it easy for man to fulfill natural obligations is the most basic purpose of government; this is what the Regents' prayer did for New York students. Contrary to Justice Black, the Regents did not set up a church such as Protestantism, Judaism or Catholicism by this prayer; it did not establish Christianity or Mohammedanism; it did not set up any religion. What it did was to recognize the religious obligations of men as men, of students as human beings.

In the eyes of Madison and the Founding Fathers this natural religion was antecedent to Christianity and was established by God, from whom men get rights and obligations. The Fathers were not men to quibble over simple words; in the Declaration they stated their rights as "self-evident" and inalienable; for these natural rights and the government's obligation to respect them, when put in simple terms, they might fight, they would not discuss. The Regents' prayer has similar connotations; it puts the basic right and obligation of students relative to homage due the Creator in the simplest evident terms. To deny the obligation of students (or all men) to make this prayer is to deny the natural obligation of prayer itself; this is the contradiction of what Madison implied. To make it more acceptable to the public, the New York prayer was voluntary in the schools; the students were not forced to participate, even though according to the Fathers' principles prayer is really a duty which ought to be obeyed by all. . . .

What the Supreme Court did was to enter the realm of natural rights and obligations, a forbidden area according to the deepest principles of the Founders. What the Regents did was to enable students to more easily fulfill a natural obligation. Justice Black said, "There can be no doubt the New York state prayer program officially establishes the religious beliefs embodied in the Regents' prayer."[17] In the eyes of Madison and the Founders the obligation to pray (and the Regents' prayer is the minimum of possible prayer) comes from nature antecedent to government; the Regents' prayer was established by nature, not New York state. It is Justice Black's misinterpretation of Madison's principles as written in the *Remonstrance* which makes painful reading for anyone who will read what Madison actually said.

According to the Founders' principles an act of government which interferes with natural rights or obligations is void. In the days of Madison and Jefferson the abuse of power came more often from the legislative branch of government than from either the Supreme Court or executive branch. George Mason, author of the

Virginia Bill of Rights, expresses the Fathers' thesis in words aimed at legislatures, but it applies also to abuse of judicial power:

"Now all acts of legislation apparently [evidently] contrary to natural rights and justice are in our laws and must be in the nature of things, considered as void. The laws of nature are the laws of God, whose authority can be superseded by no power on earth. A legislature must not obstruct our obedience to Him from whose punishments they cannot protect us. All human constitutions which contradict His laws we are in conscience bound to disobey. Such have been the adjudication of our courts."[18]

The legal thinking of the Founding Fathers indicates that the Supreme Court's decision banning the New York Regents' prayer is of itself void since the Court was entering an area beyond its jurisdiction, the area of natural rights and duties. In the words of Madison:

"It is a duty of every man to render to the Creator such homage, and such only, as he believes to be acceptable to Him. This duty is precedent both in order of time and degree of Obligation, to the claims of Civil Society. Before any man can be considered as a member of Civil Society, he must be considered as a subject of the Governor of the Universe."[19]

Had the Regents composed a specifically Protestant (or Catholic, or Jewish, or Mohammedan) prayer, this might have been construed as a step toward establishing a religion in the sense of the Founding Fathers, therefore against the First Amendment. But it is impossible to accept Justice Black's decision, given in the name of the Supreme Court majority, as against the First Amendment, and still be faithful to the principles of the men who gave us our Constitution. The Regents' prayer, composed in language which reflects natural religion in its simplest terms, and yet practiced in such a way that no student was forced to participate in its use, corresponds totally to the Fathers' principles as to what ought to be done. At the same time they would have gone, did go, further, to foster the

206

students', the people's, the nation's, dependence on God. They wanted the government to cooperate with all religions equally, to establish none, that students learn their religious obligations toward the Creator.

## The Supreme Court And Natural Law

The Supreme Court is at the apex of the American legal structure; its decisions shape the structure, and since law is a vital force in society, the Court determines in great measure what direction American society will take. That the Court would be the final authority for the meaning of the Constitution was held as natural and essential by Fathers such as Hamilton and Marshall, even if not put in so many words in the document. It is a court's prerogative to state the meaning of law to these men; this was not a function of legislature or executive. Jefferson held that since this was not written in the Constitution, the legislature or executive had as much right to interpret the real meaning of the Constitution as did the courts; therefore the Supreme Court under Marshall was usurping authority when it asserted itself as the final arbiter of the meaning of the Constitution.

Marshall and Hamilton won out. Our common-law tradition, inherited from England and Hamilton's reasoning in Federalist Paper No. 78, were too sound to be pushed aside:

"The interpretation of the laws is the proper and peculiar province of the courts. A constitution is, in fact, and must be, regarded by the judges as a fundamental law. It must therefore belong to them to ascertain its meaning, as well as the meaning of any particular act proceeding from the legislative body. If there should happen to be an irreconcilable variance between the two, that which has the superior validity ought, of course, to be preferred; in other words, the constitution ought to be preferred to the statute, the intention of the people to the intention of their agents."[20]

Realizing the key importance of the judiciary in maintaining a constitutional form of government Hamilton in the same paper argued magnificently for the independence of the courts, and for the tenure of judges during "good behavior" — which means life tenure under ordinary conditions. He maintained that since the judiciary was by nature the weakest of the three branches of government (the executive dispenses the honors and holds the sword of the community, the legislature commands the purse and prescribes the rights and duties of the citizens) there was the least danger that the courts would abuse the Constitution. Hamilton thought that individual oppression might now and then proceed from the courts, but the permanent liberty of the people could never be endangered from this quarter.

We have almost 200 years of history to judge whether Hamilton's optimism concerning the integrity of the courts to work within the Constitution and its spirit was justified. On the whole it is reasonable to conclude he was right. We have remained a free people. In comparison with other nations our people have had the protection of law against arbitrary government to an extent that we are the envy of people of other lands. We are not thrown into jail at the whim of dictators; concentration camps have not existed to bolster totalitarian theories or practices. We can sue the government itself to get justice through the courts. The writ of *habeas corpus* is an ever-living protection for personal freedom. We take for granted so many benefits of our constitutional government as enforced by the courts that only a deliberate meditation on our system compared to what has happened and is happening in other lands can faintly bring the truth home to us.

But we would be naïve and even dishonest if the instances of cancerous miscarriage of justice through courts not upholding the Constitution in letter or spirit were not admitted. The court protection of segregation, the legal indignities imposed because of race, the human suffering involved, are all too close to maintain that the ideals written into the Constitution by the Fathers (or the authors of the Thirteenth, Fourteenth and Fifteenth Amendments) were fulfilled by judges in a manner sufficient to meet Hamilton's optimistic prophecies.

The problem can be pinpointed by examining the history of the Supreme Court. It abused its power as final authority over the Con-

208

stitution by the Dred Scott decision; in this decision, by declaring the Missouri Compromise unconstitutional after it had in some way stopped the expansion of slavery (exactly what the Founding Fathers intended when they drafted and accepted the Constitution), the Court precipitated the Civil War. The Supreme Court abandoned the natural-law philosophy which undergirded the Constitution in the thought of the Founding Fathers when it imposed its *laissez-faire* criterion on state and congressional statutes from 1877 until 1937. In doing this it effectively changed the meaning of the Constitution (something only the people have a right to do) and caused immeasurable suffering to working people and unmeasured injustice to the public. The Court destroyed the purpose of the Thirteenth, Fourteenth and Fifteenth Amendments, designed to protect the human rights of the newly freed slaves, by voiding the successive laws passed by Congress to enforce the amendments. At the same time it twisted the Fourteenth Amendment into a vehicle to protect the "rights" of corporations. An examination of Dred Scott, *laissez-faire* jurisprudence and the three amendments show the Court's abuse of the Constitution.

To understand what the Supreme Court did in 1858 by the Dred Scott decision and why the abandonment of the Founders' philosophy of law after 1877 meant constitutional interpretation which changed the structure of American law and pointed the nation in a direction which injured human dignity and destroyed inalienable rights, it is necessary to compare the theory of law which replaced the Fathers' theory with that held by the Court.

Charles L. Black, Jr., made the basic comparison in his book, *The Two Cities of Law:*

"On the ground of man's public life, two shapes of law may be discerned — sometimes in mutual complement, sometimes in contrast.

"First, there is the law that prevails in society. Courts decide cases and give reasons for their decision. Statutes are printed and read. Precedents are recorded and lawyers' ingenuity may devise. . . . This law that palpably prevails in each nation may be called 'positive law.'

"Second, as misty as a Chinese painter's mountain, but as insistently there as the Chinese painter makes his mountain seem, is another shape of law — the image of law as men in their time think law ought to be. . . . We are compelled to seek the shape of right law. By taking up this quest, we may be transgressing the canons of scientific positivism, but if we do not take it up we strip ourselves of the insignia of humanity. And so from the earliest inscriptions in pyramid tombs down to the latest article in the Yale Law Journal, . . . we try and always have tried not only to know the law as it is but also to discern, however dimly and uncertainly, what it may be that justice requires of law.

"This search for light in law has taken many forms. Recurrently through Western history, the name 'natural law' has been given to the projected image of law as it ought to be. Artistotle and Cicero wrote of a law of nature, against which human positive law was to be measured. Aquinas brought the concept within his mighty synthesis. Grotius built it into the foundations of modern international law. John Locke made the idea a perdurable part of liberal thought in England, whence it crossed the Atlantic to enter our own Declaration of Independence, in that document's opening appeal to 'the Laws of Nature and of Nature's God.' . . . 'Natural law' thought permeates the epochs of our intellectual tradition."[21]

Since 1887 there has been no natural law for the Supreme Court to guide it in the interpretation of the Constitution, the document which came into being to implement the demands of natural law.[22] For the Supreme Court there is only positive law, man-made law. Holmes put it in his own terms: law is a prediction of what the courts will decide, and its immediate rule is what is expedient for the community. The thought that there are rules written in the nature of man by his Creator to tell him how he should relate to his neighbor, that he ought to tell the truth, that he should not steal his neighbor's goods or his wife, that he should not kill an innocent person, that he should respect another man's inalienable right to liberty, that freedom of conscience belongs to each human being, that each human being has a dignity which must be respected by men and governments — all these tenets of the natural law, under-

210

stood by the Fathers to be the foundation of civil law, have not existed for the Supreme Court since 1887. And we should remember that these tenets of natural law were really more clear in the Fathers' minds than the description given it by Black above: the Fathers held that the Judeo-Christian interpretation of morality was the true interpretation of natural law, and in its main obligations, if not its finer points, the Founders were in agreement. To them it was much more clear than the Chinese painter's mountain.

In the place of natural-law guidelines to interpret the Constitution the Supreme Court on the surface relied on positive, written law. The problem is that the Constitution itself is the principal written law, and after this the precedents of previous Court decisions. In practice, to paraphrase Chief Justice Hughes, the Constitution means what the Supreme Court says it means. We have here what in logic would be called a vicious circle — in the common man's language, a booby trap. The great ideal of the Founding Fathers was that we have a government of laws, not men. But if the Constitution is only what the Supreme Court says it is (and the Court has reversed itself many times as succeeding generations of Justices imposed their private criteria to interpret the document) we have *par excellence* a government of men, not laws.

It matters not that these Justices are "nine old men" presumably beyond the reach of politics. The very purpose of our written Constitution was to have a fundamental law (guided by the objective moral law written in man's nature) which would govern not only the people, who could change it only with difficulty, but the legislature, the executive, the courts — all of whom are merely creatures of the Constitution. The injustices and suffering caused by far too many Supreme Court decisions beginning with the Dred Scott decision in 1858 and compounded by succeeding Courts since 1887, the gyrations which constitutional law has undergone during these years, were due in the greatest measure to the Court's substituting private and temporary criteria for the natural-law criteria presupposed by the Fathers when they gave the Constitution to the nation.

## The Dred Scott Decision

In the Dred Scott decision the Court majority in effect denied that all men are created equal, that there is an inalienable right to liberty, that slavery is an evil. These principles which the Fathers took from natural law the Founders had compromised, but with reason to believe and hope that the vicious institution would die a natural death. Chief Justice Taney in his opinion (each Justice wrote separate opinions) rewrote the laws of nature; the intrinsic dignity and equality of all human beings simply because they are human, so much a part of the natural law according to the Fathers, was replaced by Taney's natural law in which one part of the human race was naturally subject to another. . . . He revised history and claimed that the Fathers held blacks intrinsically inferior, naturally a subject race. He even wrote that the Declaration of Independence justified his judgment![23] Taney implied that blacks could never become citizens of the United States, could never have the protection given citizens by the Constitution. . . .

The Supreme Court spoke neither for the Fathers nor for the American people of their own generation. The Court actually expected that its decree, its fiat, would make slavery respectable and permanent. It acted upon the principle that the Constitution means what the Supreme Court says it means. . . . Had the Court gone back to the natural-law ideals of the Founders in its interpretation of the Constitution it would not now have the stain painted by history: a Supreme Court decision precipitated a chain of events which cost millions of American lives and almost destroyed the Union.

## Social Darwinism

The next great defection by the Supreme Court from the Founders' natural-law criteria for interpreting the Constitution occurred definitively during the years 1886-1887. Justice Field had for a decade in his dissenting opinions been advocating social Darwinism and its correlative *laissez-faire* economic principle that the prosperity of people and nation depended on total business freedom from government supervision or control. In 1886 the Court majority took the first step toward implementing Field's theories: in Santa Clara vs. Southern Pacific it declared that a corporation was a person within the meaning of the Fourteenth Amendment. In 1887 through Mugler vs. Kansas the Court reversed one of Marshall's great doctrines given in 1819 in McCulloch vs. Maryland that the wisdom of a regulative act was a question for the legislature's judgment.[24] In a few more years, by 1900, the Court was judging the constitutionality of state and Congressional legislation on the grounds of its "reasonableness," that it be *reasonable in the judgment of the Court*.[25] The Court had thus usurped the legislatures' rights to decide on the wisdom of its acts; and in place of natural-law criteria which demanded that laws seek justice for each human being, only those laws were "reasonable" which corresponded to *laissez-faire* economic theory, the new "natural law" of the Courts.

Briefly, according to the Founding Fathers, according to the "Laws of Nature and Nature's God" ". . . all men are created equal, . . . are endowed by their Creator with certain unalienable Rights, that among these are Life, Liberty and the pursuit of Happiness. That to secure these rights, Governments are instituted among Men, . . ." But from 1887 on the Supreme Court swept away the natural-law principles of the Fathers; the object of law was not to promote human dignity, equality and justice, but to foster prosperity by *laissez-faire* economics, to make sure the fittest would survive — even when the vast majority of the weak would suffer.

## Supreme Court Racism Against Natural Law

Along with the *laissez-faire* economic principles associated with social Darwinism there were racist aspects. According to natural law all men are created equal; not equal in talents or physical strength obviously, but equal in their human nature and the dignity which should flow from it. Men by nature are intrinsically higher than animals; they are endowed with intellect and free will, with a spiritual nature which can suffer psychological wounds when not treated with respect. The talents each has should have opportunity to develop. The mind is made for the knowledge it has the ability to grasp; from man's free will derives his right to liberty, to control his own destiny within the moral law impressed upon his nature by God. According to the Founders' principle of natural law, governments ought to foster these human gifts.

That the Fathers compromised by not fulfilling the rights due their slaves who belonged to the same human family as their masters is sadly true. That the Founders recognized slavery to be an evil institution because it violated the human dignity of the blacks is also true; it was not until the 1820s that theories to justify slavery began to spread in the states saddled with it. The nation paid the price of compromise and moral blindness by the blood of the Civil War.

After the war three amendments were added to the Constitution which were aimed at guaranteeing the human and civil rights of the freed blacks. The Thirteenth Amendment destroyed the institution of slavery. The Fourteenth gave full citizenship and equal protection of the laws, plus protection of life, liberty and property to the freedmen. The Fifteenth Amendment said that the right to vote shall never be denied or abridged because of race, color, or previous condition of servitude. The power to enforce these amendments by appropriate legislation was given to Congress.

Through a series of decisions between 1876 and 1884 the Supreme Court nullified the purpose of these amendments by invalidating almost all of the laws passed by Congress to enforce them. Rodell sums it up:

"Through the 1870's and 1880's, the Court imperiously and impatiently swept aside almost all these so-called Civil Rights Acts, either by flatly branding them unconstitutional — no matter that the Constitution had been amended precisely to achieve what these laws were aimed to achieve — or by using legalistic chop-logic to 'interpret' them out of effective existence. . . . Amidst this judicial vandalism, one crumb was tossed to the Negroes in the form of a ruling that they could not be kept off juries just because they were Negroes — a ruling so obviously abstract and futile, in the light of Southern practices, that no effort was made by the Court to give it real effect for over fifty years."[26]

One can only say that the Court made a mockery of traditional constitutional law by these decisions. During the years from 1875-1890 the blacks were quiescent; under the leadership of Booker T. Washington, a truly great man, they tried to improve themselves humbly and become better workers. Education had always been segregated, and so were the churches by the blacks' own desire; but down to 1890 there was practically no segregation in public transportation or elsewhere. Then under the leadership of demagogues using the poor whites (sharecroppers on the bottom of the social and economic heap, who seemed to need a group even lower than themselves to keep their morale) Jim Crow laws came into effect. Blacks were forced to segregate on passenger trains and lavatories; there were Jim Crow sections on streetcars and buses, Jim Crow entrances to circuses, factories and the like. White nurses were forbidden to attend black patients in hospitals and vice versa; black barbers were forbidden to cut the hair of white women and children. The degradation of human dignity simply because of race became legalized. . . .[27] And the Supreme Court gave its constitutional blessing in 1896 via Plessy vs. Ferguson; the Court held that:

". . . It was reasonable for a State to require, in the interest of minimizing occasions for race friction, that white and colored persons travelling by rail be assigned separate coaches, the quality of the accommodations afforded the two races being substantially equal; and in due course the same ruling was extended to publicly-supported institutions of learning."[28]

And so the Court substituted its own criteria for what blacks had a right to in place of the criteria of natural law. The equal dignity due to human nature was replaced by legalized indignity which left deep scars on the black psyche, and the whole nation pays today in race tension.

According to the historian Samuel Eliot Morison the darkest days for black America were between 1890 and 1920. The humiliation of these days was purely racist, directly attacking the dignity of part of the human race simply because of color; in contrast the humiliation of slave days had been linked to an evil institution recognized as such by the conscience of the nation. By the 1950s many blacks had improved their lot in life, and many whites recognized the intrinsic indignity of segregation as a legalized institution. To the lasting credit of the Warren Court the Chief Justice spoke for a unanimous decision of the Justices in Brown vs. Board of Education (1954):

"To separate them (black children in grade and high schools) from others of similar age and qualifications solely because of their race generates a feeling of inferiority as to their status in the community that may affect their hearts and minds in a way unlikely ever to be undone. . . . We conclude that in the field of education the doctrine of 'separate but equal' has no place. Separate educational facilities are inherently unequal."[29]

Thus after almost sixty years of suffering and indignity a Supreme Court decision undid part of the harm inflicted by a previous Court. And the American Bar Association in its annual report had this to say about the Warren decision:

"The new jurisprudence constitutes, rather, a recognition of human beings, as the most distinctive and important feature of the universe which confronts our senses, and the function of law as guaranteeing that preeminence. . . . In a scientific age it asks, in effect, what is the nature of man, and what is the nature of the universe with which he is confronted? . . . Why is a human being important; what gives him dignity; what limits his freedom to do whatever he likes; what are his essential needs; whence his sense of injustice?"[30]

The Founding Fathers wrote our laws and Constitution on the presupposition that human beings were the most important feature of the universe, and they thought they were writing a Constitution which would guarantee that preeminence for all time. They answered for their posterity once and for all the questions put into the modern-law journal: why a human being is important, why he has dignity, what limits his freedom, what are his essential needs, and from whence comes his sense of injustice. Had the Supreme Court members not abandoned their answers for sixty years a Warren Court would not have had to correct such basic injustice.

But lower courts, in time sustained by the Supreme Court

under Chief Justices Warren and Burger, apparently stepped beyond the intention if not the letter of the Constitution by making decrees as to how desegregation was to be carried out. The Court leaped beyond its judicial function into legislative type acts which included busing among other things. Justice Black in an unprecedented interview in 1969 observed in retrospect that he felt "the Court should have decided Brown I (Brown No. 1) like any other law case, make its decision, and let the other branches of government figure out how to vindicate the rights established by the decision rather than to endeavor to do it through the judicial process."[31] Two years later Justice Burger would review the Court attempt to solve the problem by its own decrees and lay on the table the dismal record which occasioned Justice Black's comment.

From the evidence given in the foregoing it can be said that at three crucial times in history the Supreme Court turned away from the Founders' philosophy that the natural law is the foundation and guide for American constitutional law: first in the Dred Scott decision of 1858, then in the series of decisions beginning in 1886 which enthroned social Darwinism as the Court philosophy to be implemented by *laissez-faire* criteria for judging the constitutionality of Congressional and state statutes. Finally in the series of cases during the 1870s and 1880s the Court nullified the purpose of the Thirteenth, Fourteenth and Fifteenth Amendments, which was to insure the human dignity of the freedmen by protecting their civil rights; and by the decision of Plessy vs. Ferguson in 1896 the Court legalized racial segregation, the culminating blow to the human equality required by natural law.


## The Blackmun Decision And Natural Law

But by far the most drastic abandonment of the natural-law philosophy of the Founders occurred in 1973 when seven Justices on the Burger Court adhered to the decision written by Justice Blackmun striking down the anti-abortion laws in which all fifty states had been designed to protect the life of unborn human beings. Previous decisions injured the natural rights to liberty, to equality and dignity, to health and property protection: the Black-mun ruling was aimed at the right to life itself.

The deepest conviction of the Founders was that they were establishing the American nation on the laws of nature and of nature's God. From these laws came the human rights which anteceded all civil law. Thus it was put in the Virginia Bill of Rights, June 12, 1776:

"A declaration of rights made by the representatives of the good people of Virginia, assembled in full and free convention; which rights do pertain to them and their posterity, as the basis and foundation of government.

"1. That all men are by nature equally free and independent, and have certain inherent rights, of which, when they enter into a state of society, they cannot by any compact deprive or divest their posterity; namely, the enjoyment of life and liberty, with the means of acquiring and possessing property, and pursuing and obtaining happiness and safety. . . ."[32]

Natural law is the foundation of civil law. Natural rights anteceded civil powers. No legitimate government can be set up which would divest men of their inalienable rights; no generation can make an agreement which would give a government the power to take these rights away from posterity. And the first right which comes from natural law is the right to life. Always, as in this Virginia Declaration, the Founders listed it first; before liberty, property, the pursuit of happiness.

The state and national constitutions were drafted to specify how the respective governments were to implement natural law, to protect natural rights. When the Constitution of the United States was drafted in 1787, it included some protection for natural rights, but not in the clear terms desired by the people. Pressure from the people forced the First United States Congress under Madison's leadership, in 1789, to draft the first ten amendments, our national Bill of Rights. The purpose of these amendments was to specify in legal terms how the national government was going to protect the natural rights to life, liberty, property, freedom of conscience, speech, press, to justice in criminal and civil trials, to human dignity. . . . To call these rights merely civil, merely constitutional, is to dynamite them. Never, in the eyes of the Founders, do basic rights come from the government, from civil law. Constitutional law merely specifies how the protection of basic rights is to be practiced in American society.

The constant reference to these rights as constitutional rights, without characterizing them as natural to man is, by omission, a denial of the natural law which is their true origin. The omission is the studied habit of the Supreme Court since the 1880s; previous Courts were not afraid to state:

"It is among the duties of society to enforce the rights of humanity. . . ." (Justice Johnson, for the majority against Marshall, 1827)[33]

Nor was the Court afraid in 1874 (Loan Association vs. Topeka):

"It must be conceded that there are such rights in every free government beyond the control of the State. A government which recognised no such rights, which held the lives, the liberty, and the property of its citizens subject at all times to the absolute disposition and unlimited control of even the most democratic depository of power, is after all but a despotism."[34]

Unfortunately, these strong words of the Supreme Court of 1874 must be applied to the Supreme Court of 1973. By a 7 to 2 majority (Justices White and Rehnquist dissenting) in the companion cases of Roe vs. Wade and Doe vs. Bolton by the Blackmun decision the Court presumed to act as if there is no law more fundamental than civil law, as if there are no rights beyond the control of a free government, beyond the control of the state. There is no suggestion in the decision of the obligation of government to protect the primordial right of the Founding Fathers, the right to life of each human being: the mere reference would indicate the limitations of all government in accordance with the Founding Fathers.

219

But by apparently solving the cases on constitutional words alone there is the implicit assertion that there is no natural law, only positive, man-made law, which the Court is now trying to adjudicate.

## The Blackmun Decision:
## The Constitution Is Merely Positive Law

Justice Blackmun, in his opening words of the decision which struck down state anti-abortion laws, shows the Court's awareness that the problem of the right to life of human unborn stirred American people to the depths:

"We forthwith acknowledge our awareness to the sensitivity and emotional nature of the abortion controversy, of the vigorous opposing views, even among physicians, and of the deep and seemingly absolute convictions that the subject inspires. One's philosophy, one's experiences, one's exposure to the raw edges of human experience, one's religious training, one's attitude toward life and family and their values and the moral standards one establishes and seeks to observe, are all likely to influence and to color one's thinking and conclusions about abortion.

"In addition, population growth, pollution, poverty, and racial overtones tend to complicate and not to simplify the problem.

*Our task, of course, is to resolve the issue by constitutional measurement free of emotion and predilection.* We earnestly seek to do this, and, because we do, we have inquired into, and in this opinion, place some emphasis upon, medical and medical-legal history and what that history reveals about man's attitudes toward the abortive procedure over the centuries. We bear in mind, too, Mr. Justice Holmes' admonition in his now vindicated dissent in Lochner v. New York:

" *'It (the Constitution) is made for people of fundamentally differing views,* and the accident of our finding certain opinions natural and familiar or novel and even shocking ought not to conclude our judgement upon the question whether statutes embodying them conflict with the Constitution of the United States.' "[35]

220

And later on in the decision:

"The appellee and certain *amici* argue that the fetus is a 'person' within the language and meaning of the Fourteenth Amendment. In support of this they outline at length and in detail the well known facts of fetal development. If this suggestion of personhood is established, the appellant's case, of course, collapses, for the fetus' right to life is then guaranteed specifically by the Amendment."[36]

"Our task is . . . to resolve the issue by constitutional measurement free of emotion and predilection." "(The Constitution) is made for people of fundamentally different views. . . ." "If this suggestion of personhood is established . . . the fetus' right to life is guaranteed specifically by the (Fourteenth) Amendment." We have here the classic attitude of men who believe only in positive law, written law. The issue can be settled by constitutional measurement; the words of the Constitution somehow generate the answers to all legal problems. . . . But in practice "the Constitution means what the Supreme Court says it means"; in practice the Court decides according to its own predilection, states its opinion in constitutional terms; this *is* the constitutional law which the lower courts follow. There is a practical dilemma in this approach: the Court has been known to reverse itself in cases one year apart, and many times has reversed itself in history, each succeeding Court supposedly following the words of the Constitution. . . . What really did the written Constitution mean?

Blackmun's citation of Holmes is also inept. Holmes' famous dissent from his colleagues both rebukes them for violating his interpretation (also positivistic) of constitutional law and misinterprets the meaning of a constitution according to the Founders' principles. Holmes rightly indicated that even by the rules of positivism his colleagues were violating the American Constitution in Lochner vs. New York for "(the Constitution) was made for people of fundamentally different views," but they were imposing their own view (in this case social Darwinism and *laissez-faire* economic theory) on the Constitution to the exclusion of other ways of interpreting and implementing it. What right did their view have to exclusive authority when it was in no sense included in the words or agreed upon by great segments of the people who did not think it to be the one possible application or meaning of constitutional law? The written word of the Constitution certainly gave no clue that *laissez-faire* economic theory was included.

But Holmes also misinterprets the nature of a constitution in the Founders' thought. The Constitution *was* made for people of fundamentally different views: there were deep differences between some of the religious groups, v.g., Congregationalists, Episcopalians, Catholics, all of whom were to be protected by the same Constitution. The differences between those who wanted a powerful central government in distinction to those who favored a more or less loose federation of states were not small. The Constitution compromised over the institution of slavery because there were profound differences concerning this evil among those who intended to make one nation by the Constitution. . . . But, and this is where Holmes' statement that "(the Constitution) is made for people of fundamentally different views" is false, and the statement's application by the Supreme Court in the Blackmun decision is inept: the American people who ratified the Constitution did have some basic principles in common, principles understood to be the foundation of the Constitution — the duties and obligations from natural law which were to be implemented by the Constitution.

The Constitution was not only "made for people of fundamentally different views," it was made also for people who as a whole had many areas of total agreement, who understood these areas of agreement were the basis of the new Constitution; these were the moral principles of the natural law which had universal acceptance by the founding generation. The Supreme Court in the Blackmun decision moved these zones of agreement into the region of fundamental differences noted by Holmes. The Court then gave new meaning to the words of the document to justify an attack on the most basic right which the Constitution was expected to protect by the universally accepted moral principles: the right to life. It is a classic example of changing the meaning of law by mere reinterpretation.

Holmes was against this because it violates any constitution; it makes a written constitution meaningless. The Fathers were against such practices because they held some principles of law were too sacred to be changed by any human government, and they worded the Constitution to make it easy to implement this sacred natural law.

According to the Founders' principles the Blackmun decision is bad law founded on bad philosophy, because to Blackmun moral principles are merely subjective, and vary with each person:

One's philosophy, one's experiences, one's exposure to the raw edges of human experience, one's religious training, one's attitude toward life and family and their values and *the moral standards one establishes* and seeks to observe, are all likely to influence and to color one's thinking and conclusions about abortion."[37]

We must remember that Blackmun is making observations about the primordial right held sacred by the Fathers, the right to life. Abortion concerns this right and its application to unborn human beings. The whole context of the Justice's remarks assert that to him there are many opinions about abortion, no objective standard which should bind all men. His assertion is the direct opposite of the principles upon which the Constitution was built. To Blackmun the right to life of the unborn is "established" by each individual for himself; to the Fathers the right to life of each human being was established for the whole human race by the Creator. . . . Blackmun uses the word "establish" in a very different sense from the Founders; they "established justice" by the Constitution; justice is an objective condition in society when the inalienable rights of each human being are respected by fulfilling the requirements of the Constitution. . . . If unborn human offspring are human beings they have this right to life, and the Constitution demanded that it be not taken away without due process of law.

Perhaps it can be summed up: The Founding Fathers wed the Constitution to natural law, to unchanging human nature. The Supreme Court gave its marital embrace to positive, man-made and changing law. It also put itself into the ill-fated position of deciding how that law would be interpreted and changed in accordance with what the Court itself decided. . . . And in making a decision against the right to life of some human beings it has stirred the deepest indignation the Court has experienced since it ruled against the right to liberty of some human beings in the Dred Scott decision.

Using the criteria of the Founding Fathers the Supreme Court by the Blackmun decision violated three principles held by them to be the foundation of American constitutional law: 1. The Court treated the Constitution as if it were positive law, merely a written law that does not presume natural law which is its foundation and which furnishes guidelines for its proper interpretation. 2. The Constitution was meant to implement the principles stated in the Declaration of Independence. The primordial right stated in the Declaration, flowing from the natural law, is the right to life of all human beings. Overwhelming scientific proof exists that the unborn offspring of human parents must be classified as human beings in the sense of the Declaration; but the Court not only ignored the proof, it violated the canons of judicial interpretation which requires a Court to settle such a fact before trying to adjudicate a case. 3. The Court came to the conclusion that human unborn are not persons within the meaning of this term in the Constitution; but according to the Fathers' use of the word in the document it is certain that they must be classed as persons, therefore worthy of the protection due to life given by the Fifth and Fourteenth Amendments: "No person . . . shall be deprived of life . . . without due process of law."

## The Blackmun Decision:
## Human Unborn Are Non-Human Beings

The first error of the Blackmun decision according to the doctrine of the Founding Fathers, one that permeates its reasoning, is that the Constitution is merely positive law rather than the American specification, or application, of the natural law. This was treated in the above paragraphs.

The second great error of the decision is that the Court failed to settle the crucial fact of the case, whether unborn human off-spring are truly human beings (therefore with an inalienable right to life by the Founders' principles) and then adjudicated as if they were non-human.

Concerning the Blackmun decision Prof. Robert M. Byrn of Fordham University School of Law states:

"The refusal to resolve the threshold question of fact at the outset is the crucial error of *Wade*. There is a 'long course of judicial construction which establishes as a principle that the duty rests on this Court to decide for itself facts or constructions upon which federal constitutional issues rest. . . .' (Nap v. Illinois, 360 U.S. 264, 272)

"The Court noted, as justification for its refusal to resolve the crucial factual issue, that '[when] those trained in the respective disciplines of medicine, philosophy, and theology are unable to arrive at any consensus, the judiciary, at this point in the development of man's knowledge, is not in a position to speculate as to the answer.' The Court then concluded that 'we do not agree that, by adopting one theory of life, Texas may override the rights of the pregnant women that are at stake.' But what was at stake for the unborn child was not a 'theory' of life; it was the fact of life. This lack of consensus, to which the Court referred, is not a lack of consensus on the fact of existence of human life at all stages of gestation — that is established beyond cavil by medical science — but conflicting theories of the value of human life already in existence. That value judgement was made over one hundred years ago, on a constitutional level and as part of binding law, by the framers of the Fourteenth Amendment. A 'consensus is not relevant.' 'One's right to life . . . depend(s) on the outcome of no elections.' "[38]

Prof. Byrn refers to the Fourteenth Amendment since this is the amendment which applies to the states the principles of the Founding Fathers relative to the right to life. Since the philosophy of law and human rights as interpreted by the Founding Fathers or the framers of the Fourteenth Amendment is the same, it is immaterial whether one refers to the Fathers or the framers of the Fourteenth Amendment.

225

In effect the Court sidestepped a conclusion to be drawn from the modern scientific data which indicate that a human life exists from the first moment of conception, from the moment the union of sperm and ovum forms the zygote. Scientifically it is certain that there is a continuum from this point of time until the human life leaves the body at the moment called death. It is amazing in this day and age: the Supreme Court to justify its opinion cited the historical confusion concerning the nature of human life which existed in bygone centuries, showed the consequent confusion in law relative to the protection to be given this life, then on this basis proceeded to strip the unborn of the protection of existing state laws while bypassing modern scientific data.

The Blackmun decision itself relates some of the history and part of the scientific data:

*"The Position of the American Medical Association:*

"The antiabortion mood prevalent in this country was shared by the medical profession. Indeed, the attitude of the profession may have played a significant role in the enactment of stringent criminal abortion legislation during that period (nineteenth century).

"An AMA Committee on Criminal Abortion was appointed in May, 1857. It presented its report, 12 Trans. of the AMA 73-77 (1859), to the Twelfth Annual Meeting. That report observed that the Committee had been appointed to investigate criminal abortion 'with a view to its general suppression.' It deplored abortion and its frequency and it listed three causes 'of this general demoralization':

" 'The first of these causes is a wide-spread popular ignorance of the true character of the crime — a belief even among mothers themselves, that the fetus is not alive until after the period of quickening.

" 'The second of the agents alluded to is the fact that the (members of) the profession themselves are frequently supposed careless of fetal life. . . .

" 'The third reason of the frightful extent of this crime is found in the grave defects of our laws, both common and statute, as regards to the independent and actual existence of the child before birth, as a living being. These errors which are sufficient in most instances to prevent conviction, are based, and only based, upon mistaken and exploded medical dogmas. With strange inconsistency, the law fully acknowledges the fetus in utero and its inherent rights for civil purposes; while personally and as criminally affected, it fails to recognize it, and to its life as yet denies all protection.'

"The Committee then offered, and the Association adopted resolutions protesting 'against such unwarrantable destruction of human life,' calling upon state legislatures to revise their abortion laws and requesting the cooperation of state medical societies 'in pressing the subject.'

"In 1871, a long and vivid report was submitted by the Committee on Criminal Abortion. It ended with the observation (that), 'We had to deal with human life. In a matter of less importance we could entertain no compromise. An honest judge on the bench would call things by their proper names. We could do no less. . . .' "[39]

In other words, the data of science in the mid-nineteenth century indicated that the unborn offspring of a pregnant woman was human; that "quickening," the old common-law sign of fetal life when the mother could feel the child move, was not the scientific sign for the beginning of human life; and that legally the states acted to protect the offspring as human beings during the whole time of pregnancy. Thus, Robert M. Byrn, Professor of Law at Fordham University, states:

"Whatever may be said of the common law and the early nineteenth century, it is evident that in the period from 1859 to 1871, spanning a war fought to vindicate the essential dignity of every human being and the subsequent ratification of the Fourteenth Amendment in 1868, the anti-abortion mood prevalent in the United States can be explained only by a desire to protect live human beings in the womb from the beginning of their existence. When the Fourteenth Amendment was ratified in 1868, the law of at least twenty-eight of the thirty-seven states of the United States incriminated abortion acts prior to 'quickening' — two by common law,

227

and the remainder by statute. In the next fifteen years, one additional state (Colorado) entered the United States and at least seven more states incriminated pre-quickening abortional acts.

"As previously indicated, the overwhelming weight of authority is to the effect that at least one of the purposes of these statutes was the protection of unborn children at all gestational stages. . . ."[40]

The attitude that unborn human life must be protected by law lasted for the next hundred years, until the pro-abortion drive of the 1960s. Until 1967, essentially all fifty states prohibited induced abortion except to protect the life of the pregnant woman.

But the greatest tragedy occurred when, in 1967, the House of Delegates of the American Medical Association adopted "a stated policy of opposition to induced abortion" except where there is a "documented medical evidence of a threat to the health or life of the mother," or that a child "may be born with incapacitating physical deformity or mental deficiency"; rape and incest cases were also included as exceptions. While this was far stricter than the later stand of the Supreme Court, in practice (especially when "health" of the mother included mental health) it becomes abortion on demand. In practice it was a sad reversal of Hippocratic ideals. It was the reversal of a principle upon which our civilization is built, that the right of all human beings to life is equal. The helplessness of the unborn child does not change the principle that its right to life is equal to the right of the mother to her life. The American Medical Association in the nineteenth century stood firmly on the fact that life in the womb is human life. The twentieth-century delegates had much more conclusive evidence of the same fact, that fetal life is human and that each fetus is a unique and individual human being. But the advance in science was accompanied by a confusion of ethics among many members of the medical profession and a decay of ethics among others.

The present conclusion of science which indicates there is more reason now for anti-abortion laws than in the nineteenth century can be summed up in the words taken from an article by Bart T. Heffernan, M.D., and entitled "The Early Biography of Everyman": *"The unborn offspring of human parents is an autonomous human being."* (Emphasis author's.)

We quote some of the information given by Dr. Heffernan which leads to this conclusion:

"From conception the child is a complex, dynamic, rapidly growing individual. By a natural and continuous process the single fertilized ovum will, over approximately nine months, develop into the trillions of cells of the newborn. The natural end of the sperm and ovum is death unless fertilization occurs. At fertilization a new and unique individual is created which, although receiving one-half its chromosomes from each parent, is really unlike either.

"The events that follow fertilization [of the human ovum] are self-generated by the individual under the guidance of his new and absolute unique hereditary plan. The new combination of chromosomes sets in motion the individual's life, controlled by his own individual code [genes] with its fantastic library of information projected from the past on the helix of deoxyribonucleic acid or DNA. . . .

"About seven to nine days after conception, when there are already several hundred cells of the new individual formed, contact with the uterus is made and implantation begins. Blood cells are formed by seventeen days and a heart as early as eighteen days. This embryonic heart, which begins as a simple tube, starts irregular pulsations at twenty-four days, which, in about one week, smooth into a rhythmic contraction and expansion.

"Straus et al have shown that the electrocardiogram (ECG) on a 23mm embryo (7.5 weeks) presents the existence of a functionally complete cardiac system and the possibility of a myoneural or humeral regulatory mechanism. All the classical elements of the adult ECG were seen. . . .

"By the end of the twentieth day the foundation of the child's brain, spinal cord and entire nervous system will have been established. By the sixth week after conception this system will have developed so well that it is controlling movements of the baby's muscles, even though the woman may not be aware that she is pregnant. . . .

"Shettles and Rugh describe this first month of development as follows:

" 'This then is the great planning period, when out of apparently nothing comes evidence of a well-integrated individual who will form along certain well-tried patterns, but who will, in the end, be distinguishable from every other human being by virtue of ultramicroscopic chromosomal differences.'

"By the beginning of the second month, the unborn child, small as it is, looks distinctly human. Yet, at this time, the mother may still not be aware that she is pregnant.

"[The question Shettles and Rugh pose is]: 'When does the embryo become human?' The answer is that it *always* had human potential, and *no other*, from the instant the sperm and the egg came together because of its chromosomes.

"By the end of the seventh week we see a well proportioned small scale baby . . . it bears the familiar external features and all the internal organs of an adult, even though it is less than an inch long and weighs only 1/30 of an ounce.

"At the end of the eighth week no further primordia will form; everything is already present that will be found in a full-term baby. As one author described this period: 'A human face with eyelids half closed as they are in someone who is about to fall asleep. Hands that soon will begin to grip, feet trying their first gentle kicks.'

"From this point until adulthood, when full growth is achieved, somewhere between twenty-five and twenty-seven years, the changes in the body will be mainly in dimension and gradual refinement of the working parts."[41]

Because there has been a great deal of semantics in the abortion controversy, and because the Blackmun decision is careful in implying that prenatal human life is only "potential" human life, it is well to examine the meaning of Shettles and Rugh in the above quotation: " 'When does the embryo become human?' The answer is that it *always* had human potential, and *no other*, from the instant the sperm and the egg came together because of its chromosomes." The meaning of "potential" here is different from the Supreme

Court's use of "potential" to imply the non-humanity, or even non-life of the unborn.

Following the January 22nd Supreme Court decision, Dr. Landrum Shettles wrote a letter to the *New York Times* (February 14th, 1973):

"Concerning when life begins, a particular aggregate of hereditary tendencies (genes and chromosomes) is first assembled at the moment of fertilization when an ovum (egg) is invaded by a sperm cell. This restores the normal number of required chromosomes, 46, for survival, growth, and reproduction of a new composite individual.

"By this definition a new composite individual is started at the moment of fertilization. However, to survive, this individual needs a very specialized environment for nine months, just as it requires sustained care for an indefinite period after birth. But from the moment of union of the germ cells, there is under normal development a living, definite, going concern. To interrupt a pregnancy at any stage is like cutting the link of a chain; the chain is broken no matter where the chain is cut. . . . To deny a truth should not be made a basis for legalizing abortion."[42]

Landrum B. Shettles, M.D.
The Presbyterian Hospital
New York, Feb. 5, 1973

One final bit of evidence. In October, 1967, the First International Conference on Abortion met in Washington, D.C. Approximately sixty major scientific authorities from the fields of medicine, ethics, law and social sciences participated as consultants in this symposium. After several days of intense discussions, the medical group, made up of twenty geneticists, biochemists, physicians, professors, research scientists, etc., came to a near unanimous conclusion (one dissension):

"The majority of our group could find no point in time between the union of sperm and egg, or at least the blastocyst stage, and the birth of the infant at which we could say this was not

231

human life." (Blastocyst stage occurs approximately one week after fertilization and would account for twinning.) ". . . The changes occurring between implantation, the six week embryo, six month fetus, a one week old child, or a mature adult are merely stages of development and maturation."[43]

The scientific data that a pregnant woman carries a new, unique, individual human life (the data which the Supreme Court chose to ignore), is overwhelming. Byrn in a note quotes the authority Andre Hellegers, M.D.: "I don't know of one biologist who would maintain the fetus is not alive. . . . Today we are employing euphemisms to pretend that human life is not present. This stems from the fact that we are not quite ready to say, yes, there is human life but it has no dignity. . . . There is the consensus on the starting point of life, without any question."[44]

## The Blackmun Decision: Human Unborn Are Non-Persons

The third crucial error of the Blackmun decision is that the Court came to the conclusion that human unborn are not persons within the meaning of this term in the Constitution. The way our Founding Fathers used this word in the document indicates it to be certain they must be classed as persons, therefore worthy of the protection due to human life given by the Fifth and Fourteenth Amendments:

"No person . . . shall be deprived of life . . . without due protection of law."

All the Founding Fathers who met to frame the Constitution in 1787 believed that men had inalienable natural and moral rights which a just government must protect. Curiously, they did not put this into legal terms, into a bill of rights which would protect the people (and the states). To many of their fellow citizens this was an unforgivable flaw in their work. In every state the absence of a bill of rights drew opposition, and three of the most powerful states (Massachusetts, New York and Virginia) ratified the Constitution

232

with, at least, the tacit understanding that a bill of rights would be added.

The first great work of the new United States Congress was to propose a bill of rights to the states for addition to the original Constitution. James Madison, friend and confidante of Jefferson, led the fight for these first ten amendments. By those who drafted them, these amendments were meant to be legal implementations of moral rights which belong to men by nature. When the Fifth Amendment stated, "No person . . . shall be deprived of life . . . without due process of law," it spelled out the legal guidelines for the protection of the natural right to life: the Constitution itself and the common and statute law of England which the colonists brought with them when they came to America. This is "due process" according to an 1855 Supreme Court decision; and when the Fourteenth Amendment was added in 1868 it applied "due process" protection of life to the states.

It can be said with certainty that in the Constitution "person" means first of all a human being, because the framers so understood it. The criterion which the Supreme Court used to deny legal personhood to an unborn human being in the Blackmun decision becomes legal legerdemain when judged in the light of history. We deal here with a focal point in the decision as Justice Blackmun indicates:

"If this suggestion of personhood is established, the appellant's case, of course, collapses, for the fetus' right to life is then guaranteed specifically by the Fourteenth Amendment."[45]

"The Constitution," the Court then stated, "does not define 'person' in so many words. Section 1 of the Fourteenth Amendment contains three references to 'person.' The first, in defining 'citizens,' speaks of persons born or naturalized in the United States. The word also appears both in the Due Process Clause and in the Equal Protection Clause. 'Person' is used in other places in the Constitution: in the listing of qualifications for representatives and senators, Art. I, No. 2, cl. 2 and No. 3, cl. 3; in the Apportionment Clause, Art. I, No. 2, cl. 3; in the Migration and Importation provision, Art. I, No. 9, cl. 8. . . . But in nearly all these instances, the use of

233

the word is such that it has application only postnatally. . . . None indicates, with any assurance, that it has any possible prenatal application. . . . All this, together with our observation, *supra,* that throughout the major portion of the nineteenth century prevailing legal abortion practices were far freer than they are today, persuades us that the word 'person,' as used in the Fourteenth Amendment, does not include the unborn. . . ."[46]

The Court will not accept the word "person" for a human unborn, but unhesitatingly and often uses the word "fetus" to specify such unborn. However, a fetus is by definition "an unborn or unhatched vertebrate *after attaining the basic structural plan of its kind,* and specifically a developing human from usually three months after conception to birth."[47] (Emphasis author's.) Thus a fetus is the scientific term for a human unborn when it is recognizably human, in other words, an unborn baby.

In the critical point at issue the Justices concurring in the Blackmun decision arrived at a definition of "person" which included born human beings but not unborn living offspring of human parents, for the reason that the Constitution does not define "person" while often using the term when apparently postnatal situations are referred to. Of course this is the usual use of the term: ". . . Neither shall any person be eligible to that office [President] who shall not have attained to the age of thirty-five years. . . ."[48] Thirty-five years is a reasonable minimum age for the person who will hold the most important office in the land. An unborn baby cannot run for President. But The fifty-year-old man who in actuality becomes a candidate for the presidency is the same person as he was when a fifteen-year-old adolescent, the same person who was a five-year-old child, the same person who once was a five-month-old baby, the same person who was once a five-month-old fetus.

"The migration or importation of such persons as any of the states now existing shall think proper to admit, shall not be prohibited by the Congress prior to the year one thousand eight hundred and eight, but a tax or duty may be imposed on such importation, not exceeding ten dollars for each person."[49] We do not think that the iniquitous slave trade specialized in pregnant women; one would not expect the constitutional Fathers to be troubled about unborn slave infants. Almost all laws are of necessity made for persons in a postnatal situation. It proves nothing that the Constitution, a brief fundamental law, does not immediately seem to refer also to prenatal situations.

In this line of reasoning the Supreme Court seems to imply that the Constitution had no historical background, that it dropped out of the sky fully worded, fully sentenced and paragraphed, with its meaning self-contained; all one has to do is cite one section of the document to explain another. It just did not happen this way.

Nor should the Court expect definitions in the Constitution. In the original document only one word is defined: "Treason against the United States shall consist only in levying war against them, or in adhering to their enemies, giving them aid and comfort."[50] The Court cites a second instance of definition, in the Fourteenth Amendment: "In defining 'citizen' (the Amendment) speaks of 'persons born or naturalized in the United States.' "[51]

Thus the Constitution is not self-explanatory, and definitions of terms are almost nonexistent in the original document. If one wants to know its meaning the logic of the situation calls for a dictionary, one which would give the historical use of "person" at the time the word was put into the Constitution.

The *New English Dictionary on Historical Principles,* edited by Dr. James A. H. Murray, published in 1905 by Oxford Clarendon Press in twenty-two volumes, gives the meaning of English words with quotations of their use for more than 600 years. "Person" in its first and etymological meaning is defined as a character in a play; this is certainly not the constitutional meaning. Next, at the time of the Founding Fathers, the late eighteenth century, the word "person" meant an individual human being — man, woman, or child; or emphatically, a human being as distinguished from a thing or animal. And the dictionary quotes from Blackstone, Commentary II, ii, 16: "The objects of dominion or property are things as contradistinguished from persons." Thirdly, "person" can mean the living body as distinct from clothing, and examples of restricted or colloquial use of "person" are given. In the fourth classification Murray gives the legal meaning of "person," again citing Blackstone, Commentary I, i, 123, 1765: "Natural persons are such as the God of nature framed us; artificial [persons] are such as are created and devised by human law for the purpose of society and government; which are called corporations or bodies politic."

In the second and fourth classifications we have the key to the meaning of the word "person" in the Constitution. It can be used in the sense of an individual human being — man, woman, or child; and/or emphatically a human being as distinguished from a thing or animal. At the time of the Founding Fathers the lack of biological knowledge prevented them from understanding the full humanity of the unborn, as developed above; but implicitly the unborn are included in the definition of "person": a human unborn offspring is certainly not a thing or an animal.

The dictionary quotations from Blackstone are of crucial importance here, both because of the influence of lawyers in framing the Constitution and because it is itself a legal document. Blackstone's Commentaries were the bible of the eighteenth-century lawyer.

The Constitutional Convention included twelve active lawyers and one retired lawyer among its fifty-five members, and a few more than half had studied law at one time or other. It also included plantation owners and large-scale farmers, merchants, political officeholders, small farmers, a doctor and an educator. There were graduates of six American colleges, and one each had attended Oxford, St. Andrews in Scotland, and St. Omer's in Belgium.[52] The Constitution was accepted by the American people as a whole after almost a year of debate. It was a document which had the precision lawyers could give to its wording but was meant for all the people. It was not so technical that the average citizen was not supposed to understand it. "We the People of the United States . . . do ordain and establish this Constitution for the United States of America." As a nation matures and applications of such a fundamental legal document become almost endless, the need for specialists in the courts, both lawyers and judges, multiplies. But never should such a document be so construed, or misconstrued, that an ordinary citizen can conclude that one of its fundamental principles is distorted by means of semantics.

A reference to a modern English dictionary such as *Webster's Collegiate* will show that the uses of the word "person" have not changed in 200 years. The meaning is the same as when used by the Founding Fathers: a "person" is a human being as distinguished from an animal or thing; and in law we can have a "body of persons, corporation, partnership, or other legal entity recognized by law as the subject of rights and duties."[53]

When the framers of the Constitution used the word "person" they meant human beings, and by implication unborn human beings also. The Constitutional Convention's farmers, merchants, plantation owners, and even the doctor, used English as ordinary citizens. They knew words could have both explicit and implicit meanings. The lawyers would be quite clear in their minds that the legal meaning of "person" could imply corporations. ... It was their ordinary, everyday language that the Founding Fathers put into the Constitution. They did not try to define these ordinary words; nor could they have foreseen that the Constitution would be strained out of context, or that, because the specific situations they legislated for applied to born persons, their principle of the inalienability of the right to human life would never apply to other persons, other human beings. It is unworthy of the Supreme Court to rely on semantics in this life-or-death situation.

## The Supreme Court And Natural Rights

In one sense it is superfluous to discuss natural rights in the light of the philosophy of the Founding Fathers relative to Supreme Court decisions during the past 100 years. By interpreting the Constitution merely as positive, man-made law, and constantly bypassing the possibility that there is a law written in the nature of man which the Constitution was drafted to uphold, the Court has destroyed all natural rights. Natural rights are based on natural law; if there is no law of nature to guide and rule mankind, there are no inalienable rights to life, liberty, the pursuit of happiness, justice, freedom of conscience, the others named or unnamed by the Fathers.

The Supreme Court has substituted legal, civil rights of its own choosing in place of the rights held sacred by the Fathers; and these rights are read from or into the Constitution by the Court. In a great number if not in the majority of practical cases these legal, civil, constitutional rights do protect the American people in their basic natural rights. The Fathers who drafted the Constitution knew which rights were natural and inalienable, and they protected these rights by the specific wording of the sections of the Constitution which were to show how these rights were to be respected in American society. For example, human beings have a right to justice: in our tradition justice is best achieved by trial by jury, so Article III, Section 2, No. 3, of the Constitution states:

"The trial of all crimes, except in cases of impeachment, shall be by jury; and such trial shall be held in the State where the said crimes shall have been committed; but when not committed within any States, the trial shall be at such place or places as the Congress may by law have directed."[54]

Again, human beings have a natural right to freedom of conscience; the Fathers knew that this was most often breached by government interference with religion, so the First Amendment of the Bill of Rights decrees:

"Congress shall make no law respecting an establishment of religion, or prohibiting the free exercise thereof; . . ."[55]

Because the Founding Fathers understood so well the rights which were due human nature, and because we inherited English common law which if not always adequate did develop within a Judeo-Christian consciousness of human dignity and human rights, our Constitution to an amazing perfection implemented natural rights by specifically worded provisions. Because of the genius of the Founding Fathers very often the Supreme Court follows specific provisions which make the Court's civil rights coincide with true natural rights. But because the Court for the past century abandoned the Fathers' root principles of natural rights which had blos-

238

somed into particular constitutional rights, and because a generally worded Constitution cannot provide specifically for the myriad types of cases which arise in a complicated and changing society, the Court also very often read into or out of the Constitution the legal rights which were subjective to the particular Justices when sitting; their personal opinions decided what was good for the American people.

Sadly and perhaps subconsciously the Court often decided for the group they stood for or favored: the Court decided by *laissez-faire* policies in favor of the "rights" of wealth and business against labor and the consumer, for the "rights" of (prejudiced) whites against blacks, for those of pregnant women who wanted to dispose of their unborn children against the children. When a Court believes only in positive law and is applying a Constitution written in general terms it can make that Constitution say just about anything it wants. This is, tragically, what happened. Chief Justice Hughes, between his terms on the Supreme Court, said it:

"We are under a Constitution, but the Constitution is what the judges say it is."[56]

We have become a government of men, not of laws.

Two conditions made tolerable the practice of deriving all American rights from the Constitution as interpreted by the Court rather than from human nature. As stated above, there is so much wisdom in our Constitution and American law as founded on natural law that ordinarily when applied it protects natural human rights. And secondly, the judges of the nation's highest tribunal usually represented the dominant force in society, if not the majority; or often represented the dominant spirit where the laws went into effect, v.g., the unhappy white supremacy prejudice which backed segregation when Plessy vs. Ferguson was handed down. "Tolerable" here means "tolerated"; the Supreme Court interpretations of the Constitution did not cause revolution. But the rights of minority groups which the Constitution was meant to protect were often trampled upon. In theory, therefore, interpretation of the Constitution as mere positive law left the American people merely

239

with civil rights; in practice many, but not all, natural rights were protected. It is important to keep before our minds what the Fathers actually intended to achieve by the Constitution.

## Inferences Of Founders' Natural Rights Vs. Supreme Court Civil Rights

The principles and inferences of the natural-rights philosophy of the Founding Fathers may be summarized as follows:

All human beings are equal in their nature, not of course in talents, strength, health, intelligence, etc.; but because of equal human nature there is a basic equality between rich and poor, black and white, strong and weak, young and old, which must be recognized in law.

Due to the equal quality of humanness, each human being has certain inalienable rights such as the rights to life, liberty, property, pursuit of happiness, justice, freedom of conscience, and so forth.

The inalienable rights cannot be ceded. A man cannot morally give up his right to life by committing suicide, for example. One generation cannot cede the inalienable rights of a future generation, v.g., by committing posterity to slavery.

Each human being must respect the equal rights of others.

The individual is central, all-important. Government exists to protect the rights of individuals, not vice versa. Governments are established to make it easier for individuals to pursue legitimate happiness.

But men need each other; they are social by nature. They need the protection of society. Receiving that protection, individuals are committed to fostering the common good, and they agree to use their rights within legally accepted boundaries.

For the Federalists especially, the right which the government must be most careful to protect in practice is the right of an individual to his honestly owned property, since by owning property a human being is secure and free to pursue his happiness. In practice a property owner will be more stable and reliable than a propertyless person and can be better trusted to run the government. He has a higher stake in a peaceful, stable, prosperous community. *This is not the survival of the fittest* since the weakest in society has a right to the protection of his inalienable right to life, health, property, pursuit of happiness; and there is an order of priority in rights.

The right to life is the primordial right, antecedent by nature to all other rights.

Practically all of these principles and inferences of the natural-rights philosophy of the Founders were nullified at one time or another by the Supreme Court.

The first principle that the Fathers imbedded into law, as a result of their natural-rights thinking, is the basic equality of all human beings. As worded by Chief Justice Taney the Dred Scott decision handed down by the Supreme Court in 1857 is perhaps the most blatant example of the Court's denial of human equality. The other concurring Justices filed separate opinions. It is well to remember that the Court had not yet abandoned the natural-law principles of the Founders, and that the Fathers had compromised on the issue of slavery while founding the nation on the principle of human equality. Taney thus distorts the Declaration of Independence:

"It is difficult at this day to realize the state of public opinion in relation to that unfortunate race (blacks), which prevailed in the civilized and enlightened portions of the world at the time of the Declaration of Independence, and when the Constitution of the United States was framed and adopted. . . .

"They had for more than a century before been regarded as beings of an inferior order; and altogether unfit to associate with the white race, either in social or political relations; and so far inferior that they had no rights which the white man was bound to respect; and that the negro might justly and lawfully be reduced to slavery for his benefit. . . .

"The language of the Declaration of Independence is equally conclusive. . . ."[57]

The Dred Scott decision did much to precipitate the Civil War; the war was the answer to a troubled American conscience which

241

could not reconcile slavery with the basic equality of all human beings, could not reconcile itself with an institution which kept one race subject to another. The war should have guaranteed the equality of men for all time. The Thirteenth, Fourteenth and Fifteenth Amendments were added to the Constitution to establish this basic equality. The Supreme Court during the 1870s and 1880s nullified the amendments, thereby wasting the blood spilled in the war. But it was the 1896 Court decision in Plessy vs. Ferguson, settling the question of segregation in the South for the next sixty years, which legally established inequality on the blacks in its most obnoxious manner. There is the smell of hypocrisy in the majority opinion as written by Justice Henry B. Brown:

"We consider the underlying fallacy of the plaintiff's argument to consist in the assumption that the enforced separation of the two races stamps the colored race with a badge of inferiority. If this be so, it is not by reason of anything found in the act, but solely because the colored race chooses to put that construction upon it. . . . The argument also assumes that social prejudices may be overcome by legislation, and that equal rights cannot be secured to the Negro except by forced commingling of the two races. We cannot accept this proposition. If the two races are to meet upon terms of social equality, it must be the result of natural affinities, a mutual appreciation of each other's merits, and a voluntary consent of individuals. . . . If the civil and political rights of both races be equal one cannot be inferior to the other civilly or politically. If one race be inferior to the other socially, the Constitution of the United States cannot put them upon the same plane."[58]

The lone dissenter, the first of the two Justices named John Marshall Harlan, was a voice crying in the wilderness of an unredeemed Court:

". . . But in the view of the Constitution, in the eye of the law, there is in this country no superior, dominant, ruling class of citizens. There is no caste here. Our Constitution is color-blind, and neither knows nor tolerates classes among citizens. In respect of

242

civil rights, all citizens are equal before the law. The humblest is the peer of the most powerful. The law regards man as man, and takes no account of his surroundings or his color when his civil rights as guaranteed by the supreme law of the land are involved. . . ."[59]

This is Jeffersonian reasoning.

The second principle of the Fathers which they implicitly wrote into the law by the specific articles of the Constitution was the acknowledgment that certain inalienable rights existed. Thus the right to justice was to be guaranteed by jury trial; the right to freedom of conscience by the First Amendment prohibiting a nationally established religion; the rights to property and life were protected by due process of law guaranteed by the Fifth Amendment.

The most sweeping denial of inalienable rights and the obligation of the law to protect them occurred when the Supreme Court espoused social Darwinism as its theory to judge the constitutionality of congressional and state statutes. It accomplished this by using *laissez-faire* economic criteria to determine the reasonableness of the respective enactments. William H. Marnell analyzes what happened by tracing the Court's attitude back to some of its sources:

"The full pattern of American Philistinism is thus revealed in Sumner (William Graham Sumner, an extremely influential Yale professor of political and social science, 1872-1910). The utilitarian objective underlies all his argumentation and gives it an appropriate moral coloration; our only justifiable concern is the rise of civilization with the concomitant blessings that rise will confer on all its members. Civilization will rise so long as civilization is based on classical economics; observes that the goal is a material one; recognises that virtue is to be measured in terms of material gain; protects the entrepreneur, who is the cornerstone of society, by strict observance of *laissez-faire;* and never loses sight of the quasi-Calvinistic assurance that the rich man is God's anointed. There was something about Sumner, perhaps his personal inheritance and perhaps his inheritance as an American, that made him prefer the self-reliant small businessman to the blatant millionaire whom the system was producing so successfully in the post-Civil War era, but Sumner accepted the Fisks and Goulds as products of the system, reflecting that at the best we are on the road to perfection. Such concepts as natural rights and human equality are part of the outworn folklore of a romantic past; the scientific study of folkways reveals that all rights are man-made products of the mores of society, subject to change as society develops, and the entire tenor of social Darwinism rebuts the romantic fallacy of human equality. Liberty and property are one and inseparable, progress and the acquisitive instinct are Siamese twins. Government exists to protect one's liberty to exercise his acquisitive instincts in the accumulation of property and thus to forward the progress of civilization. All that really is needed is a properly educated and disciplined legislature to write this philosophy into law, and a properly educated and disciplined Supreme Court to read it in. . . .

"The Supreme Court began to show the requisite training and discipline about 1870, as the influence of the most dedicated social Darwinian in Court history, Stephen J. Field (1816-1899), began to make itself felt. . . . Justice Field did it with the eloquence of an Old Testament prophet, nor is there reason to doubt that when he proclaimed the doctrine of *laissez-faire* in a phraseology indebted in part to Isaiah and in part to Thomas Jefferson he honestly believed that he was speaking in full accord with divine revelation. . . ."[60]

What Marnell is indicating is that the Supreme Court abandoned the natural-law philosophy of the Founding Fathers, the same Founders who gave us the Constitution as the criterion for its interpretation, and substituted social Darwinism and *laissez-faire* economic theory in its place. The Court did this with no mandate from the people. The people through state legislatures and Congress kept pressing for legislation to protect natural human rights. The legislatures never became "properly educated and disciplined" to enact social Darwinism into law; the Supreme Court read it into law by declaring unconstitutional state statutes passed to protect the rights of workingmen, or Congressional legislation to the same effect or designed to curb the ever-growing trusts and monopolies. The Court abandoned Washington, Jefferson, Madison; in their place were Sumner, Spencer, their own version of Darwin.

Justice Holmes pointed out part of the fallacy:

". . . This case is decided upon an economic theory which a large part of the country does not entertain. . . . The Fourteenth Amendment does not enact Mr. Herbert Spencer's Social Statics. . . . But a constitution is not intended to embody a particular economic theory, whether of paternalism and the organic relation of the citizen to the State or of *laissez-faire*. It is made for people of fundamentally differing views. . . ."[61]

According to the principles of the Founding Fathers the individual is central; government exists first to protect the inalienable rights of the individual and then to foster the common good so that each person may pursue his happiness in a legitimate way. The Supreme Court in applying *laissez-faire* economics, forbidding national and state governments the power to exercise even a control of business necessary for the common good, wreaked havoc with the rights of the common man to life, liberty and the pursuit of happiness. The Court did this usually by its interpretation of the Fourteenth Amendment: corporations were legal persons under the law, and neither Congress nor state legislatures could deprive them of property without due process of law, or interfere with their right to make contracts — no matter how unfair these might be to defenseless workers or unsuspecting consumers.

Sometimes in pursuing *laissez-faire* policies the Court would defang legislative acts meant to control monopolies by interpreting the Constitution in a way to eliminate the legislative power itself. The Court nullified Congress' Sherman Anti-Trust Act in the first important case to rise under it, the Sugar Trust case in 1895, because the clause in the Constitution gave Congress the power to regulate interstate commerce, but the Sugar Trust, which manufactured ninety-eight percent of the sugar refined and sold in the United States, was engaged in manufacture and not commerce! Control of commerce belonged to Congress, but manufacture to the states.[62] Sometimes the Court ruled that legislation meant to protect workers (v.g., minimum-wage regulations) interfered with the workers' freedom to make contracts, and were therefore invalid under the Constitution.[63]

Specifically, the Court created civil barriers under the Constitution which nullified the natural rights of human persons, the rights which the Founding Fathers wrote the Constitution to protect. Thus, the right to life was affected, to cite an example, in this manner:

Under the police powers of the states belongs the right as well as the obligation to protect the health of the citizens. To put it another way, if health conditions are dangerous in practice the right of each citizen to his life is in danger. In 1908 the Court overruled Congress on making the railroads pay for avoidable accidents to employees. Some years later the Court nullified a Congressional minimum-wage law for women workers in the District of Columbia, a law supported in Congress as protective of health and morals. Holmes as usual made a pointed dissent:

"The end, to remove conditions leading to ill health, immorality and the deterioration of the race, no one would deny to be within the scope of constitutional legislation. . . . When so many intelligent persons, who have studied the matter more than any of us can, have thought that the means are effective and are worth the price, it seems to me impossible to deny that the belief *reasonably* may be held by *reasonable* men."[64]

In the same era child labor was a social cancer, a national disgrace. In 1913 it was estimated that twenty percent of the children age ten to fifteen in America were earning their own living. One thinks of boys separating coal from slate in Pennsylvania or West Virginia breakers; of ten-year-old girls making artificial flowers or cigars in New York City tenement sweatshops; of the 5,000 girls between ten and twelve in Southern cotton mills. In Alabama children could work sixty hours a week; in Georgia there was a gentleman's agreement between mill operators that children should not work more than sixty-six hours per week! Yes, twelve hours per day, snatch lunch while watching your machine. . . .[65] But *laissez-faire* economic theory said this was good for the nation. . . .

"Nevertheless, when in 1916 Congress endeavored to break up a widespread traffic in child-made goods, by forbidding the transportation of such goods outside the State where produced, it was informed, in the case of Hammer v. Dagenhart, by a closely divided Court, that it was not regulating commerce among the States but was invading 'the reserved powers of the States,' meaning thereby the power of the States over the employer-employee relationship in productive industry. . . . What is more, as the decisions stood at that date *both* Congress and the States were forbidden to prohibit the free flow of the products of child labor from one State to another — the former on the ground that it would be usurping power reserved to the States; the latter on the ground that they would be usurping Congress's power to regulate commerce!"[66]

If the *laissez-faire* policy of the Court attacked the right of each human being to his or her life it also undermined the right to liberty. " 'Liberty' at the common law meant little more than the right not to be physically restrained except for a good cause."[67] To the Founding Fathers, of course, liberty meant much more; it was the totality of legitimate freedom that Patrick Henry wanted when he said, "Give me liberty, or give me death." The Supreme Court during its social Darwinism days acted to curb the natural and legitimate freedom of Americans and in its place substituted its own brand of "freedom." In 1908 when the Court overruled Congress' efforts to make the railroads financially responsible for avoidable accidents it also denied the workers the freedom to help themselves. Congress had passed a law to make it a crime for a railroad to fire a worker for belonging to a union, or to hold a worker to the "yellow dog" contract in which a worker anxious for a job had signed a promise not to join a union. . . . "Unconstitutional," declared the Court. . . .

However, in place of the personal liberty (which in the eyes of the Founding Fathers belonged to men because of the dignity of human nature), the Court created a new constitutional "freedom of contract" which permitted employers to abuse the natural right of employees to a fair wage and just working conditions; v.g., minimum-wage laws were declared invalid because they interfered with

247

the "freedom" of a worker who needed a job to accept substandard conditions, and the "freedom" of an employer to force employees to accept inhumanly low wages.[68] With *laissez-faire* theory their guiding light, the Court declared this "freedom" to make unjust contracts to be guaranteed by the Fourteenth Amendment. But eventually the Court had to reverse itself — and in New Deal days ended up with precisely the human rights and freedoms the principles of the Founding Fathers required. But meanwhile, instead of adhering to the objective standards of the Fathers or Congress' interpretation of freedom, the Court was insisting on its own subjective criteria as to what freedoms the American people were to have:

"About seventy-five years ago, however, the Court, following the urging of influential members of the American Bar and the lead given by certain of the State courts, adopted the view that the word 'liberty' as used here (in common law) and in the Fourteenth Amendment was intended to protect the 'freedom of contract' of adults engaged in the ordinary employments, especially when viewed from the point of view of would-be employers. Then in 1925 the Court took the further step of extending the term as it is used in the Fourteenth Amendment to certain of the rights, described as 'fundamental' which were already protected against the National Government by the more specific language of the Bill of Rights, among these being freedom of speech and press. Later, the Court, responding to the social teachings of the New Deal, came practically to dismiss the conception of 'freedom of contract' as a definition of 'lberty' and to substitute for it a special concern for 'the rights of labor', its right to organize, and to strike and picket so long as too obvious violence was avoided.

"In brief, this clause, for a time (roughly from 1900-1937) was employed frequently to challenge the *substantive* content of legislation or in other words to require that Congress exercise its powers 'reasonably', that is to say, *reasonably in the judgment of the Court....*"[69]

Social Darwinism, *laissez-faire* economics, denied the human rights to life and liberty. It was also a denial of the right to property. This is a paradox, for social Darwinians seemed always to be on the side of property owners. Yet *laissez-faire* theory is essentially different from that which leads to the protection given property owners by natural-rights founding principles.

The Founding Fathers believed that it belonged to man's nature to acquire property, that it was morally his when honestly acquired. If a man catches a fish, it is his; if he shoots a deer, it belongs to him. Society has a right to make rules for the acquiring of land; but when a man does fulfill the requirements and has planted his crops, they are his. . . . However, the principle of *laissez-faire* denies moral rights which come from nature; there are only mores which can change with custom.

To *laissez-faire* devotees what leads to economic and social efficiency is the survival of the fittest among competing men. A man can work all his life to build his oil business, but if a monopolistic oil refiner like John D. Rockefeller could force railroads to give him cheaper rates than competitors and drive all smaller rivals to the wall, this would be good for the country because bigness leads to efficiency. If Andrew Carnegie could keep his workers at a low wage the nation would prosper because steel could be produced at a lower price to the consumer (if Andrew Carnegie wanted to pass the lower price on). While the ideal of the Fathers was to lead to many self-sufficient property owners, the ideal of *laissez-faire* economic theory was business efficiency; the worker or weak competitor be damned so long as the fittest survived.

What the Supreme Court did in espousing *laissez-faire* economics was to give theoretical and practical justification to the law of the jungle in economic relationships. When Chief Justice Marshall got out of hand in protecting property rights he was reminded by his colleagues who overruled him that:

"It is among the duties of society to enforce the rights of humanity, and both the debtor and the society have their interest in the administration of justice, and in the general good, interests which must not be swallowed up and lost sight of while yielding attention to the claim of the creditor. . . ."[70]

249

Such a debtor would be merely an incident in guaranteeing the survival of the fittest for social Darwinians. . . . But the inalienable rights to life, liberty and the pursuit of happiness must in a just society be balanced against the right of a man to his property. To a Supreme Court governed by natural-rights philosophy there is a natural check on the avarice of property owners; under *laissez-faire* adjudication there is none. The two theories are essentially different.

Social Darwinism also had racial overtones as Marnell noted. It was the violation of personal freedom in the enforced segregation decreed by the Plessy vs. Ferguson decision which made it so obnoxious to Justice Harlan:

"Railroad corporations of Louisiana did not make discrimination among whites in the matter of accommodation for travellers. The thing to accomplish was, under the guise of giving equal accommodations for whites and blacks, to compel the latter to keep to themselves while travelling in railroad passenger coaches. No one would be so wanting in candor as to assert the contrary. The fundamental objection, therefore, to the statute, is that it interferes with the personal freedom of citizens. . . . If a white man and a black man choose to occupy the same public conveyance on a public highway, it is their right to do so, and no government, proceeding alone on grounds of race, can prevent it without infringing on the personal liberty of each."[71]

## The Supreme Court And The Compact

There is no historical doubt that the Founding Fathers who drafted the Constitution in 1787 and the people who accepted it were establishing a new political compact which was to be binding on government and people. From the Mayflower Compact instituting a political society for the Pilgrims when they landed in a new world, and the various covenants which put the New England towns into existence, to the constitutions for such states as Virginia and Pennsylvania in 1776, or Massachusetts in 1780, the American people had gained practical experience in setting up governments by compact. The constant succession of writings to justify the struggle against Great Britain which culminated in independence show the Founders' reliance on the principle that just government rests on using its powers in accordance with an understood agreement of the people; practice and theory had to be one in the American mind. Because the British government had broken its compact with them, the colonists were convinced they had sufficient grounds for resistance. The "Declaration of Resolves" of the First Continental Congress in 1774 stated:

"That the inhabitants of the English Colonies in North America, by the immutable laws of nature, the principles of the English Constitution, and the several charters or compacts, have the following rights:
"1. That they are entitled to life, liberty, and property, and they have never ceded to any sovereign power whatever, a right to dispose of either without their consent. . . ."[72]

Of course it is the Declaration of Independence which puts the principles of the founding generation in their most perfect form:

"We hold these truths to be self-evident, that all men are created equal, that they are endowed by their Creator with certain unalienable rights, that among these are life, liberty, and the pursuit of happiness. That to secure these rights, governments are instituted among men, deriving their just powers from the consent of the governed. That whenever any form of government becomes destructive of these ends, it is the right of the people to alter or to abolish it, and to institute new government, laying its foundation on such principles and organizing its powers in such form as to them shall seem most likely to effect their safety and happiness. . . ."[73]

Putting their theory into practice they created a nation by the most famous compact in history:

"We the People of the United States, in order to form a more perfect Union, establish Justice, insure domestic Tranquility, provide for the common defence, promote the general Welfare, and secure the Blessings of Liberty to ourselves and our Posterity, do ordain and establish this Constitution for the United States of America."[74]

A compact is an agreement, a contract between people. The Constitution of the United States defines the terms under which the American people agree to live as a political society, it establishes the government which is to rule that society and ordains the powers which that government is to have. The officers of the government take an oath to uphold the Constitution; this is the guarantee the people have that they will not be abused. To achieve the purposes of the Constitution the people cede to the government certain definite powers and enjoin the methods by which the powers are to be used. If the government is acting within its powers and according to the rules established by the Constitution the people must obey even unpopular laws; the government has the power to enforce its legitimate acts. But a constitution is meaningless if the government, or any of its branches, can violate the compact and claim legality in unconstitutional actions. The Declaration of Independence was precise: ". . . To secure these (inalienable) rights, Governments are instituted among Men, deriving their just powers from the consent of the governed, . . ." It is the consent of the people which establishes the compact, the Constitution; only acts in accord with their given consent are truly legal.

But underlying the compact are the "Laws of Nature and of Nature's God." For the Fathers, no compact could destroy the moral law, no constitution could nullify the Ten Commandments. The inalienable rights which the government must protect, which came from the moral law, could never be ceded to any government either for the generation making the compact or for posterity.[75] No people could validly consent to such a cession. This was totally understood, precisely expressed in the Declaration of Independence and many other documents. Within the Constitution were stated the methods whereby future generations could change the structure, increase or diminish ceded powers; but the natural moral law underlying the Constitution could not be ceded or changed by any man or generation.

The organs of government, in their specific makeup and powers, are creatures of the Constitution. The Founding Fathers rejected the age-old method of placing the powers necessary to any government — the legislative, executive, judicial — in the hands of one or a few men. The Founders rejected monarchy and/or oligarchy. Long experience had taught that excessive concentrated power leads to tyranny. Thus the Constitution provided:

"All legislative Powers herein granted shall be vested in a Congress of the United States, which shall consist of a Senate and House of Representatives." (Art. I, Sect. 1)

"The executive Power shall be vested in a President of the United States of America. . . ." (Art. II, Sect. 1)

"The judicial Power of the United States, shall be vested in one supreme Court, and in such inferior Courts as the Congress may from time to time ordain and establish. . . ." (Art. III, Sect. 1)

The Constitution does not literally invest the Supreme Court with the power of declaring acts of Congress, the President, or the states invalid under its provisions, but before its acceptance by the people Hamilton in Federalist Paper No. 78 said this had to be its meaning. The Courts must interpret the law; the Constitution is the fundamental law of the land; if any act of the other branches of government contravene it, the Courts must rule in favor of the Constitution. This has been the accepted practice since Marshall's famous 1803 decision in Marbury vs. Madison.

Yet this is a key point: if the Courts established by the Constitution exceed their constitutional power their acts are invalid no less than those of Congress, the President, or the states when these branches exceed theirs. The Courts are creatures of the Constitution. In practice, since the Supreme Court makes the final decision on constitutionality of acts, it is this Court which assumes final responsibility where the meaning of the Constitution is concerned. And here is the booby trap: if the Supreme Court decrees an action of another branch of government constitutional or the reverse, there is no higher constitutional authority to say *No*. And historically it has also happened often that constitutional authorities of greater learning, and perhaps of higher character than the Justices of the majority whose vote decided the case, have judged the Court to be exceeding *its* authority in handing down decisions which could not be defended by legitimate constitutional principles.

One must ponder the implications of a Supreme Court constitutional decision which is bad constitutional law because it has been handed down by prejudiced or incompetent Justices. One hesitates to use the word corrupt, and history indicates a singular freedom from such on the highest Court; but biased and incompetent judges there have been, and decisions which cannot be justified by sound constitutional scholarship, which have harmed the nation or played havoc with human dignity and human rights, have been aplenty. The cost in human suffering as a result of the Dred Scott decision, or due to social Darwinism and *laissez-faire* prejudices, cannot be estimated. Subjectively the Justices were probably convinced they were men of honor; objectively history can convict them of a greater violation of American law than Watergate. In this case it would be the Constitution itself twisted to mean not what the Founders meant, not what the words imply, not what the people agreed to, but what any number from five to nine men desired to impose on the country. In essence it means that the Supreme Court has many times violated the compact, the foundation of our civil structure.

This could probably never have happened during the era of the Founding Fathers because the American people as a whole understood the nature of the compact and the Constitution which they agreed to, and its violation would have been too apparent. It did happen after the Civil War and many times since. One reason would be that the Constitution had worked so well the people took it for granted. Again as Court cases became overwhelming in number and more technical it would be difficult for any but lawyers to see the flaws in some Supreme Court decisions, and sadly the profession seems not to have measured up to its responsibility to protect the Constitution. A third explanation is that the people were so distracted with the superabundant growth and rapid changes in the nation and society that they could not notice all that was going on. The country as a whole was flourishing in spite of the Supreme Court. And, of course, the bulk of Supreme Court decisions did have reasonable principles to justify them.

According to the principles of the Founding Fathers the political compact upon which American society was founded put the government under contract with the people to respect certain natural rights and to perform its legitimate functions in accordance with the powers granted in the written Constitution. The compact could therefore be broken or violated in two ways:

The first involved the government or any of its branches invading the sphere of inalienable rights, the rights which belonged to the people antecedent to any government whatever. These were the natural rights to life, liberty, the legitimate pursuit of happiness, property, and other truly existing but not fully listed rights. The Ninth Amendment states:

"The enumeration in the Constitution, of certain rights, shall not be construed to deny or disparage others retained by the people."

The second way for the government to break the compact with the people implied by their acceptance of the Constitution was for government officials to violate the written terms of the document. The most important written provision was the separation of powers within the government. The Declaration of Rights which was Part I of the Constitution of Massachusetts (1780) gave the principle as understood by the Founders:

"In the government of this commonwealth, the legislative department shall never exercise the executive and judicial powers, or either of them: the executive shall never exercise the legislative and judicial powers, or either of them: the judicial shall never exercise the legislative and executive powers, or either of them: to the end it may be a government of laws and not of men."[76]

Some of the natural rights protected by the Constitution and

255

capable of violation by the Court are easily mentioned. The right to life was the primordial right of each human being; without this all others are illusory, and it was always mentioned first by the Founders. The right to liberty was fought for by the Americans in the Revolution; they would be freemen, not slaves. It was unfortunately compromised relative to the blacks, but with some reasonable hope that slavery would die a natural death. The right to the pursuit of happiness was to be governed by the moral law; all were free to fulfill themselves so long as they did not infringe the rights of God or other men. The right to property, that what a man honestly owned was *his*, subject only to his disposition, was considered also natural; taxation without representation was immoral. Freedom of conscience was often listed as a prime natural right. Not listed, but specifically implied, was the natural right to justice.

Not listed, but an example of a natural right always understood, would be the right to marry; probably also the rights to emigrate, so often practiced by the Americans. These rights were antecedent to all government; they belonged to men as men. The most vicious breaking of the compact to the Founders was government interference with these rights; this was what the Revolution was all about. Following are instances in which the Supreme Court violated the compact:

In the Dred Scott decision of 1858 the Court by a 7 to 2 decision attempted to saddle the country permanently with the iniquitous institution of slavery, the prime denial of the natural right to liberty.

By a succession of decisions nullifying the Thirteenth, Fourteenth and Fifteenth Amendments in the 1870s and 1880s, culminating in the Plessy vs. Ferguson decision in 1896, the Supreme Court violated the natural freedom and dignity of the blacks and degraded them by imposing segregation on them.

The Court by espousing social Darwinism and applying *laissez-faire* criteria as the determinant of the constitutionality of laws affecting workingmen and the consuming public, the Court discarded without the consent of the people the concept of natural law and natural rights which had given birth to the Constitution. This type of decision-making continued, with a few intermissions, from 1887 to 1937. The Court prevented Congress and state governments from passing and enforcing laws which would have protected working people in their natural rights to life, health and the legitimate pursuit of happiness.

The natural rights to freedom of conscience and the possibility of fulfilling the natural obligation to pray were violated when the Court in 1962 struck down the New York State Regents' prayer which permitted the children to voluntarily participate in school prayer of the simplest nonsectarian kind.

Intrinsically the worst breaking of the compact is the most recent. In 1973, via the 7 to 2 Blackmun abortion decision which invalidated state laws protecting the lives of unborn babies, the right to life was violated. Among the Founding Fathers this natural right was always listed as the first of the rights which government must protect. Its violation destroys the primordial right of the human baby and in its place manufactures the right to privacy of the mother from the so-called "penumbras" or marginal areas of the Bill of Rights. This turns the whole thinking of the Founding Fathers upside down.

It must be remembered that the people never agreed to new criteria to interpret the Constitution, never agreed to social Darwinism as the national philosophy. The people never agreed to have a new yardstick to measure their rights in place of the natural-rights philosophy of the Founders. Natural-law philosophy was never rejected by the American people. In times of crisis they have always reverted to it in practice even when their leaders gave it no adequate formulation in words.

### The Supreme Court Breaks The Compact By Violating The Words Of The Constitution

According to the principles of the Founding Fathers, the second type of breaking the compact by the Supreme Court lies in its violation of the separation of powers written into the Constitution. Sometimes this type of violation occurred joined to a violation of natural rights. In following *laissez-faire* economics, so harmful to the natural rights of worker and public, the Supreme Court often made legislative decisions, so much so that Justice Brandeis was to coin the phrase "super-legislature" to describe his colleagues. That is, in seeking the betterment of the country in their own eyes, the Justices would make legislative decisions rather than restrict them- selves to merely judicial reasoning as to the constitutionality of stat- utes: the Court majority struck down statutes using constitutional phrasing but in reality struck them down because, in their judg- ment, Congress or state legislatures passed unwise decisions.

"Thus the Court has never exercised its censorship of legisla- tion, whether national or State, more energetically than during the half century between 1887 and 1937, when its thinking was strongly colored by *laissez-faire* concepts of the role of government. This point of view, translated into congenial constitutional doctrines, like that of 'liberty of contract' and the exclusive right of the States to govern industrial relations, brought hundreds of State laws to grief, as well as an unusual number of Congressional enactments. Two persistent dissenters from this tendency where Justices Holmes and Brandeis, both of whom thrust forward maxims of judicial self- restraint in vain. The Court had converted judicial review, declared Justice Brandeis, into the power of a 'super-legislature,' while Jus- tice Holmes complained that he could discover 'hardly any limit but the sky' to the power claimed by the Court to disallow State acts 'which may happen to strike a majority' of its members 'as for any reason undesirable.' "[77]

In 1969 another instance of breaking the compact seems to have been suggested by Justice Black. In a veiled way Black men- tioned the failure of the Courts when attempting to solve the segre- gation problem by school busing, a type of decision which is essen- tially legislative rather than judicial:

"It was this dismal record (the results of school busing) which led Justice Black in an unprecedented television interview to ob- serve that in retrospect he felt that the Court should have decided *Brown I* [Brown No. 1] like any other law case, make its decision,

258

and let the other branches of government figure out how to vindicate the rights established by the decision rather than to endeavor to do it through the judicial process. . . ."[78]

The border line between a legislative and judicial decision is sometimes hard to distinguish. The Court intended to enforce equity for the blacks by destroying state-imposed school segregation which the Supreme Court held denied the equal protection of the laws for all required by the Constitution; and judgments of equity do belong in courts. But in our society the legislatures are supposed to solve social problems, not the courts. Such decisions are therefore legislative in character, and the spirit of the Constitution if not the letter puts the responsibility on the legislatures.

By the Founders' principles a far worse violation of natural rights, which included also an infraction of the constitutional separation of powers, occurred in the 1973 Blackmun decision legalizing abortion. The right involved is the right to life itself. In his dissent Justice Rehnquist notes:

"But the Court's sweeping invalidation of any restrictions on abortion during the first trimester is impossible to justify under any standard, and the conscious weighing of competing factors which in the Court's opinion apparently substitutes for the established test is far more appropriate to a legislative judgement than a judicial one. . . .

"The decision here to break the term of pregnancy into three distinct terms and to outline the permissible restrictions the State may impose in each one, for example, partakes more of judicial legislation than it does of a determination of the intent of the drafters of the Fourteenth Amendment."[79]

There is a terminology being used now to describe the Supreme Court which, judged by the principles of the Founding Fathers, is unhappy in its implications. Succeeding Courts are "activist" or governed by "judicial self-restraint" according to their attempts to solve social problems or not. Tresolini describes the situation:

"As will be seen . . . the Warren Court, with few exceptions, has consistently defended individual freedoms. The acknowledged

259

leader of the civil libertarians on the Warren Court is Justice Black, who has been ably supported by Justices Brennan, Douglas, and the Chief Justice himself. These 'judicial activists' believe that the Court must play a positive role in the protection of civil liberties. They seek to promote social welfare and to protect American freedom from erosion by partisan legislative bodies and executive officers. Justice Black and his supporters thus view the Court as the ultimate guardian of constitutional rights. Justice Felix Frankfurter, who retired in 1962, headed another bloc on the Court which advocated a policy of 'judicial self-restraint.' He and his supporters believe that the primary responsibility for governing lies with the people and their duly elected officers. They feel that the Court must take a back seat to legislative bodies lest the freedom of the people to govern themselves be hampered by 'judicial legislation'. . . ."[80]

"Activist" and "judicial self-restraint" are terms which indicate the Supreme Court has come to practices not justified by the Founders' principles of what the Supreme Court should do. If there were no "activists" advocating judicial legislation there would be no need for followers of "judicial self-restraint." The Court was never intended to be a legislature, or a solver of social problems. Congress and the States were to pass laws for the common good; if these statutes violated natural justice or the Constitution the Supreme Court had the power to declare them unconstitutional. But to the legislatures go the power of legislating.

We are a government of the people, by the people, for the people. The people make the laws through their legislatures; that the people have a hearing is insured by committee hearings, by lobbying groups, by publicity through press, TV, radio. When Supreme Court Justices insulated from the people, with life tenure so that they do not have to answer to the people, and without the tools required by the democratic process, decide what is best for a nation of 210 million people, there is a subversion of the democratic process. The country then has a government of men, not laws; worse, of an oligarchy of from five to nine men, whatever the Court majority happens to be in a particular decision.

The "activist" Justices are in a position to impose their private philosophies on the nation — which is exactly what has happened during the past hundred years, except for the brief intervals when judicial self-restraint ruled. During this time a few men saddled the country with *laissez-faire* economic policies, to the detriment of the great mass of workers, farmers and consuming public; these were the Justices who became a "super-legislature" in the terms of history. They thought they were bringing prosperity to the country. More recent members of the Warren Court were "activists" to correct the racial injustices imposed by the same *laissez-faire* Courts. Had the *laissez-faire* Darwinians not violated the natural rights of the blacks the Warren Court would not have had to be considered "activist" in correcting these injustices; they could have been justified in their acts simply by realizing that they were restoring the natural justice required by the principles of the Founding Fathers. But because they also were "activist" in mentality they by decree imposed legislation to correct the injustice; they ordered busing instead of merely striking down the unjust segregation laws. Busing may or may not be the best means to correct injustices caused by school segregation; but it is not for the Court to decide.

The Burger Court was "activist" in its procedure with the abortion cases of Roe vs. Wade and Doe vs. Bolton. Permissive abortion was being debated throughout the nation, and after an initial momentum, apparently the people were rejecting it by upholding the tradition of the state laws which protect the right to life of the unborn. In 1972 by referenda in Michigan and North Dakota pro-abortion laws were turned back; in the same year New York and Pennsylvania legislatures after much publicity and committee hearings rejected their liberal abortion laws only to have vetoes of the actions by Governors Shapp and Rockefeller. But on January 22, 1973 the Supreme Court cut off the national debate on abortion by invalidating all state anti-abortion laws, in effect attempting to make the problem moot. The Court was "activist" in a decision which rivals only the Dred Scott ruling of the preceding century when the Taney Court attempted to lock slavery on the nation by nullifying the Missouri Compromise. Justice Byron White in a dissenting opinion said that the decision was "an improvident and extravagant exercise of judicial power," and:

261

"The upshot is that the people and the legislatures of the 50 States are constitutionally disentitled to weigh the continued existence of the fetus on the one hand against the spectrum of possible impacts on the mother on the other hand."[81]

The Supreme Court in Roe vs. Wade and Doe vs. Bolton made itself not only a "super-legislature" and cut off the power of state legislatures to act; in this case it cut off the capability of the people to influence legislation in an area of the deepest moral concern, the life or death of unborn human beings. The effect on the democratic process was devastating. It can in no way be reconciled with a "government of the people, by the people, for the people."

## The Supreme Court And Virtue

The final principle of the Founding Fathers, which with unshaken confidence they were convinced would generate a strong and happy society, was the maxim that there is a necessary connection between the virtue of the people and the strength of the society. Some states wrote the principle into their constitutions by requiring public instruction in religion and morality and making provision for the public worship of God, v.g., Massachusetts and New Hampshire. Virginia merely summed it up in her Bill of Rights:

"15. That no free government, or the blessings of liberty, can be preserved to any people, but by a firm adherence to justice, moderation, temperance, frugality and virtue, and by frequent recurrence to fundamental principles."[82]

George Washington was not eloquent in speech like his fellow Virginian, Patrick Henry, or a master of words as was his other fellow statesman, Thomas Jefferson; but he had an eloquence which flowed from the sincerity of his heart. His formal education might be thought of today as perhaps high-school training. However, Washington was a reader, and collected 900 books for his library. He mixed with and learned from the educated men of his time.

Above all he was a man of experience; the sufferings of life proved to be his great teacher. From the early hardships endured while surveying Indian country in western Virginia through the agony of Valley Forge and the war years he experienced what it means to have personal character. He believed religion and morality were the foundation of private and national character. He was consistent in the convictions expressed in his first inaugural address spoken to the Senate and House of Representatives on April 30, 1789:

"In these honorable qualifications (of his listeners) I behold the surest pledges that as on one side no local prejudices or attachments, no separate views nor party animosities, will misdirect the comprehensive and equal eye which ought to watch over this great assemblage of communities and interests, so, on another, that the foundation of our national policy will be laid in the pure and immutable principles of private morality, and the pre-eminence of free government be exemplified by all the attributes which can win the affections of its citizens and command the respect of the world. I dwell on this prospect with every satisfaction which an ardent love for my country can inspire, since there is no truth more thoroughly established than that there exists in the economy and course of nature an indissoluble union between virtue and happiness; between duty and advantage; between the genuine maxims of an honest and magnanimous policy and the solid rewards of public prosperity and felicity; since we ought to be no less persuaded that the propitious smiles of Heaven can never be expected on a nation that disregards the eternal rules of order and right which Heaven itself has ordained; and since the preservation of the sacred fire of liberty and the destiny of the republican model of government are justly considered, perhaps, as *deeply,* as *finally,* staked on the experiment intrusted to the hands of the American people."[83]

The "republican model of government" is, of course, the American democracy; we use more commonly today the word "democratic" to mean a government of the people, by the people, for the people. Democratic government was indeed an experiment in Washington's day: practically all contemporary governments were monarchies, and whether the American experiment would last, only time would tell. But if it were going to last it would have to be built on "the pure and immutable principles of private morality" ... for there was "an indissoluble union between virtue and happiness; between duty and advantage; between the genuine maxims of an honest and magnanimous policy and the solid rewards of public prosperity and felicity. . . ."

We have recently passed through months which have taught us that the government is in danger when "the principles of private morality" have been dishonored by men in high position: Watergate. But we do not advert to the fact that we have other national problems because a secular society has fairly well obscured the necessary connection between private morality and a healthy society so evident to the Founding Fathers. "Law and order" — the debate goes on: how tough does the police force have to be, how severe the courts, if the ordinary citizen is to regain confidence that he is safe even in his own home? But there would be no problem of "law and order" if the quality of virtue were higher in society, if the dope problem were minuscule, if juvenile delinquency were not a scandal, if our rate of crime and violence were not a disgrace before the world. If order does not come from the hearts of the citizen, if overprevalent crime tones society rather than widespread decency, order must be imposed from without. When democracies decay, ordinary people have been known to welcome dictatorship: imposed order. The elementary fact is that a democracy cannot perdure unless its people maintain a high standard of virtue; the more widespread the freedom allowed in society, the greater the need for virtue among the people. It would be a tragedy of history if this nation finally proved that democracies are at best temporary; Washington saw so clearly that "the preservation of the sacred fire of liberty and the destiny of the republican model of government are justly considered, perhaps, as *deeply*, as *finally*, staked on the experiment intrusted to the hands of the American people."[84]

The "Father of his Country" was sure that the United States would perdure as long as the virtue of its citizens remained at a high level.

The conclusion to be drawn from the Founders' principle that private virtue and the strength, vitality of political society are indissolubly joined is that it is a civic duty to foster private virtue.

## The Court Destroys Virtue By Bad Example

This leads us to the specific problem: What has the Supreme Court contributed to the private and public morality of the country which will enable it to perdure? Justice Brandeis gives a first principle for maintaining virtue among the people:

"Our government is the potent, the omnipresent teacher. For good or ill, it teaches the whole people by example. Crime is contagious. If the government becomes a lawbreaker, it breeds contempt for law; it invites every man to become a law unto himself; it invites anarchy. To declare that in the administration of the criminal law the end justifies the means — to declare that the government may commit crimes in order to secure the conviction of a private criminal — would bring terrible retribution. . . ."[85]

The power of example, especially bad example, is a vital point to ponder. But we should not limit bad example to the executive department enforcing law. The big politician taking bribes teaches the ward leader to get his. The politicians who make campaign promises and write off their fulfillment as "campaign promises" have destroyed the faith of many Americans in the government itself; national polls show this. The thought is widespread that success in politics at a high or low level means abandoning ordinary moral standards.

The Supreme Court has not given the bad example of open corruption, nor can personal corruption be charged against the hundred Justices who have sat on the bench since the founding of the Republic. Subjectively they may well have been honorable men. Yet in reading the history of the Court it is reasonable to conclude that the Court has at times given very bad example to the country, objective bad example which is not ordinarily described in these terms. The legal profession is in trouble today; it cannot agree on a definition of law itself, and does not seem to know its own identity or function in society. Could not one cause be that young lawyers know bad Supreme Court decisions stick, are accounted as good law (they will be enforced) although their origin has at times been known to be foul? Cannot the dilemma forced on the profession by such decisions be one reason for its present disarray? The motto over the portico of the most stately edifice in Washington, the Supreme Court building, reads: *Equal Justice Under Law.* The true purpose of law in society is justice, yet a short passage written by a professor of law at Yale University describes one well-known period of Supreme Court history:

"They [the Supreme Court Justices] were a different group of men in 1886 than they were in 1877. And, although the interstate commerce clause was their *technical* device for protecting the railroads from regulation in 1886, the soon-to-come perversion of the due process clause to judicial defense of *laissez-faire,* in prosperity or depression, was telegraphed by the politico-legal temper of the Court's new and business-minded members.

"Meanwhile, the Justices had been busily perverting the plain intent of the Fourteenth Amendment — and the Fifteenth too — in another and even more indefensible fashion. Through the 1860s and 1870s, Congress had passed a series of laws designed to put teeth in the otherwise empty words of the post-War Amendments, by imposing criminal penalties on anybody who deprived the Negroes of any personal or political rights, including 'the equal protection of the laws,' which the Amendments were supposed to guarantee. Then, through the 1870s and 1880s the Court imperiously and impatiently swept aside almost all of these so-called Civil Rights Acts, either by flatly branding them unconstitutional — no matter that the Constitution had been amended precisely to achieve what these laws were aimed to achieve — or by using legalistic chop-logic to 'interpret' them out of effective existence. A federal statute that made it a crime for any state official to stop citizens from voting was vetoed by the Court as too far-reaching, and hence an improper invasion of state's rights — since the Fifteenth Amendment only forbids the states to stop people from voting 'on account of race, color, or previous condition of servitude.' (Actually, the statute did use the phrase, 'on account of race and color,' so the Court, by a weird contortion of words, had to hold that the statute meant more than it said in order to hold that, by meaning that much, by going that far, it was unconstitutional.) In another Negro voting case, the Court refused to let some Louisiana state officials be punished under Federal law for their violent maltreatment of Negro would-be voters — simply because of a tiny technical slip in the wording of the indictment. Said the Court, quite straight-faced: 'We may suspect that race was the cause of the hostility, but it was not so averred.' On a broader and equally callous scale, the Justices gave a green light for the future to the brutality and terrorism of the Ku Klux Klan, by over-throwing a federal statute deliberately meant to curb the Klan — on the ground that the protections and guarantees of the Fourteenth Amendment could be enforced (if at all) only against state acts, not against the acts of private persons. Amidst this judicial vandalism, one crumb was tossed to the Negroes in the form of a ruling that they could not be kept off juries just because they were Negroes — a ruling so obviously abstract and futile, in the light of Southern practices, that no effort was made by the Court to give it real effect for over fifty years."[86]

Here is the Court defeating the essential end of law: justice, equal justice, for all. How can a profession have self-respect when its highest authority defeats the end of the profession? Does this bad example from the top not help to explain why many lawyers use the law, with all its technicalities, to absolve clients from just obligations? This is the opinion of much of the public concerning the legal profession. And how can virtue which, according to the Founding Fathers, must exist if a democratic society is to grow in strength, be present in society if its legal base is anti-virtue, and of a vicious nature? A widespread disrespect for law is a cancer in a free society; either the cancer is excised or the democracy must become authoritarian to force men to do what is right.

Were the bad example of the Supreme Court a thing totally of the past there would be no problem; in a subtle, insidious way it is a thing very much of the present. The most frightening example of bad Court decisions happened in 1973 when the Blackmun ruling struck down the laws in all fifty states which had hitherto protected the lives of unborn children. Its only parallel in history was the Dred Scott decision that helped precipitate the Civil War.

There is no charge here of personal dishonor or subjective guilt directed at the seven Justices who voted this decision. The confused thinking within the legal profession on the nature of law itself, thinking which has pervaded the profession for a century and which the Justices breathed in with their law-school training, produced finally a monstrous decision on the level of Dred Scott. The anti- and pro-slavery emotions before the Civil War accounts for those Justices thinking it honorable, and good for the country, to hand down a decision which would have saddled slavery on the nation forever. The positivistic principle that law does not have to be moral, that law is anything enforced by the courts, can justify in judicial minds anything that satisfies the current power structure or current popular trends.

In principle, positivistic judges can justify anything. In the Dred Scott decision the inalienable right to liberty of a race was infringed; in Justice Blackmun's decision the inalienable right to life itself for unborn human beings was destroyed. Both decisions violate the principles of the Founding Fathers that there is a law higher than positive, man-made law, a law which protects each human being in his inalienable rights and that with this law all court decisions, all legislation, must correspond. It is the objective breaking of this natural moral law, the intrinsically bad example of the Blackmun decision, which concerns us here, not the subjective righteousness of the Justices who handed down the ruling.

Justice Blackmun states in Roe vs. Wade:

"One's philosophy, one's experiences, one's exposure to the raw edges of human experiences, one's religious training, one's attitudes toward life and family and their values, and the moral standards one establishes and seeks to observe, are all likely to color one's thinking and conclusions about abortion. . . . Our task is, of course, to resolve the issue by constitutional measurement free of emotion and predilection. . . ."[87]

268

Justice Blackmun is following a positivistic principle that man-made law alone is sufficient to decide the right to life of the unborn. In this case it is the Constitution, but, of course, the Constitution devoid of the objective principles of morality understood by the Fathers as the basis of all law. In its place we have the Constitution as interpreted by Justice Blackmun and his colleagues. Other individuals may have "one's philosophy, one's experiences, one's exposure to the raw edges of human existence, one's religious training, one's attitude toward life and family, and the moral standards one establishes" (as if sound morality is not objective and the same for all); to Blackmun and the Justices who voted with him it is enough to "resolve the issue by constitutional measurement free of emotion and predilection. . . ."

In other words, to solve the abortion problem, legality is enough; some may be troubled by religious training, others by the moral standards (?) they set up, but the Court can bypass all this and proceed to make the momentous decision of life and death for millions of human beings on man-made law alone as to whether abortion is legal or not, i.e., legal by their interpretation of the Constitution. It is a shocking example of legality being placed above morality. Morality is totally bypassed; in the practice of society human rights need depend only on legality, Supreme Court legality.

This is bad example to the country in its most arrant form. The Founding Fathers built the country on a moral law which they held binds all men; they fought Britain on the conviction that their inalienable rights to life, liberty and the legitimate pursuit of happiness, among other things, were objective rights which all decent men must recognize, and they had such a "decent respect for the opinions of mankind" that they placed their principles before the world with a full willingness to risk their "Lives, . . . Fortunes . . . sacred Honor." But the Justices who voted with Blackmun did not even try to ponder the morality of this life-and-death decision. In practice legality is all that matters. The subtlety of this dereliction makes it far more reprehensible than Justice Brandeis' concern over evident problems such as wiretapping or police brutality. Likewise, the irrefutable bad example of Watergate will pass away; it was a disgraceful sin of commission, but temporary. However, the Supreme Court's sin of omission is more devastating. The absence of even an attempt to solve the deepest of moral problems, then proceeding to hand down a decision as if the problem were not there, gives the great example to the nation that one can act merely on legality, that morality does not matter. This example dynamites the virtue which the Founders held was necessary to the nation.

"Bad example for the country" is not simply a phrase to air and forget. It is elementary ethics that legality and morality are not the same. The vote of a legislature cannot change a lie into truth; the decision of a Court cannot make rape an honorable act. Legalizing abortion does not make abortion moral. The problem remains: is it moral to kill an unborn human being?

The subtle bad example of the Court violating one of the most fundamental moral principles of Western civilization undermines the morality of many individual Americans. Because abortion requires study to understand the problem; because there have been countless shallow statements that "a woman's body is her own" (but she carries within herself another's body when seeking abortion) or "only wanted children should be born" (most children are wanted, all should be by the individual or society, after birth); or "there are too many people in the world" (as if the violent killing of the unborn is a proper solution) — it is easy for untrained minds to think that what the prestigious Supreme Court decides is legal must also be moral. The teen-ager, the distraught, uneducated, overburdened mother, can and does take legality with its origin (the Supreme Court) as a moral guide in this traumatic experience of life. One can doubt that any of the Justices who voted for permissive abortion would say that legality makes morality; but it is safe to say that in practice the Court decision has settled the moral problem for thousands who follow through to have an abortion.

If the executive department becomes a lawbreaker in fighting crime, according to Justice Brandeis it breeds contempt for law; if the Supreme Court rides roughshod over a moral principle upon which American civilization was built, the inalienable right to life of each innocent individual, can its example be less devastating than that of the executive department? Its offense is merely more subtle, less apparent to the untrained, but more harmful because of this.

270

With no attempt to solve a deep moral problem, the nature of the human rights of the fetus (by definition a fetus is an unborn human baby), the Court willed the death of those who are not protected by the ethics of the doctor or the natural morality of the mother. Legality can never make morality, but in the American tradition it was expected to be the witness to it. Nevertheless, for countless untrained or unconscionable persons, legality becomes a quick rule for morality.

## The Court Raises A Barrier To Virtue: School Secularism

A democratic society, according to the Founding Fathers, can be strong only if its people are virtuous. One can injure morality in others not only by bad example but also by more positive action. The Fathers were convinced that education is sound only when joined to moral and religious training:

"Religion, morality, and knowledge, being necessary to good government and the happiness of mankind, schools and the means of education shall be forever encouraged."[88]

The Congress under the Articles of Confederation which passed the above provision of the Ordinance of 1787 had two years previously decided their practical means for securing this sound education:

"There shall be reserved the lot no. 16 of every township for the maintenance of public schools within the said township; . . ."[89] (This amounted to about eighteen acres for every square mile of a township.)

The founding generation was quite positive in fostering religion and morality. Thus the Pennsylvania Constitution, adopted September 28, 1776, stated:

"44. A school or schools shall be established in each county by

271

the legislature, for the convenient instruction of youth, with such salaries to the masters paid by the public as may enable them to instruct youth at low prices: and all useful learning shall be duly encouraged and promoted in one or more universities.

"45. Laws for the encouragement of virtue, and the prevention of vice and immorality, shall be made and constantly kept in force, and provision shall be made for their due execution: And all religious societies or bodies of men heretofore united or incorporated for the advancement of religion or learning, or for other pious and charitable purposes, shall be encouraged and protected in the enjoyment of the privileges, immunities, and estates which they were accustomed to enjoy, or could of right have enjoyed, under the laws and former constitution of this State."[90]

The Constitution of New Hampshire, June 2, 1784, declared:

"VI. As morality and piety, rightly grounded on evangelical principles, will give the best and greatest security to government, and will lay in the hearts of men the strongest obligations to due subjection; and as the knowledge of these, is most likely to be propagated through a society by the institution of public worship of the DEITY, and of public instruction in morality and religion; therefore, to promote these important purposes, the people of this state have a right to impower, and do hereby fully impower the legislature to authorize from time to time, the several towns, parishes, bodies-corporate, or religious societies within this state, to make adequate provision at their own expense, for the support of public protestant teachers of piety, religion and morality. . . ."[91]

It is within this background of the necessity of education joined to morality and religion as a base for civil society that the Fathers drafted the Constitution, that the public debated it, that the states adopted it. To use the Constitution to block the necessary interaction of the three would be a monstrous thought to the founding generation. It is from this background of this necessary connection that the Supreme Court must be judged when one considers whether the Court is fostering the virtue, the morality which is needed for a democratic society.

272

The Constitution was drafted without a bill of rights. The people were so upset about this that some states accepted the Constitution on condition that a bill be added. This is the origin of the first ten amendments.

The founding generation as a whole did not think it wrong to have established churches. The Constitution of South Carolina, adopted in 1778, read:

"The Christian Protestant religion shall be deemed, and is hereby constituted and declared to be, the established religion of this State. . . ."[92]

Connecticut did not disestablish until 1818, Massachusetts until 1833. What the Americans did not want is for one church to be established nationally in preference to all the others. So the First Amendment read:

"Congress shall make no law respecting an establishment of religion or prohibiting the free exercise thereof; . . ."

According to the oldest authoritative commentator, Justice Story, who sat on the bench with Marshall, the clause forbids Congress from giving *preferential* treatment to any particular religion or sect, but he regarded Congress as still free to prefer Christianity to any other religion. To Cooley in his *Principles of Constitutional Law* the clause forbids "the setting up or recognition of a state church [v.g., the Episcopalian Church in England], or at least the conferring upon one church of special favors and advantages which are denied to others."[93]

According to a second theory, voiced in a letter sent in 1802 to a group of Baptists in Danbury, Connecticut, by Thomas Jefferson, the purpose of the amendment was to build "a wall of separation between Church and State." In 1879 to Chief Justice Waite, speaking for a unanimous Court, Jefferson's statement was "almost an authoritative declaration of the scope and effect of the Amendment."[94] A vivid, literary phrase from a gifted writer, voiced in a letter and not a considered legal document, had become a dogma for the Supreme Court. But in a much more authoritative document, Jefferson's second inaugural address, three years after the Danbury letter, he expressed a very different interpretation of the First Amendment: "In matters of religion, I have considered that its free exercise is placed by the Constitution independent of the powers of the general government." Justice Story sums up the problem and solution:

"An attempt to level all religions, and to make it a matter of state policy to hold all in utter indifference would have created a universal disapprobation, if not universal indignation. . . . The real object of the Amendment was to exclude all rivalry among Christian sects, and to prevent any national ecclesiastical establishment which should give to a hierarchy the exclusive patronage of the national government."[95]

In spite of this the wall grew in height and breadth as succeeding Courts quoted and used Jefferson's figure of speech, especially in the decisions which secularized the public-school system. In addition to this it should not be forgotten that Jefferson was not one of the drafters of the First Amendment, nor was Madison, his confidant, its author. James Madison was the leader in securing Congressional approval for the First Amendment, but it went through six versions in its wording until it satisfied Congress as a whole, including representatives from states which had established churches. When one realizes that the makeup of the House of Representatives consisted of fifty-two Federalists and twelve Anti-Federalists, while in the Senate there were twenty Federalists and not one single Anti-Federalist, and that the Federalists especially held to the proposition that religion and morality must be taught in the schools, it is evident that the drafters of the amendment never intended nor envisioned that the national separation of church from state would result in a separation of religion and morality from education.

We discussed above the implications to the virtue of the people due to the bad example set by the Supreme Court when the Court majority voted with Justice Blackmun to strike down state laws protecting unborn human beings — without even examining the morality of abortion. But it is in its unhistorical use of the First Amendment's prohibition on Congress from making any laws regarding an establishment of religion to prohibit cooperation between the public schools and local churches in the matter of teaching religion (and morality based on religion) that the Court raised a positive barrier to the teaching of virtue and morality to children in public schools. The Court applied the prohibition to the states via the Fourteenth Amendment. The school district of Champaign, Illinois, guided by state statute, had set up a program whereby at the request of parents children could be taught by ministers of their own faith for one-half hour each week, in the public schools and during school hours. The Court voided the plan in the McCollum decision.

In a later case the Court allowed students to be dismissed early from school for instruction in their own churches. The difference in cooperation permitted seems at first merely of degree. In practice it makes it much more difficult to adequately teach children the principles of morality necessary to be a good citizen; and it totally secularized the public-school system. There is no doubt that the Fathers considered it necessary to teach morality and religion as an integral part of education; to demean the importance of morality and religion and to hinder their adequate teaching by the cumbersome separation caused by the released-time system is to destroy their principle and purpose.

How impossible the Court's action is to reconcile with the practice of the Fathers, who took for granted Bible teaching in the public schools and often hired the local minister as the local school teacher! But the Court read this out of (or into?) the Constitution. This was positive action on the part of the Supreme Court which impaired the growth of morality among the citizens; results are around us in the increase of juvenile delinquency, of the dope problem, of crime. To the Fathers only virtue among citizens can make a democracy flourish; and the time to teach virtue, to guide morality, to develop character, is during the formative school years.

Bible teaching, with indoctrination, was the ordinary teaching program in the "common" (later public) schools when the Founding Fathers lived. Yet in 1963 Justice Clark delivered a majority opinion of the Supreme Court that voided a Pennsylvania statute which read:

"At least ten verses from the Holy Bible shall be read, without comment, at the opening of each public school on each school day. Any child shall be excused from such Bible reading, or attending such Bible reading, upon the written request of his parent or guardian."[96]

We must look at the forest, not the trees. It is impossible to think that the Founding Fathers intended the First Amendment to be used to destroy the connection between Bible religion, morality and education in the American system of training good citizens, and in its place to establish the anti-religion of secularism. It is quite easy for the Court to repeatedly deny it is establishing secularism as the state religion as far as tax-supported schools are concerned. The constant omission of religion as a cornerstone of the country, and morality founded on religion (and really all morality is based on religion) as a necessary ingredient of good citizenship, is secularism in full practice. To secularists God and religion are not necessary, and have no bearing on practical life. The child who never in his or her education hears a connection between concrete religious doctrines and morality is by omission being taught secularism as a way of life. By the principles of the Founders this can only lead to disaster. Thus Washington stated:

"Of all the dispositions and habits which lead to political prosperity, religion and morality are indispensable supports. In vain would that man claim the tribute of patriotism who should labor to subvert these great pillars of human happiness — these firmest props of the duties of men and citizens. . . . And let us with caution indulge the supposition that morality can be maintained without religion. Whatever may be conceded to the influence of refined education on minds of peculiar structure, reason and experience both forbid us to expect that national morality can prevail in exclusion of religious principle."[97]

To Washington "refined education" may be sufficient "on

276

minds of peculiar structure"; it would never be sufficient for national morality. But the Supreme Court has imposed this "refined" (read "secular," without religion) education on all public-school children, by means of the Constitution. The Court is positively interfering with the acquiring of the virtue and morality necessary to good citizens. This is more than bad example. . . . It would be well to read the dissenting opinions of Justices outvoted in different cases as the Court established secularism as the religion of tax-supported schools; in the Abington case the dissenting opinion of Justice Stewart is eloquent in its clarity. It reminds one how often the dissents of Justices Holmes and Brandeis were later proven to be better constitutional law than the opinions of the majority, and how much the people suffered until Brandeis' and Holmes' conclusions were accepted.

# EPILOGUE

"Much has been said in recent years about a leadership crisis, even a leadership vacuum. Surely the appearance at the birth of the nation of a constellation of statesmen of first-rate abilities prompts the query as to why such a cluster of leadership talents has never appeared again in the American skies. Talented individuals to be sure; but as a group even the remarkable team of Webster, Clay, and Calhoun pales in comparison."[1]

Professor Richard B. Morris of Columbia University, chairman of the American Historical Association's Committee on the Commemoration of the Bicentennial, voices the judgment of professional historians. It can be added with confidence generated by historical facts that no generation understood so well the nature of government, or the importance of a sound philosophy of society in the production of a strong nation and happy people, as the founding generation. The Founding Fathers and the founding generation left to their posterity a capital investment in philosophical principles and practical structure of government upon which the most powerful and freest nation in history was built. Are we who live at present going to pass this American heritage on to posterity? Or are we going to fritter away both capital and income?

We are blind if we do not recognize the signs of decay in American society. We are foolish if we are not willing to learn from history that internal decay foretells the end of a nation or civilization. We are dishonest if we are not willing to look at our faults. An examination of conscience means just this: one looks for faults, not for virtues, in one's character. It is a method for improvement which for the moment bypasses the virtues present. The acknowledgment of sin is the first step to correction, to improvement. It is far more sensible to look for the signs of decay, the sins of omission and commission in society and government, and to try to correct them, than to be deceived by material progress or lulled to sleep because there are also evidences of vitality.

Watergate is an obvious sign of decay; the general public reaction is an evidence of vitality. But Watergate is only the topmost of many instances of absentee ethics in government. Because of the number of lawyers involved it is also symptomatic of a widespread lack of ethics in the legal profession. Individual lawyers do not lack ideals but the whole profession is plagued with the principle that there is no connection between law and morality.

Other leadership groups also show signs of decay. There has been a constant lowering of moral standards in the communications media. The idea that crime can be spread by the way it is reported, or that individual and family morality, private and public morality have a relationship to what the TV and radio industry feeds daily to tens of millions of children (and adults) — this idea has not awakened a widespread sense of responsibility within the media. Crime *is* on a terrifying ascent; family life *is* breaking down; juvenile delinquency *is* on the increase. We are the most literate great nation in history, and also the most materialistic. Is this the product to be expected of our school systems? If we were shortly to be faced with a national crisis equal to World Wars I and II, would our willingness to self-sacrifice be sufficient for national salvation in this post-Vietnam era? Have the churches worked together in a spirit of ecumenism to bring our people closer to the same God we all worship? Are we ready to overcome inbred prejudices? How much of the materialistic outlook within American society today is due to the failure of the churches?

But, of course, no nation need be lost as long as a new generation is forming. Ideals belong to youth; even the rebellion of the youth of the 1960s, the anti-war protests, the communes and the violence, were signs of youth rebelling against a materialistic and selfish society. It was the means taken by the young to overcome the evils that are frightening — the mob reaction on the campuses, the dropping-out of society, the terrorism. If the youth had had better leadership from the generation running the colleges and universities, the media and government, would the young have gone in such irrational directions? If the leaders were devoted to the founding ideal that all men are created equal and have inalienable rights derived from their humanness, if the leaders were inspiring exam-

279

ples of the Judeo-Christian standards of morality, would the youth have lashed out so blindly in so many directions?

All sections of the national leadership are to blame for the loss of ideals and principles upon which the Founding Fathers built the nation and which they considered necessary for its continuing vitality, its very existence. But if it is possible to pinpoint the group which might have dammed the flood of secularism which inundated American society during the past century, it is the legal profession. Lawyers are, of course, a product of the schools, of the churches, of the mass media, of society; perhaps it is not fair to convict them of such responsibility. They drifted along with the materialistic society of which they are a part.

The legal profession, however, is a nervous system for society; it controls so many of its vital actions that it tones the whole body. Out of the 535 Senators and Representatives in the 93rd Congress, there were 288 lawyers. The executive department, from the President through the teeming bureaucracy, is guided by law and lawyers. State and city governments are also toned, if not dominated, by lawyers. All the judges must be lawyers. Business and labor are guided by their legal departments. Covertly or overtly lawyers are part of the decision makers in banking, insurance, manufacturing, commerce. The man in the street enters the lawyer's office at the crucial points of his life, in making or settling wills, accident claims, transfers of property, encounters with law and government.

Of the seven greatest Founding Fathers, five were lawyers — Jefferson, Hamilton, Adams, Jay, Madison (never formally admitted to the Bar, but a legal scholar and constitutional lawyer on the genius level); Washington and Franklin were the laymen. Lincoln, the second "Father to his Country," was a lawyer.

The Founding Fathers enshrined their principles in the legal structures they set up. Their principles were the ideals of the lawyers of the first century of national existence; it is the second century, the post-Civil War era that has witnessed the evident decay in American society. Had the legal profession not gone along with the change in the interpretation of American law and permitted positivism to replace the natural-law principle that the human individual with inalienable rights is central to American society, the drift toward secularism could have been checked in vital areas, at crucial times.

The American system of education would not now be secularized; race problems would not have grown to race hatreds; the workingman would have been treated with justice, and the poverty-stricken with human dignity. The incidence of crime would not be so high. The gross lack of decency in the entertainment field could have been checked by lawyers who believed there is a distinction between liberty and license. Perhaps they could have influenced editors and news commentators to observe the same distinction: freedom of speech does not extend only to the prohibition of faking the call "fire" in a crowded theater. The soul of liberty is not the spirit of license. Obscenity is not difficult to recognize for people who keep within the Judeo-Christian tradition of the Founding Fathers; it becomes blurred when lawyers quibble. . . .

The sad reality is that the legal profession does not recognize its proper function, its own dignity in society; it should be the guardian of justice and the protagonist of the common good, for all true laws are meant to protect justice and further the common good of society. If the legal profession were true to itself it could have, to a very great extent, checked the downward trend all around it. Had the profession kept in mind that it is as much responsible for the state of justice in society as the medical profession is for health or the clergy for morality, the tone of society in America would have been far more humanitarian in the truest sense of the word. If the 375,000 lawyers of the country recognized their own dignity, lived up to their responsibilities, this nation of 210 million people would not now be showing signs of decay.

America has a tradition from the Founding Fathers that the purpose of government is justice and the common good; the tradition was codified into law, in the state and national constitutions. The people yearn for justice and the placing of public good above private interest. The American people still believe in morality, that legality does not make morality, that liberty and license are not the same. If the legal profession were adequate to its task of leadership, lawyers would be formulating the desires of the people in terms understandable to them, in natural law and human-rights phraseology; and the profession would be implementing the yearnings of the people by putting the soul back into American law.

But if the legal profession has failed to lead the people toward justice through law, if lawyers as a group have failed to recognize their function in society or their true dignity, the failure at the top of the profession has been more evident and more disastrous. At the apex of the profession is the Supreme Court. In reaching the zenith of prestige and authority Justices have by the criteria of the Fathers often descended to the nadir of lawlessness and immorality. This is said of objective actions, not of subjective dispositions. The hundred Justices who have sat on the Court in the past 185 years have as a group been superior to the rank-and-file politicians in freedom from corruption. To use an analogy there is a world of difference between the doctor who makes an honest mistake, who unknowingly orders a death-dealing medicine compared to the medical felon who prescribes a poison. But history shows that Justices led by emotion or the prejudices of a particular generation have by the standards of the Founding Fathers undermined the Constitution; they have defeated the purposes intended by the men who drafted it and the understanding of the people who accepted it.

It is well to realize that this is but part of the picture; there have been tens of thousands of Court decisions which did fulfill the purpose of the Constitution and the laws made under it. But the violations of the ideals and purposes of the Founders by the Court have injured vital areas of the common good. Watergate is temporary, and Congresses come and go; the effects of Supreme Court decisions, sound or unsound, trivial or dangerous, last from generation to generation. And one cannot assess the impact of present Court decisions unless past history is kept in mind.

The five elements with which the Founders connected the welfare of the country are God, natural law, natural rights, compact and virtue. The attitude of the Court towards these constitutes the Fathers' criteria for judging the highest judicial body.

## God

The Fathers were convinced that basic human rights were inalienable because they came from God, the Creator. If there is no God, there are no rights; atheism cannot supply men with any reason why might does not make right, why the law of the jungle should not prevail, and can furnish no foundation to oblige men to be good. But in spite of lip service to the proposition, "We are a religious people whose institutions presuppose a Supreme Being," the Court has acted as if there were no Supreme Being. This is implicit in such a decision as the Blackmun ruling which struck down the laws in fifty states protecting the lives of unborn human beings. The first right which comes from the Creator according to the Declaration of Independence is the right to life. The Declaration states that governments are instituted to protect this right; it was the philosophy of the Declaration which the Constitution was to implement. The Court in the Blackmun decision was not even remotely concerned with the possibility that each human life is sacred and its protection is a God-given obligation of governments. . . . More directly against God, the Court has made itself the great advocate of secularism.

The Supreme Court has made it impossible for government and church to cooperate in leading children to the knowledge of God, a knowledge presupposed as necessary for good citizens, for as the Court truly did say, "We are a religious people whose institutions presuppose a Supreme Being." The most obvious secularizing decisions were McCollum vs. Board of Education and Abington School District vs. Schempp. It is helpful to study the dissenting opinion of Justice Stewart in Abington and of Justice Reed in McCollum to see if these Justices do not reflect the standards of the Founding Fathers far better than the opinions of the majority in these cases.


## Natural Law

The second ideal of the Founding Fathers violated seriously by the Supreme Court is the principle that a natural law was given to mankind to guide human relations, that this law is the foundation of civil law, that civil law must never contradict it. The words of

George Mason, the author of the Virginia Bill of Rights, are terse, strong:

"Now all acts of legislation apparently contrary to natural rights and justice are in our laws and must be in the nature of things, considered as void. The laws of nature are the laws of God, whose authority can be superseded by no powers on earth. A legislature must not obstruct our obedience to Him from whose punishments they cannot protect us. All human constitutions which contradict His laws we are in conscience bound to disobey. Such have been the adjudication of our Courts."[2]

The Supreme Court for the past century has acted as if this natural moral law does not exist. In the fifty years between 1887-1937 when social Darwinism was its philosophy and *laissez-faire* economics its criterion of constitutionality, without the permission of the people the Court substituted this philosophy and this theory of economics in place of the Founders' natural law. The harm to the working people and consuming public was incalculable. . . . The Blackmun decision in particular exemplifies the Court's constant omission of natural-law moral criteria. The Founding Fathers were convinced that civil law must correspond to moral law; the Supreme Court during the recent past has become a law unto itself by permitting the legal taking of innocent life.

## Natural Rights

From natural law the Fathers derived natural rights, the inalienable rights to life, liberty, pursuit of happiness, property, justice, the various freedoms. Because of a disregard of a true concept of natural law the Supreme Court made decisions which destroyed natural rights. The Founders, unfortunately, compromised on the right to liberty; on principle they should have struck at the heart of slavery, but as an institution it was enmeshed in the economic and societal life of the South; they saw it weakening and had reason to hope for its natural death. The Fathers as a group detested it; but

284

the Supreme Court by the Dred Scott decision of 1857 would have saddled the nation with it forever. The country paid for this violation of the natural right to liberty of the blacks with the blood of the Civil War.

The Court wounded the right of working people to justice during its half century of *laissez-faire* policies; the suffering caused to the poor, to children, to women employees, when the Court struck down protective legislation of Congress and the states, is hard to estimate. The Supreme Court decision in Plessy vs. Ferguson (1896) clamped legalized segregation on the South and for sixty years denied blacks their natural rights of freedom and human dignity. We are paying now in the coin of race tensions and prejudice; injustice to any minority brings an accounting sooner or later.

In 1973 the Supreme Court attacked the ultimate right held sacred by the Founders, the right to life itself. If the government can take away innocent human lives or authorize private citizens to do so at will, essentially we have totalitarianism; there is no protection left for the individual, for all other rights depend on the right to life. It seems absurd to think the highest Court in the land would decree that the right to privacy of one human being is superior to the right to life of another; but the Blackmun decision was such a decree. The only decision with which this can be compared to some extent is Taney's Dred Scott ruling: in the Dred Scott decision the right to liberty was attacked; but it is the right to life itself that has been denied in the Blackmun decision. There is so much irrationality in this violation of the Founders' principles that parts of American law are in shambles.

How can a reasonable man make a distinction between a baby one day before birth and the same human being one day after? Yet if a doctor with the acquiescence of the mother kills it within the womb a day before natural birth he performs a legal act, has the protection of Supreme Court law; if the doctor destroys it one day after natural birth he will be held for murder. Or how can one justify the destruction, inherent in the Blackmun decision, of the father's rights as to whether his flesh-and-blood child shall live? By nature indeed the mother is the host to the child, provides for nine months its protection and nourishment; but the origin of the unborn human being is equally from the father, who by nature has an equal responsibility and right with the mother toward the life and welfare of his offspring. By a God-like decision the Court in Blackmun swept this all aside. ... Natural rights are nonexistent in present Court outlook; in their place are only those rights which the five to nine Court majority will permit Americans to have.

## Compact

To the Founding Fathers the origin of a particular government is a compact among a definite group of people. The American contribution to this principle was the written compact, the written constitutions of state and nation. The compact was under God's law; the people could devise particular means to insure their rights and happiness under constitutional government, subject only to the limits placed by natural moral law. Thus the American people insured freedom of conscience on a national level by forbidding the national government to establish a national church; they insured justice in criminal cases by a constitutional requirement of trial by jury. They opted for governments with triune devisions of power: legislative, executive, judicial.

The Supreme Court is a creature of the national Constitution, subject to it. Only the people have the power to change the Constitution; this is basic. As society changes there must be changes in law; the Fathers foresaw need for changes in the Constitution and wrote into it the method of its change: it can be adapted through amendments recommended by two-thirds of the House and Senate, ratification by three-fourths of the states, or by national and state conventions. Changes must go back to the people by these methods; it is beyond the ordinary legislative power of Congress to change the Constitution. The Supreme Court was given no power to amend the Constitution; nor was the President. The Supreme Court has the power to interpret the Constitution. The powers given Congress, the Supreme Court and the executive branch were broad; but not broad enough to make essential changes in the Constitution.

American courts inherited from English courts the power to

286

change law: "I used to say to my students that legislatures make law wholesale, judges retail" (Justice Frankfurter as a Harvard law professor). But the Justices were considered to have guidelines in the slow process of making common law fit new situations: since they were sitting in courts of justice, they implicitly went back to natural law, natural justice, to guide this natural growth of the law. The written constitutions were also to give American judges this guidance; judges were to have no power to violate natural moral law or the constitution under which they operate. The preamble to the U.S. Constitution states:

"We, the People of the United States, in Order to form a more perfect Union, establish Justice . . . do ordain and establish this Constitution for the United States of America."

The people intended to establish justice; this was the fundamental purpose for which they established this Constitution. Justice was objective, just as the written Constitution was an objective compact. Justice is a state of affairs which exists when each man respects the rights of his fellowman, especially his basic natural rights. As a cardinal virtue, a hinge virtue which affects other human relationships, justice is defined as "the moral virtue which inclines the will to render everyone his due or his right according to some measure of equality."[3] It is always subject to the natural moral law; no man can ever have a right to rape a woman, to torture a child, lead children into evil, to lie under oath, to directly kill an innocent human being.

Natural justice which flows from natural law was what the Fathers intended to establish by means of the Constitution. This implies that the basic rule for interpreting the Constitution is the natural moral law. Constitutional law was to grow in accordance with natural law, sound morality. At the same time natural justice was to be achieved in accordance with the Constitution; Americans were to attain justice ordinarily by jury trial, not merely by the adjudication of judges. This was implicit in the compact which made the states one United States; *e pluribus unum,* the inscription on our coins, is very apt.

In concrete instances how differently the Supreme Court has

287

operated, how violently it has broken the compact of the people! To interpret the national Constitution the Court substituted whole new guidelines when it made social Darwinism its standard in place of the natural moral law; it amended the Constitution by using its wording in decisions rendered, but changed the meaning and the direction in which the Constitution was meant to grow. Instead of the individual human being with inalienable rights protected by the Constitution the nation saw giant corporations fostered as fulfilling the social Darwinist theory that the fittest should survive.

It must be remembered also that the Supreme Court is a creature of the Constitution:

"The judicial Power of the United States shall be vested in one supreme Court, and in such inferior Courts as the Congress shall from time to time ordain and establish. . . ." (Art. III, Sect. 1)

But previously the document states:

"All legislative Powers herein granted shall be vested in a Congress of the United States, which shall consist of a Senate and House of Representatives." (Art. I, Sect. 1)

If there were any principle which Americans wanted to establish in their compacts it was that there should be a separation of powers between legislative, executive and judicial branches. Thus the national and state constitutions incorporated this division of powers. It is just as much a violation of the Constitution when the Supreme Court takes over legislative functions which belong to Congress as it would be for the executive to exercise court functions, v.g., by consigning a man to jail without trial.

Our courts do have an inherited legislative function, to preside over the growth of common law in accordance with sound morality. But if a legislature passes a law in accordance with natural-law morality and the individual constitution involved, it supersedes a court interpretation; law can grow naturally under court decisions, but radical legislation belongs to legislatures. The Supreme Court has repeatedly violated this principle; that is the origin of the term "activist" court, when during a certain era a particular set of Justices are prone to go beyond their rightful prerogatives and make decisions which are legislative in character. One of the many instances of this type of Supreme Court violation of the Constitution is exemplified by Justice Rehnquist's dissent in the Blackmun decision:

"But the Court's sweeping invalidation of any restrictions on abortion during the first trimester is impossible to justify under that standard, and the conscious weighing of competing factors which the Court's opinion apparently substitutes for the established test is far more appropriate to a legislative judgement than to a judicial one.... The decision here to break the term of pregnancy into three distinct terms and to outline the permissible restrictions the State may impose in each one, for example, partakes more of judicial legislation than it does of a determination of the intent of the drafters of the Fourteenth Amendment. . . ."[4]

The Court, having violated the natural-law guideline which was to keep constitutional decisions within natural-law ethics, also violated the separation of powers which the Fathers wrote into the Constitution.

The Supreme Court majorities when infringing on legislative authority have often thought they were helping the nation; the Justices apparently in good faith were acting as "activist" social reformers — even apparently the social Darwinians. History shows how much harm Justices in good faith can do when they do not permit legislation to go through the legislative process, through the give-and-take of committees, of lobbying, of public opinion and pressure; in a word, when the Justices change the Constitution by reading into it what they want. Legislation belongs to legislatures; social reforms should be supervised by the people through the democratic process. We are a government of the people, by the people, for the people.

The Court falls into a trap similar to that of the entire legal profession when it eschews its natural function, which is to achieve justice in society through law. Contrary to Justice Holmes, the Supreme Court should not separate justice from law: *Equal Justice Under Law* reads its motto over the colonnaded entrance to the

289

Court building in Washington. The purpose of law is justice. Justice is the reality which comes first; laws are made to attune with it. The true dignity of the Supreme Court Justices is not to be "activist" social reformers (this belongs to others), but to see that justice is attained in accordance with constitutional and natural-law directives. The Court is the guardian of the Constitution as given by the Founding Fathers and framers of the various amendments; this is an awesome responsibility, an exalted dignity. In avoiding or not recognizing its true function the Court demeans itself; and in the process of not achieving its function it pits the judgment of from five to nine men against the wisdom of the democratic process and has, repeatedly, harmed the nation in so doing.

## Virtue

The last element which the Founding Fathers considered necessary for the strength and permanence of the nation was the necessity of virtue in people and government. The Supreme Court has contributed in a definite way to the virtue of the people by good example; there has been a high consistency of personal integrity, subjective goodness on the part of the hundred Justices who have sat on the highest bench. Objectively the record in many concrete instances is quite the opposite; the Court has given bad example, too. Lawyers know that the Constitution has been changed in meaning by the Court; it is easy for lawyers to fall into the principle that law is merely the prediction of what the courts will decide when they see it happening on the high bench ("the Constitution means what the Supreme Court says it means").[5]

This is the undermining of law; it can explain why lawyers are content to use any technicality to win their cases, though justice suffers.

A whole profession surely has been injured by Supreme Court example in this. And it cannot have helped the people to become more moral when they suffered under the injustices of the *laissez-faire* Courts, the racist generations of Justices. But more directly the Court has injured the virtue of the people by its secularizing decisions which prevented religion and morality based on religion from being taught in the public schools — though this had been the tradition of the country from the beginning. It gave scandalous example when it substituted legality for morality in the Blackmun decision. The Court has truly violated the Founders' ideals that a strong nation must be built on a moral people when its example, its concrete attitude and resultant decisions, hindered implementation of morality among the people.

At this point of time all preceding problems come into perspective in the Blackmun decision. In this 7 to 2 ruling the Supreme Court violated every principle which the Founders held vital to the nation: dependence on and obedience to God, guidance from the natural law, reverence for basic human rights, the obligation of the Court to respect the Constitution as the people's compact, the essential need for virtue in a democracy. All these ideals and principles the Fathers took from Western civilization as interpreted by the Judeo-Christian tradition; we are dealing with a civilization and tradition 3,500 years old. This generation must make its decision whether it wants to maintain this American civilization as given by the Fathers or whether it intends to enter a different path guided by Court-decreed secularism, man-made morality. If the present Court would examine its conscience and face the problem in all its depths we can hope for a reversal of the Blackmun decision: previous Courts have reversed themselves. This means an act of great humility, great honesty.

But meanwhile the people cannot wait for the Court to act. In this Bicentennial era the people are faced with the clearest decision concerning American civilization and the nature of law and morality since Dred Scott and the Civil War. The movement to enact a new amendment to the Constitution to reverse Blackmun is merely facing the question: is the right to life a right basic to American civilization, a right which comes from God and is founded on sound morality, or can the nation survive on man-made rules? The acceptance of an amendment to the Constitution to once again give legal protection to unborn human lives will be the people's answer. This generation will make the choice between Washington, Jefferson and Lincoln — or Burger, Blackmun and Brennan.

# appendix

Appendix

# SOME THOUGHTS TO PONDER

There is no doubt that the legal profession is in trouble. An Associated Press dispatch which appeared in the *Philadelphia Inquirer* of February 24, 1975, bore the headline: U.S. COURTS LABELED 'BUSH LEAGUE.' The origin of the term came from a speech of Chief Justice Warren E. Burger to the midyear meeting of the American Bar Association. Justice Burger complained that the federal courts were being used as "bush league" training grounds for neophyte prosecutors and public defenders who leave after a short time for more lucrative private practice.

Mr. Burger was quoted as saying:

"The standards for selection . . . of these lawyers on whom the system of justice depends should be made sufficiently attractive so that the federal courts will not continue to be used as a 'bush league' facility to train trial lawyers for private practice. . . . No other developed country operates with the casual attitude we exhibit toward the need of qualified advocates on both sides of the table in the administration of criminal justice."

Chapters 13 and 14 of this book dealt with some of the problems of the present-day legal profession; Chief Justice Burger's remarks are but another observation on the situation. It is useful to compare Abraham Lincoln's attitude toward his profession, and his advice to would-be lawyers, with the present state of affairs. Lincoln was a very successful lawyer in his home state of Illinois in spite of the humble words and homespun way of developing his thoughts. One cannot doubt that if his principles were in more evidence today the legal profession and the country would be better for it. This is what Lincoln had in his "Notes for a Law Lecture" (c. 1850):

I am not an accomplished lawyer. I find quite as much material for a lecture in those points wherein I have failed, as in those wherein I have been moderately successful. The leading rule for the lawyer, as for the man of every other calling, is diligence. Leave nothing for to-morrow which can be done to-day. Never let your correspondence fall behind. Whatever piece of business you have in hand, before stopping, do all the labor pertaining to it which can then be done. When you bring a common-law suit, if you have the facts for doing so, write the declaration at once. If a law point be involved, examine the books, and note the authority you rely on upon the declaration itself, where you are sure to find it when wanted. The same of defenses and pleas. In business not likely to be litigated, — ordinary collection cases, foreclosures, partitions, and the like, — make all examinations of titles, and note them, and even draft orders and decrees in advance. This course has a triple advantage; it avoids omissions and neglect, saves your labor when once done, performs the labor out of court when you have leisure, rather than in court when you have not. Extemporaneous speaking should be practised and cultivated. It is the lawyer's avenue to the public. However able and faithful he may be in other respects, people are slow to bring him business if he cannot make a speech. And yet there is not a more fatal error to young lawyers than relying too much on speechmaking. If any one, upon his rare powers of speaking, shall claim an exemption from the drudgery of the law, his case is a failure in advance.

Discourage litigation. Persuade your neighbors to compromise whenever you can. Point out to them how the nominal winner is often a real loser — in fees, expenses, and waste of time. As a peacemaker the lawyer has a superior opportunity of being a good man. There will still be business enough.

Never stir up litigation. A worse man can scarcely be found than one who does this. Who can be more nearly a fiend than he who habitually overhauls the register of deeds in search of defects in titles, whereon to stir up strife, and put money in his pocket? A moral tone ought to be infused into the profession which should drive such men out of it.

The matter of fees is important, far beyond the mere question of bread and butter involved. Properly attended to, fuller justice is done to both lawyer and client. An exorbitant fee should never be claimed. As a general rule never take your whole fee in advance, nor any more than a small retainer. When fully paid beforehand, you are more than a common mortal if you can feel the same interest in the case, as if something was still in prospect for you, as well as for your client. And when you lack interest in the case the job will very likely lack skill and diligence in the performance. Settle the amount of fee and take a note in advance. Then you will feel that you are working for something, and you are sure to do your work faithfully and well. Never sell a fee note — at least not before the consideration service is performed. It leads to negligence and dishonesty — negligence by losing interest in the case, and dishonesty in refusing to refund when you have allowed the consideration to fail.

There is a vague popular belief that lawyers are necessarily dishonest. I say vague, because when we consider to what extent confidence and honors are reposed in and conferred upon lawyers by the people, it appears improbable that their impression of dishonesty is very distinct and vivid. Yet the impression is common, almost universal. Let no young man choosing the law for a calling for a moment yield to the popular belief — resolve to be honest at all events; and if in your own judgement you cannot be an honest lawyer, resolve to be honest without being a lawyer. Choose some other occupation, rather than one in the choosing of which you do, in advance, consent to be a knave.

*Collected Works of Abraham Lincoln*
Roy Basler, editor

# CHAPTER NOTES

## *Chapter 1*

1. Bob Lancaster, columnist, *Philadelphia Inquirer,* June 24, 1974.

2. *Man-Made Morals: Four Philosophies That Shaped America,* William H. Marnell, Doubleday & Co., Inc., Garden City, NY, p. 137.

3. Richard B. Morris, Professor of History, Columbia University, from an interview published in *U.S. News & World Report,* Copyright, 1974, U.S. News & World Report, Inc., (issue of July 8, 1974), p. 66.

4. Ibid.

## *Chapter 2*

1. William O. Douglas in Zorach vs. Clauson (1952), text from *Church and State in American Law,* John J. McGrath, ed., Bruce Publishing Co., Milwaukee, WI, 1962; also *We Hold These Truths,* John Courtney Murray, S.J., Sheed & Ward, New York, NY, 1960, p. 42.

2. *The Farmer Refuted,* Alexander Hamilton, New York, NY, 1775, pp. 5-6.

3. Jefferson's Va. Rep., 109. Robin vs. Hardaway, and Mason cites *Coke's Report of Bonham's Case* and Calvin's case.

4. *Rights of the British Colonies Asserted and Proved,* James Otis, London, England, 1765, pp. 10-13.

5. *Documents of American History,* Vol. I, Henry Steele Commager, ed., F.S. Crofts & Co., New York, NY, 1946, pp. 92, 95.

6. Ibid., p. 107.

7. Ibid., p. 173.

8. *Church and State in American Law,* supra, p. 388.

## Chapter 3

1. *Foundations of American Constitutionalism,* Andrew C. McLaughlin, Fawcett Publications, Inc., New York, NY, 1961, pp. 67-68.

2. Ibid., p. 94.

3. Thomas Jefferson in a letter to Henry Lee, 1825; from *Thomas Jefferson on Democracy,* Saul K. Padover, ed., New American Library, Inc., New York, NY, p. 13.

4. *The Natural Law,* Heinrich A. Rommen, B. Herder & Co., St. Louis, MO, 1947, pp. 12-13.

5. *The American Philosophy of Law,* Francis P. LeBuffe, S.J., and James V. Hayes, Crusader Press, New York, NY, 1947, p. 71.

6. *The Natural Law,* supra, p. 23.

7. Gaius (Institutes I, 1), in *The American Philosophy of Law,* supra, pp. 72-73.

8. Ibid., p. 73.

9. Romans 2:13-16, *New American Bible,* St. Joseph Edition, Catholic Book Publishing Co., New York, NY.

10. Aquinas, in *The American Philosophy of Law,* supra, pp. 74-75.

11. Ibid., p. 77.

12. *Two Treatises on Government,* John Locke, excerpt from *Living Ideas in America,* Henry Steele Commager, Harper & Row, Publishers, New York, NY, 1964, p. 120.

12a. *Cambridge Modern History,* Vol. VIII, entitled *United States,* New York, NY, 1907, p. 189.

13. *The Farmer Refuted,* Alexander Hamilton, New York, NY, 1775, p. 5.

14. *Works,* Vol. I, Pt. 1, Ch. III, James Wilson; quoted in *The American Philosophy of Law,* supra, p. 85.

15. *Documents of American History,* Vol. I, Henry Steele Commager, ed., F.S. Crofts & Co., New York, NY, 1946, p. 66.

16. Ibid., p. 83.

## Chapter 4

1. *Rights of the British Colonies Asserted and Proved,* James

Otis, from *Sources and Documents Illustrating the American Revolution,* Samuel Eliot Morison, ed., Oxford University Press, Inc., New York, NY, 1965, p. 5.

2. Ibid., pp. 32-33.

3. *Documents of American History,* Henry Steele Commager, ed., F. S. Crofts & Co., New York, NY, p. 103.

4. Ibid., p. 107.

5. Thomas Jefferson's letter to F. W. Gilmer, from *Thomas Jefferson on Democracy,* Saul K. Padover, ed., New American Library, Inc., New York, NY, p. 17.

6. Thomas Jefferson to DuPont de Nemours, 1816, ibid., p. 18.


## Chapter 5


1. *Foundations of American Constitutionalism,* Andrew C. McLaughlin, Fawcett Publications, Inc., New York, NY, 1961, p. 67.

1a. Ibid., pp. 26-27.

2. Ibid., p. 34.

3. Ibid., p. 35.

4. Ibid., p. 35.

5. *Conscience Versus Law,* Jeremiah Newman, Franciscan Herald Press, Chicago, IL, 1971, p. 74.

6. *We Hold These Truths,* John Courtney Murray, S.J., Sheed & Ward, New York, NY, 1960, Image Book edition (Doubleday & Co., Inc.), p. 44.

7. *Conscience Versus Law,* supra, pp. 78-79.

8. *Sources and Documents Illustrating the American Revolution,* Samuel Eliot Morison, ed., Oxford University Press, Inc., New York, NY, 1965, pp. 8-9.

9. *Documents of American History,* Vol. I, Henry Steele Commager, ed., F. S. Crofts & Co., New York, NY, 1946, p. 56.

10. Ibid., p. 66.

11. *Sources and Documents Illustrating the American Revolution,* supra, pp. 119-120.

12. *Documents of American History,* supra, p. 79.

13. *The Federalist Papers,* Andrew Hacker, ed., Pocket Books, Inc., New York, NY, 1971, pp. 121-123.

## Chapter 6

1. *Thomas Jefferson on Democracy,* Saul K. Padover, ed., New American Library, Inc., New York, NY, p. 116.
2. *Documents of American History,* Vol. I, Henry Steele Commager, ed., F. S. Crofts & Co., New York, NY, p. 104.
3. *Sources and Documents Illustrating the American Revolution,* Samuel Eliot Morison, ed., Oxford University Press, Inc., New York, NY, 1965, p. 164.
4. *Documents of American History,* supra, p. 107.
5. *Church and State in American Law,* John J. McGrath, ed., Bruce Publishing Co., Milwaukee, WI, 1962, pp. 379-380.
6. *Documents of American History,* supra, p. 131.
7. Ibid., p. 152.
8. Ibid., p. 173.
9. *Education of the Founding Fathers,* James J. Walsh, Fordham University Press, Bronx, NY, 1935, passim.

## Chapter 7

1. The texts sampled were: *A New History of the United States,* Irving Bartlett, Edwin Fenton, David Fowler and Seymour Mandelbaum, Holt, Rinehart & Winston, Inc., New York, NY, 1969; *A History of the United States,* Richard C. Wade, Louise C. Wade and Howard B. Wilder, Houghton Mifflin Co., Boston, MA, 1971; *History of a Free People,* Henry W. Bragdon and Samuel P. McCutcheon, The Macmillan Co. in Toronto, Canada, 1969; *United States History,* Alexander de Conde, Harris L. Dante, Richard N. Currant and Scott Forseman, Atlanta, GA, 1967; *A Strong and Free Nation,* Charles Forcey, The Macmillan Co., New York, NY, 1971; *Discovering American History,* Alan O. Kownslar and Donald B. Frizzle, Holt, Rinehart & Winston, Inc., New York, NY, 1970;

*Quest for Liberty,* June R. Chapin, Raymond J. McHugh and Richard E. Gross, Field Educational Publications, Inc., Berkely Heights, NJ, 1971; *This Is America's Story,* Howard B. Wilder, Robert P. Ludlum and Harriett McCune Brown, Houghton Mifflin Co., Boston, MA, 1970. (*History of a Free People* gave an excellent but short treatment of the preamble to the Declaration of Independence and an excellent treatment of the Constitution in the opinion of this writer. Some of the books were outstanding in format; perhaps all were adequate for other topics, but they must be criticized for their inadequate treatment of the foundation of our nation.)

2. *A Short History of the British Commonwealth,* Ramsey Muir, Geo. Philip and Son, Ltd., London, England, 1954; quoted in *Discovering American History,* supra.

## Chapter 8

None.

## Chapter 9

1. *Seedtime of the Republic,* Clinton Rossiter, Harcourt, Brace & Co., New York, NY, 1953, p. 449.

2. *We Hold These Truths,* John Courtney Murray, S.J., Doubleday & Co., Inc., Garden City, NY, 1964, p. 42.

3. *Religious Situation in 1968,* Donald J. Cutler, ed., Beacon Press, Boston, MA, 1968; article entitled "Modern Secularity" by Guy E. Swanson, pp. 804-805.

## Chapter 10

1. *Seedtime of the Republic,* Clinton Rossiter, Harcourt, Brace & Co., New York, NY, 1953, p. 449.

2. *We Hold These Truths,* John Courtney Murray, S.J., Doubleday & Co., Inc., Garden City, NY, 1964, p. 51.

3. *Documents of American History,* Vol. I, Henry Steele Commager, ed., F.S. Crofts & Co., New York, NY, 1946, p. 173.

4. McCollum vs. Board of Education, in *Church and State in American Law,* John J. McGrath, ed., Bruce Publishing Co., Milwaukee, WI, 1962, pp. 171-198.

5. Editorial from *California Medicine,* "Official Journal of the California Medical Association," Vol. 113, No. 3, September 1970, pp. 67-68 (from a reprint issued by the Grand Rapids Right to Life Committee, Michigan).

## Chapter 11

1. Cf. *The First Freedom,* Wilfrid Parsons, S.J., Declan X. McMullen Co., Inc., New York, NY, 1948, pp. 54-57.

2. Text of McCollum vs. Board of Education with Justice Reed's dissenting opinion, in *Church and State in American Law,* John J. McGrath, ed., Bruce Publishing Co., Milwaukee, WI, 1962.

3. *Special Issue on Psychological Humanistic Education,* University of State of New York (Edu. Opp. Forum), p. 75.

4. *The Educating Society,* Ch. II, entitled "American Education: Success or Failure?"; Charles E. Silberman, Random House, Inc., New York, NY, 1970, p. 13. (The forty percent figure comes from an article entitled "A Special Kind of Rebellion," by Daniel Seligman, *Fortune* magazine, January 1969.)

5. *The Educating Society,* supra, pp. 24-25.

6. Reprinted from *U.S. News & World Report,* Copyright, 1974, U.S. News & World Report, Inc., (issue of June 3, 1974), p. 66.

7. Ibid., issue of August 27, 1973.

8. Ibid., issue of June 24, 1974, p. 39.

9. *New York Times,* August 28, 1974.

## Chapter 12

1. *The Educating Society,* Ch. II, entitled "American Educa-

tion: Success or Failure?"; Charles E. Silberman, Random House, Inc., New York, NY, 1970, p. 30.

2. Ibid., p. 33.

3. *America,* November 3, 1973, pp. 324-325.

4. *How True,* Thomas Griffith, Little, Brown & Co., Boston, MA, 1974, p. 126.

5. Cf. *The Constitution and What It Means Today,* Edward S. Corwin, Princeton University Press, Princeton, NJ, 1973, p. 281.

6. Ibid., pp. 281-282.

7. Ibid., p. 282.

8. *New York Times,* August 18, 1974.

9. *How True,* supra, p. 30.

10. *The Mindszenty Report,* Cardinal Mindszenty Foundation, St. Louis, MO.

11. *How True,* supra, p. 70.

12. Ibid., pp. 70-71.

13. Richard E. Behrman, M.D., in an article entitled "The Importance of Fetal Research," *New York Times,* June 9, 1974.

14. *A Sign for Cain,* Fredric Wertham, M.D., Warner Paperback Library, New York, NY (by arrangement with The Macmillan Co.), 1969, pp. 150-186. (This is a chilling and precise account of an official campaign supervised by the psychiatrists, the object of which was "the destruction of life devoid of value." Prof. Robert Havemann, a physical chemist, denouncing the euthanasia murders, said, "The patient is no longer a human being needing help, but merely an object whose value is measured according to whether his life or his destruction is more expedient for the nation. The physicians took over the function of judge over life and death. . . . They made themselves into infallible gods" [p. 160].)

15. *How True,* supra, pp. 44-45.

16. Ibid., pp. 6-7.

## Chapter 13

1. *Time,* June 3, 1974, p. 14.

2. Richard B. Morris, Professor of History, Columbia University. Reprinted from an interview published in *U.S. News & World*

*Report,* Copyright, 1974, U.S. News & World Report, Inc., (issue of July 8, 1974), p. 31.

3.*The Hidden Persuaders,* Vance Packard, David McKay Co., Inc., New York, NY, 1958, pp. 156-163.

4. *New York Times,* September 29, 1974, section "E," p. 6.

5. R. W. Apple, *New York Times'* Biographical Edition, May 1973.

6. Reprinted from *U.S. News & World Report,* article entitled "America's Lawyers: A Sick Profession?"; Copyright, 1974, U.S. News & World Report, Inc., (issue of March 25, 1974), pp. 23-28.

7. Ibid., p. 26.

8. Ibid., p. 26.

9. Ibid., p. 25.

10. Ibid., p. 28.

11. Reprinted from *U.S. News & World Report,* Copyright, 1974, U.S. News & World Report, Inc., (issue of September 23, 1974), p. 20.

12. Ibid., pp. 20-21.

13. *Philadelphia Inquirer,* September 12, 1974. (The data in this book amount to a refutation [I hope complete] of Prof. Presser's positivistic theory of American law. Presser's statement, "Further, if the legal trainee studies much in the field of American Legal History . . . he sees that resort to 'natural law' among the Puritans justified many acts of religious oppression, and an occasional witch incineration," is amazing. It is to be hoped that Prof. Presser does not teach American Legal History at Rutgers. The Puritans are notorious in history for theocratic communities, unfortunately often distorting biblical principles according to their narrow interpretation. They were following their own interpretation of supernatural law [i.e., revelation], not natural law as understood by the Founding Fathers. But the Puritans contributed mightily to American constitutional law by their practical use of the compact in setting up their colonies.)

14. *Thomas Jefferson on Democracy,* Saul K. Padover, ed., New American Library, Inc., New York, NY, pp. 28-29.

15. *Saturday Review of Literature,* December 17, 1955, article by William P. Aspell.

16. *Rights of the British Colonies Asserted and Proved,* James Otis, London, England, 1765, p. 13.

17. *Thomas Jefferson on Democracy,* supra, pp. 17-18.

18. Ibid., p. 34.

19. *The Writings of Abraham Lincoln,* Vol. V, Arthur Brooks Lopsley, ed., G. P. Putnam's Sons, New York, NY, 1923, pp. 244-245.

20. *Abraham Lincoln,* Benjamin P. Thomas, Alfred A. Knopf, Inc., New York, NY, 1965, p. 64.

21. Ibid., pp. 120-121.

22. *Documents of American History,* Vol. I, Henry Steele Commager, ed., F. S. Crofts & Co., New York, NY, 1946, p. 387.

23. Ibid., p. 388.

24. Ibid., pp. 442-443.

25. Cf. *Man-Made Morals: Four Philosophies That Shaped America,* William H. Marnell, Doubleday & Co., Inc., Garden City, NY, p. 228.

26. Ibid., p. 252.

27. Ibid., pp. 248-251.

28. *A Galley of Justice: One Man's Dream Court,* Fred Rodell, quoted in *The Reference Shelf, The Supreme Court,* pp. 64-65, from *Saturday Review,* 1958.

29. *Man-Made Morals: Four Philosophies That Shaped America,* supra, pp. 319-322.

30. *An American Primer,* Daniel J. Boorstin, ed., New American Library, Inc., New York, NY, 1968, pp. 686-687.

31. *Man-Made Morals: Four Philosophies That Shaped America,* supra, pp. 318-319.

32. *The Fundamentals of Holmes' Juristic Philosophy,* John C. Ford, S.J., Jesuit Philosophical Eighteenth Annual Convention, 1941, in Appendix to *The American Philosophy of Law,* Francis P. LeBuffe, S.J., and James V. Hayes, Crusader Press, New York, NY, 1947, p. 395.

33. *An American Primer,* supra, p. 616.

34. Ibid., p. 617.

35. *Man-Made Morals: Four Philosophies That Shaped America,* supra, pp. 317-318.

36. Ibid., p. 318.

37. *An American Primer,* supra, p. 615.

38. Ibid., p. 627.

39. *The Occasions of Justice,* Charles L. Black, Jr., The Macmillan Co., New York, NY, 1963, pp. 17-31. Quoted in *The Reference Shelf, The Supreme Court,* H. W. Wilson Co., Bronx, NY, book entitled *Law in American Society,* pp. 163-165.

40. Felix Frankfurter, quoted in *The Reference Shelf, The Supreme Court,* supra, p. 22.

41. *Mr. Justice Holmes and the Supreme Court,* 2nd edition, Felix Frankfurter, Harvard University Press, Cambridge, MA, 1961, p. 11, *Man-Made Morals: Four Philosophies That Shaped America,* supra, p. 310.

42. *The Common Law,* Oliver Wendell Holmes, pp. 35-36, *Man-Made Morals: Four Philosophies That Shaped America,* supra, p. 310.

43. *The Farmer Refuted,* Alexander Hamilton, New York, NY, 1775, pp. 5-6.

44. *The Constitution and What It Means Today,* Edward S. Corwin, Princeton University Press, Princeton, NJ, 1973, p. 173.

45. *Encyclopaedia Britannica,* 1972, article entitled "Common Law" by A. R. Kiralfi; cf. also *Encyclopaedia Britannica,* 1970, article entitled "Common Law" by T.F.T. Plucknett and T. S. Legg.

46. Cf. *Encyclopaedia Britannica,* 1972, A. R. Kiralfi's "Common Law"; cf. also *New Catholic Encyclopedia,* 1973, article entitled "Common Law" by F. E. Lucey.

47. *Encyclopaedia Britannica,* 1972, supra.

48. Ibid.

49. Alexander Hamilton in "Federalist Paper No. 78," *The Federalist Papers,* Pocket Books, Inc., New York, NY, 1971.

50. *The Two Cities of Law,* Charles L. Black, Jr., p. 153; see also Note 40, supra.

51. *The Constitution and What It Means Today,* supra, p. 173.

52. *The American Political Tradition,* Richard Hofstader, Vintage books, New York, NY, 1948, pp. 11-12.

53. *Nine Men,* Fred Rodell, Random House, Inc., New York, NY, 1955, p. 105.

54. *The Farmer Refuted,* supra, p. 5.

55. Ibid., p. 6.

56. Pennsylvania Constitution, *Sources and Documents Illustrating the American Revolution,* Samuel Eliot Morison, ed., Oxford University Press, Inc., London, England, and New York, NY, 1965, p. 175.

57. Ibid., p. 364.

58. Loan Association vs. Topeka, quoted in *The American Philosophy of Law,* Francis P. LeBuffe, S.J., and James V. Hayes, Crusader Press, New York, NY, 1947, p. 225.

59. Ibid., pp. 225-226.

60. *The Occasions of Justice,* supra, pp. 17-31.

61. Stephen P. Presser, Associate Professor of Law, Rutgers University (see Note 14, supra).

62. Reprinted from *U.S. News & World Report,* article entitled "America's Lawyers: A Sick Profession?"; Copyright, 1974, U.S. News & World Report, Inc., (issue of March 25, 1974), p. 26.

63. James Madison in "Federalist Paper No. 51," *The Federalist Papers,* Pocket Books, Inc., New York, NY, 1964, p. 125.

64. *Judges,* Donald Dale Jackson, Atheneum Publishers, New York, NY, 1974, p. 331. (N.B.: It is Jackson who says, "Law in this sense is the written and accepted body of rules that guide the society; justice is what is morally right. But justice is then a subjective determination, dependent on the morality of the beholder, whereas law is objective and codified." Justice Cardozo's statement can be fully accepted — not Jackson's interpretation, which does, however, fit Holmes'. The Founding Fathers held that the basic principles of morality were "self-evident," obvious for any sincere person, and very objective — found in human nature itself. Cf. also Supreme Court decision in Loan Association vs. Topeka [Note 59, supra].)

## Chapter 14

1. *Thomas Jefferson on Democracy,* Saul K. Padover, ed., New American Library, Inc., New York, NY, p. 64.

2. Cf. *Judges,* Donald Dale Jackson, Atheneum Publishers, New York, NY, 1974, p. 17.

3. Cf. *The Constitution and What It Means Today,* Edward S. Corwin, Princeton University Press, Princeton, NJ, 1973, p. 176.

4. "Benjamin Fletcher White, whose *American Interpretations of Natural Law* is the standard study of the subject from the colonial period to 1931, the date of publication, carefully traces the process by which belief in the natural law gradually becomes an unvoiced axiom underlying American political thought in the earlier nineteenth century." Quoted from *Man-Made Morals: Four Philosophies That Shaped America,* William H. Marnell, Doubleday & Co., Inc., Garden City, NY, 1966, p. 236.

5. "It [natural law] became accepted, and then unquestioned and finally unvoiced. It is not that Andrew Jackson, Henry Clay, Daniel Webster, and the men who wrote the state constitutions did not accept the concept of natural law and its concomitant, natural rights; they accepted them so completely, and could rely so totally on their acceptance by their fellow Americans, that they took them for granted. The very fact, however, that they took them for granted facilitated the distortion of such concepts by many who came after them. As the nineteenth century progressed, the image of Thomas Jefferson slowly faded and the image of Herbert Spencer gradually assumed its place. The abolitionists were the last important group in the nineteenth century to plead for the rights of man on the principle of the natural law. It may yet be one of the ironic judgments of history that the first important group to do so in the twentieth century are the civil rights advocates. The hundred years belong to the social Darwinians and the pragmatists." Quoted from *Man-Made Morals: Four Philosophies That Shaped America,* supra, p. 237. (Another irony is that the principle of inalienable natural rights under the heading of the right to liberty was cemented specifically by the Supreme Court treatment of the Thirteenth, Fourteenth and Fifteenth Amendments.)

6. *We Hold These Truths,* John Courtney Murray, S.J., Doubleday & Co., Inc., Garden City, NY, p. 42.

7. Text from Supplement to *Church and State in American Law,* John J. McGrath, ed., Bruce Publishing Co., Milwaukee, WI, 1962.

8. Ibid., p. 397.

9. *The Constitution and What It Means Today,* supra, pp. 269-270.

10. Ibid., p. 270.

11. *Documents of American History,* Vol. I, Henry Steele Commager, ed., F. S. Crofts & Co., New York, NY, 1946, p. 173.

12. *Report to the Massachusetts Board of Education, 1848,* Horace Mann, in *An American Primer,* Daniel J. Boorstin, ed., New American Library, Inc., New York, NY, 1968, pp. 361-362, 372-373.

13. *Church and State in American Law,* supra, pp. 400-403.

14. Ibid., pp. 135-137.

15. Cf. *The First Freedom,* Wilfrid Parsons, S.J., Declan X. McMullen Co., Inc., New York, NY, 1948, pp. 30-45.

16. *Church and State in American Law,* supra, pp. 381-382, 386.

17. Ibid., p. 400.

18. Jefferson's Va. Rep., 109, Robin vs. Hardaway, and Mason cites *Coke's Report of Bonham's Case* and Calvin's case.

19. *Church and State in American Law,* supra, p. 381.

20. Alexander Hamilton in "Federalist Paper No. 78," *The Federalist Papers,* Pocket Books, Inc., New York, NY, 1971, p. 145.

21. *The Occasions of Justice,* Charles L. Black, Jr., The Macmillan Co., New York, NY, 1963, pp. 17-31.

22. This is said with the realization that the social Darwinians on the Court apparently considered *laissez-faire* economic theory to be a "natural law." In fact it is a theory not accepted by all, even in *laissez-faire* Court days and since 1937 rejected by the Court itself. It was imposed on the country because the Court put itself above both the Constitution and natural law as seen by the Founders.

23. Cf. Dred Scott vs. Sanford (misspelled in Supreme Court records as "Sandford"), opinion of Chief Justice Taney, *Documents of American History,* supra, pp. 341-342.

24. Cf. *Man-Made Morals: Four Philosophies That Shaped America,* supra, p. 250.

25. Cf. *The Constitution and What It Means Today,* supra, p. 390.

26. *Nine Men,* Fred Rodell, Random House, Inc., New York, NY, 1955, p. 166.

27. Cf. *The Oxford History of the American People,* Samuel Eliot Morison, New American Library, Inc., New York, NY, pp. 108-109.

28. *The Constitution and What It Means Today,* supra, p. 405.

29. Ibid., p. 406.

30. *New American Commonwealth,* Louis Heren, Harper & Row, Publishers, New York, NY, 1968, p. 91.

31. *The Constitution and What It Means Today,* supra, p. 409.

32. *Sources and Documents Illustrating the American Revolution,* Samuel Eliot Morison, ed., Oxford University Press, Inc., London, England, and New York, NY, 1970, p. 149.

33. *Nine Men,* supra, p. 105.

34. *The American Philosophy of Law,* Francis P. LeBuffe, S.J., and James V. Hayes, Crusader Press, New York, NY, 1947, p. 225.

35. Justice Harry A. Blackmun in Roe vs. Wade, *U.S. Law Week,* January 23, 1973, LW 4214.

36. Ibid., 41 LW 4226.

37. Ibid., 41 LW 4214.

38. *An American Tragedy: The Supreme Court on Abortion,* Robert M. Byrn, in *Fordham Law Review,* May 1973, Fordham University Press, Bronx, NY.

39. *U.S. Law Week,* supra, 41 LW 4221, 4222.

40. *An American Tragedy: The Supreme Court on Abortion,* supra, pp. 836-837.

41. Article by Bart J. Heffernan, M.D., entitled "The Early Biography of Everyman," in book entitled *Abortion and Social Justice,* edited by Thomas W. Hilgers, M.D., and Dennis J. Horan, M.D., Sheed & Ward, New York, NY, 1972, pp. 4-7.

42. *New York Times,* February 14, 1973.

43. *Handbook on Abortion,* Dr. and Mrs. J. C. Wilke, Hiltz Publishing Co., Cincinnati, OH, 1972, p. 10.

44. *An American Tragedy: The Supreme Court on Abortion,* supra, p. 840.

45. *U.S. Law Week,* supra, 41 LW 4226.

46. Ibid., 41 LW 4226, 4227. The central part of the quotation, left out in the text, reads: ". . . In the Emolument Clause, Art. I, No. 9, cl 2; in the Electors provisions, Art. II, No. 2, cl 2 and the

superseded cl 3; in the provisions containing qualifications for the office of President, Art. II, No. 1, cl 5; in the Extradition provisions, Art. IV, No. 2, cl 2, and the superseded Fugitive Slave cl 3; in the Fifth, Twelfth and Twenty-second Amendments as well as in secs. No. 2 and No. 3 of the Fourteenth Amendment."

47. *Webster's Seventh New Collegiate Dictionary*, G. & C. Merriam Co., Springfield, MA.

48. U.S. Constitution, Article II, Section 1, clause 5.

49. Ibid., Article I, Section 9, clause 1.

50. Ibid., Article III, Section 3, clause 1.

51. *U.S. Law Week*, supra, 41 LW 4226.

52. Cf. *1787, The Grand Convention*, Clinton Rossiter, The Macmillan Co., New York, NY, 1966, pp. 114, 144, 147.

53. *Webster's Seventh New Collegiate Dictionary*, supra.

54. U.S. Constitution, Article III, Section 2, clause 3.

55. Ibid., Amendment I.

56. Chief Justice Charles Evans Hughes.

57. *Documents of American History*, supra, pp. 341-342.

58. Plessy vs. Ferguson, *American Constitutional Law*, 2nd edition, Rocco J. Tresolini, The Macmillan Co., New York, NY, 1965, p. 599.

59. Ibid., p. 600.

60. *Man-Made Morals: Four Philosophies That Shaped America*, supra, pp. 247-248.

61. Oliver Wendell Holmes in Lochner vs. New York, *An American Primer*, supra, pp. 247-248.

62. Cf. *The Constitution and What It Means Today*, supra, p. 47.

63. *Nine Men*, supra, pp. 193-194.

64. Ibid.

65. Cf. *The Good Years*, Walter Lord, Harper Bros., New York, NY, 1960, pp. 320-330.

66. *The Constitution and What It Means Today*, supra, p. 51.

67. Ibid., p. 327.

68. Cf. *Nine Men*, supra, p. 193.

69. *The Constitution and What It Means Today*, supra, pp. 327-328.

70. *Nine Men,* supra, p. 105.

71. Justice John M. Harlan in Plessy vs. Ferguson, *American Constitutional Law,* supra, p. 599.

72. *Sources and Documents Illustrating the American Revolution,* supra, p. 119.

73. Ibid., p. 157.

74. Preamble to the Constitution.

75. Cf. Virginia Bill of Rights, para. 1; also George Mason (see Note 3, Chapter 2).

76. *Documents of American History,* supra, p. 110.

77. *The Constitution and What It Means Today,* supra, p. 176.

78. Ibid., p. 409.

79. Justice William H. Rehnquist in Roe vs. Wade, *U.S. Law Week,* 41 LW 4231, 4232.

80. *American Constitutional Law,* supra, pp. 23-24.

81. Justice Byron White in Doe vs. Bolton, *U.S. Law Week,* 41 LW 4246.

82. *Sources and Documents Illustrating the American Revolution,* supra, p. 151.

83. *Documents of American History,* supra, p. 152.

84. Ibid.

85. Justice Louis D. Brandeis.

86. *Nine Men,* supra, pp. 165-167.

87. *U.S. Law Week,* supra, LW 4214.

88. *Documents of American History,* supra, p. 131.

89. *Sources and Documents Illustrating the American Revolution,* supra, p. 206.

90. Ibid., pp. 174-175.

91. *Church and State in American Law,* supra, pp. 379-380.

92. Ibid., p. 375.

93. Cf. *The Constitution and What It Means Today,* supra, p. 269.

94. Ibid., p. 270.

95. *The First Freedom,* supra, p. 43.

96. *Church and State in American Law,* supra, p. 1 of Supplement.

97. *Documents of American History,* supra, p. 173.

## *Epilogue*

1. *Seven Who Shaped Our Destiny,* Richard B. Morris, Harper & Row, Publishers, New York, NY, 1973, p. 3.

2. George Mason, from Jefferson's Va. Rep., Robinson vs. Hardaway, p. 109.

3. Cf. *Outlines of Moral Theology,* Francis J. Connell, C.S.R., Bruce Publishing Co., Milwaukee, WI, 1953, p. 102.

4. *U.S. Law Week,* January 23, 1973, 41 LW 4231, 4232.

5. Cf. *Equal Justice Under Law,* The Foundation of the Federal Bar Association, Washington, D.C., 1965, p. 10. (The words of Charles Evans Hughes, later Chief Justice of the Supreme Court, are: "We are under a Constitution, but the Constitution is what the Judges say it is.")

# INDEX

315

**Bill of Rights, U.S.**
*See* Constitution, Amendments to (First ten . . .)

**Bill of Rights for corporations**
Fourteenth Amendment — 160f.

**Black, Charles L., Jr.**
Excerpt on natural law — 171f., 179f., 186, 209f.

**Black, Justice Hugo**
Decision against prayer in public schools — 19ff., 204f.

**Blackmun, Justice Harry**
Abortion decision aimed at right to life — 219ff.
Constitution only positive law — 221
Decisions:
  Bad example for country — 269f.
  Comparable to Dred Scott decision — 285
  Violates natural rights — 258
Human unborn not human — 224f.
Inept use of Holmes quotation — 221
Prenatal life only potentially human — 230f.
Text of abortion decision — 220f.

**Blackmun, Burger, Brennan vs. Washington, Jefferson, Lincoln — 291**

**Blackstone**
Definition of person — 235f.
Law of nature — 24f., 40f., 176, 182f.

**Bonham**
The Bonham case — 176

**Bracton**
Bracton, Coke and King James I — 52f.
Common Law commentator — 52

**Brandeis, Justice Louis**
Dissents proved good constitutional law — 277
Estimation of Brandeis by William Marnell — 163f.
Government teaches by example, good or bad — 265f.

**Brennan, Justice William**
"Judicial activist" — 260

**Britain, Great** — 21f., 136, 143, 269

**Brooks, Mel**
Offensive author — 118

**Brown, Justice Henry B.**
Segregation decision — 242

**Browne, Robert**
Covenant, compact theory of society — 48f.

**Burger, Chief Justice Warren E.**
Burger vs. Washington, Jefferson, Lincoln — 291
Criticism of legal profession — 139

**Burger Court**
Activist — 261
Pro-abortion decision — 217f.

**Byrn, Robert M.**
Criticism of Blackmun decision — 225

**Calhoun, John** — 20

**Cardozo, Justice Benjamin**
Influences which affect judges — 191
Nature of a judge — 189

**Carroll, Charles**
Denounced slavery — 70
Roman Catholic signer of Declaration of Independence — 141

**Cary, Hugh L.**
Use of TV to form image — 134

**Cherokee Indians**
Robbed of land under Justice Marshall — 181

**Child labor**
Permitted by Supreme Court — 246f.

**Churches**
Churches should seek return to Founding Fathers — 85
Churches split over slavery — 87
Duty to point out that end does not justify means — 90f.
Failure of churches regarding abortion — 90
Founders' philosophy began with God — 84f.
Materialism partly due to churches — 93
Separation of church and state not meant to separate God from society — 84f.
Some churchmen change abortion judgment — 87

**Civil War**
*See* War, Civil

**Civilization**
Depends on morality — 144f.

316

**Clark, Justice Tom**
Opinion on Bible reading in public schools — 275f.

**Clay, Henry**
One of nineteenth-century galaxy of leaders — 20

**Clifford, Justice Nathan**
Dissent from Supreme Court natural-law decision — 185f.

**Coke, Chief Justice Sir Edward**
Bonham's case under James I — 176ff.
Calvin's case under James I — 40

**Communism**
American opposition based on natural rights — 81
Ethic of Communism: end justifies means — 90f.

**Compact**
Associated with covenant origin of church — 49
*Compact* and *Consent:* correlative terms — 50f.
Connecticut Fundamental Orders — 50
Consent of governed in Magna Carta — 51
Constitution, practice of compact (C.) — 51
Declaration of Independence, theory of C. — 50f.
First Continental Congress "Declaration and Resolves" — 54
Locke's version of C. — 47f.
Massachusetts, parliament under constitution — 54
Theory justifying origin of government — 47ff.

**Conscience, National examination of**
Nature, object of examination of conscience — 76f.
Points to be covered — 76f.
Subjective data proves objectivity — 77

**Constitution, Amendments to**
Amending process cumbersome — 57
Eighteenth, ratified then repealed — 144
First, misrepresentation of — 94f., 197f., 206

**Constitution (Amnds.)** — *continued*
First, oldest interpretation of — 273f.
First ten called Bill of Rights — 67, 218f.
First, text of — 238
Fourteenth, Fifteenth — 266f.
Fourteenth, philosophy same as Founders' — 225
Madison not author of First — 200f.
Thirteenth, Fourteenth, Fifteenth — 67f., 156f., 214, 242

**Constitution, U.S.**
Declaration of Independence is foundation — 19, 76, 283
Helped solve Watergate — 76
History, nature, description — 55ff.
Madison, Wilson, Hamilton: drafters of Constitution (C.) — 138
Only people can change C. — 56, 82
President Ford upholds C. — 79
Supreme Court destroys natural rights by interpreting C. as positive law and in accordance with Justices' personal philosophy — 237ff. and passim

**Constitutional Convention**
Composition of framers (1787) — 236
Framers' intention of separation of powers — 56

**Continental Congress, First**
Meets, drafts "Resolves" (1774) — 42
Text of "Resolves" — 54f., 251

**Cooley, Thomas**
Author of *Principles of Constitutional Law* — 196, 273

**Corwin, Edward S.**
Author of *The Constitution and What It Means Today* — 115f.
Child labor adjudication in 1916 — 247
Nature, history of judicial review — 176
Two theories of "establishment of religion" — 196

**Court of chancery**
Origin in England — 179

**Custer, Gen. George**
Indian desire to discern justice in law — 172

**Darwin, Charles**
Apparent undermining of traditional thought — 157f.
Theory of evolution — 158

**Darwinism, Legal**
Form of social Darwinism — 159f.

**Darwinism, Social**
Herbert Spencer's theory — 158f.
Acceptance by Supreme Court — 159f., 186f., 221f., 243, 247f., 254, 256, 284f., 288ff.

**Declaration and Resolves Text, First Continental Congress** — 54f.

**Declaration of Causes of Taking Up Arms, Second Continental Congress** — 28f.

**Declaration of Independence**
According to Declaration of Independence (D.I.) and Constitution, human person is central — 180f.
After Civil War, philosophy of D.I. ceased to be guide for Constitution — 157
Aquinas' definition of law implicit in D.I. — 150f.
Bicentennial project: return D.I. to school children — 72
Blackmun decision violates D.I. — 225
Castigation of slave trade by Jefferson left out — 70
Chief Justice Taney misinterprets D.I. — 212, 241
Civil War, affirmation of D.I. and text — 67f.
Constitutions imply that people must give consent to laws — 251f.
Doctrine of D.I. answer to Communism — 72
False interpretation of D.I. — 68f.
Ground and foundation of American government — 19, 68
Implies function of government as in preamble to Constitution — 180
Inalienable rights cannot be ceded according to D.I. — 252f.
Jefferson's explanation of sources — 35
Lincoln's adherence to D.I. — 154f., 184

**Declaration** — *continued*
List of rights — 66f.
Not taught in our schools — 68
People hold principles of D.I., not leaders — 76f.
Presupposes God — 29
Presupposes natural moral law — 148
Signers — 65f. and passim
Spells out intentions of Founding Fathers — 180f.
Succinct expression of American convictions — 80
Text of D.I. — 143, 213, 251

**Declaration of Rights**
Bill of Rights — 26f.

**Deists**
Franklin, Jefferson, John Adams — 38

**Democracy**
Experiment called "republicanism" by Washington — 264
Justice Brandeis' dictum of responsibility in democracy — 162f.

**Dewey, Thomas E.** — 120

**Dickinson, John**
Lawyer, pamphleteer, signer of Constitution — 40

**Douglas, Justice William O.**
American institutions presuppose Supreme Being — 23
Judicial activist — 260

**Dred Scott Decision** — 194, 209, 211f., 241, 254ff., 261, 268, 285

**Education**
*See* Schools
*See also* Washington (Farewell Address . . .)

**Ehrlichman, John** — 137

**Ethics**
Meeting of ethics and law — 144

**Federalist Papers**
Constitution is fundamental law — 178
Hamilton coauthor with John Jay, James Madison — 24
No. 78, Courts interpret Constitution — 207

**Federalist Party**
Morality in schools — 274
Reliance on property — 181
**Field, Justice Stephen J.**
Social Darwinism and *laissez-faire*
policies — 159, 212f., 244
**Fisk, Jim**
"Robber baron" — 157
**Fonda, Henry and Jane** — 118
**Ford, President Gerald**
Appeal to divine law — 144
Inauguration speech — 79
Pardon of Nixon — 141
**Fortescue, Chief Justice Sir John**
Definition of constitutional monarch
— 52
**Founding Fathers**
American civil society built on God
— 194
And Justice Reed's McCollum dissent
— 96
Based constitutional system on natu-
ral law — 38f., 149, 213, 224, 251,
268
Basic rights do not come from civil
law — 219, 237f.
Belief in a personal God — 28f., 38,
201
Connection between education and
morality — 271f.
Constitution is a political compact —
250ff.
Constitutional Convention — 56
Definition of law same as Aquinas' —
150f.
Established nation on principles of
Declaration of Independence — 194,
217f.
Ethics of F.F. may be used to judge
press — 122f., 127
F.F.'s principles condemn Blackmun
decision — 223f.
Greater sense of morality than pres-
ent politicians — 131f., 135
Guide for TV producers — 110
Human dignity and rights of individu-
al — 90, 149, 211f.
Human unborn are "persons" in
Constitution, contrary to Blackmun
decision — 232f.

**Founding Fathers** — *continued*

Importance of freedom of press —
127f.
Influence of John Locke — 39f., 47f.,
51f.
Insistence on religion in education —
103
Intended law to grow in accordance
with natural law — 180, 184
Intended to stop spread of slavery —
209
Justice is objective — 188
Moral law makes society possible —
119, 140f.
Natural religion antecedent to Chris-
tianity — 205
Necessity of religion and moral train-
ing — 198
No human law valid if against moral
law — 176, 206
Objective and Judeo-Christian moral-
ity — 86f., 143ff.
Obligation of government to protect
right to life — 219
Priority of rights determined by
human nature — 92
Purpose of government is justice —
281
Recognized basic national code of
morality — 131f.
Rights "retained by people" — 91
Sense of leadership vs. present politi-
cians — 129f.
Supreme Court abandonment of
F.F.'s philosophy — 157, 208f., 212,
217, 244f.
Supreme Court breaks compact —
257f.
Supreme Court decision regarding
New York prayer void — 206
Survival of democracy — 111, 128
**Founding generation**
Comparison with present generation
— 21
**Frankfurter, Justice Felix**
Advocate of "judicial self-restraint"
— 260
Legislative power of judges — 174f.,
178, 286f.

**Franklin, Benjamin**
Against slavery — 70
Among greatest of Founding Fathers
— 19
Committee to draft Declaration of Independence — 28
Deist — 38, 65
**Freedom**
Liberty vs. license — 86
**Freedom of conscience**
Jefferson's Act — 32
Separation of church and state — 86
**Freedom of the press**
Definition, analysis — 115f.
**Freund, Paul**
Return to legal philosophy of Founding Fathers — 140, 167f.

**Gaius**
Roman jurist, idea of natural vs. civil law — 37
**Garth, David**
TV consultant for Gov. Hugh Carey — 134
**George III, King**
Violated trust to Americans — 53f.
**God**
American belief in — 79
And the teaching of religion in schools — 94ff.
Existence is foundation of civil society — 23ff., 64
Founders believed in personal God of theism — 65
Right to life comes from God — 291
Supreme Court and God — 194f., 271ff., 282f.
**Gould, Jay**
"Robber baron" — 157
**Government**
Center of leadership, amorality — 129ff.
**Grant, President Ulysses**
Corrupt politics during administration — 157
**Great Britain**
See Britain, Great
**Griffith, Thomas**
"Advocacy journalists" — 120
Distortions in journalism — 124f.

**Griffith** — *continued*
Public distrust of journalists — 127
Television — 113
Writing defensively for Henry Luce — 120
**Grotius, Hugo**
Definition of natural law — 173

**Hadlow, Earl B.**
Honesty of lawyers — 139
**Haldeman, H.R.**
Advertising executive, Nixon's chief of staff — 137
**Hamilton, Alexander**
Authority of courts regarding Constitution — 56f., 178
Definition of freedom of the press — 116
Lack of confidence in people — 59
Moral obligation flows from man's nature — 66
One of greatest Founding Fathers — 19
**Hancock, John**
"Declaration of the Causes and Necessity of Taking Up Arms" — 28f.
Declaration of Independence foundation of future government — 18f.
Franklin-Hancock conversation on Declaration of Independence — 136f.
**Hand, Judge Learned**
Conversation with Justice Holmes regarding justice and law — 189
**Harlan, Justice John**
Constitution is color-blind — 242
**Harris, Louis (pollster)**
Low rating of journalists — 127
**Heffernan, Dr. Bart T.**
Development of unborn human from conception onward — 228ff.
**Henry, Patrick**
Eloquence compared to Washington's — 262
**Hippocratic Oath**
Sad abandonment by American Medical Association — 228
**Hitler, Adolph**
Justified by Nazi laws — 80

**Hobbes, Thomas**
Atheist philosopher indicted by Hamilton — 24, 123
**Holmes, Justice Oliver Wendell**
Atheist in belief (quote) — 166
Challenge to *laissez-faire* philosophy in law — 159
Contrary to Holmes, law and justice not separate — 289
Law is force — 167ff., 175, 187
Law is prediction of what courts will do — 149, 154, 174, 188
Misuse of Holmes quote by Justice Blackmun — 220f.
Separated law from justice — 189
**Hopkins, Mark**
Scholar, president of Williams College — 159
**Hufstedler, Judge Shirley M.**
Expense of civil trials — 138
**Hughes, Chief Justice Charles E.**
"Constitution is what judges say it is" — 174, 239
**Humphrey, Hubert**
Beaten by Nixon — 137
**Huston, John** — 118
**Huxley, Thomas Henry**
Biologist, apparently undermining traditional thought — 157

**Independence Hall**
Site of Lincoln's speech — 153

**James I, King**
Conversation with Lord Coke — 52
**Jay, John**
Among greatest of Founding Fathers — 19
Helped draft "Declaration of the Causes and Necessity of Taking Up Arms" — 28
**Jefferson, Thomas**
Abandoned by Supreme Court — 244f.
"Act for Establishing Religious Freedom" — 32
Alternative to Burger, Blackmun, Brennan — 291
Among greatest of Founding Fathers — 19, 138

**Jefferson** — *continued*

Deist — 38, 141
Helped draft "Declaration of the Causes and Necessity of Taking Up Arms" — 28
Justice Field's use of Jefferson — 244
Leader in separation of church and state — 85
Limitation of majority rule (quote) — 152
Political philosopher — 20, 138
Purpose in drafting Declaration of Independence — 35
Regarding freedom of the press — 115
**Johnson, Justice William**
Bankruptcy laws constitutional — 181f., 184
**Journalism**
*See* Advocacy journalism
*See also* Press

**Kareda, Urjo**
Article in *New York Times* — 177f.
**Kelley, Stanley**
Public relations men in political parties — 133
**Krogh, Egil**
Watergate figure — 131
**Ku Klux Klan**
Brutality against blacks — 267

**"Laissez-faire"** — 158 and passim
**Langton, Archbishop Stephen**
Leader in attaining Magna Carta — 51
**Law**
Definition (Aquinas and Founding Fathers) — 150f.
Law is force (Holmes) — 167ff.
**Law, Civil**
Ethical law — 142f.
Jefferson's criteria — 152f.
Judges make law — 174f.
Law is a prediction of what courts will do (Presser's interpretation of Holmes) — 149
Lincoln's criteria — 154f.
Morality cannot be legislated — 143f.

**Law (Civil)** — *continued*

Must correspond to higher (natural) law — 144f., 189f.

To Founding Fathers civil law built on inalienable rights — 45

To Locke civil law protects property rights — 47f.

**Law, Common**

History, analysis — 176f., 179f.

Relation to natural law — 176

**Law, Natural**

According to Locke — 47f.

Bad example of Supreme Court in abandonment of natural law (N.L.) in Blackmun decision — 267ff.

Civil law must correspond to natural moral law — 144, 178f.

Civil law specifies N.L. — 183

Editors and publishers and N.L. guidelines — 114, 116f.

First Continental Congress (quote) — 42, 54f.

Found in consciences of right-thinking men — 33

Founders intended American law to grow according to N.L. — 180

Founding Fathers' N.L. — 39ff., 47, 180, 191ff.

Full content found in Bible and Western tradition — 34

Function of churches in upholding N.L. — 86f.

Judeo-Christian N.L. — 38

Justice and N.L. — 287

Justice Brandeis and N.L. — 162f.

Legal profession permits positivism to replace N.L. — 280

Source of inalienable rights — 66f., 91

Supreme Court Justices abandon N.L. — 158, 192f., 207f., 256f., 284f., 288f.

Supreme Court relies on N.L. in 1874 — 185, 192f.

To founding generation — 79f., 86

To past generations — 80f.

To present generation — 80

TV, radio and N.L. guidelines — 106f.

Underlies U.S. Constitution — 251f.

**Lawyers**

Ethics of — 139f.

In Watergate scandal — 138f.

Number in Congress — 137

Number in Continental Congress — 138

Number in country — 139

Tradition as leaders — 137f.

*See also* Legal profession

**Leadership groups**

Composed of churches, schools, media, government — 84

Decay in leadership grows — 279

**Lear, Norman**

Producer of *Maude* — 109

**Lee, Richard Henry**

Supported Anglican Establishment — 201

**Legal profession**

". . . A Sick Profession" (Justice Burger) — 138

Dilemma of legal profession (L.P.): What is law? — 149ff.

Ethics of L.P. — 139f., 279

Failure at apex: Supreme Court — 282

Failure of L.P. — 281

Responsibility of L.P. — 186ff., 280

**Lenin**

Communist morality (quote) — 72

**Lincoln, Abraham**

All political principles from Declaration of Independence (quote) — 153f., 184

Analysis of cause of Civil War: slavery (quote) — 81, 155

Choice between Lincoln and present leaders — 21, 135, 291

Leader on par with Founding Fathers — 20, 129f.

Respect for moral obligation to Constitution (quote) — 155

**Livingston, Philip**

New York delegate to First Continental Congress — 28

**Lochner vs. New York**

Destroyed legislative power to judge own acts — 160

Holmes' famous dissent (quote) — 165

322

**Warren, Charles**
Authority on Supreme Court — 160
**Warren, Chief Justice Earl**
Activist in using courts to force deseg-
regation — 215f., 261
Brown vs. Board of Education deci-
sion voided segregation (quote) —
216
Credit for destroying legalized segre-
gation — 215f.
**Washington, Booker T.**
Great black leader — 214
**War, Civil**
Causes; effect on slavery — 156
Incredible result of Civil War on na-
tural-law philosophy — 157
**Washington, George**
Background, character — 262f.
Choice between Washington, Jeffer-
son, Lincoln and Burger, Blackmun,
Brennan — 291
Choice must be made between Wash-
ington and modern politicians — 21
Farewell Address vs. McCollum deci-
sion — 197
Giant among Founding Fathers — 19
Necessity of morality for welfare of
civil society (quote) — 62, 135, 262f.
Necessity of religion and morality
(quote) — 31, 63, 85, 95, 99, 197, 276
Opposed to slavery — 70f.
Supreme Court abandons Washing-
ton — 244
**Watergate**
Egil Krogh and Watergate (W.) —
131
Jeb Magruder and W. — 130
Principles of Declaration of Inde-
pendence would have prevented W.
— 76

**Watergate** — *continued*

Responsibility of communications
media for W. — 126
W. and ethics of legal profession —
139
**Webster, Daniel**
Nineteenth-century leader — 20
**Westin, Alan**
Education-research statistician — 100
**White, Justice Byron**
Dissent in Blackmun abortion deci-
sion (quote) — 261f.
Dissent in Blackmun decision — 219
**Williams College**
Source of Justice Field's philosophy
— 159
**Williams, Roger**
Rhode Island compact (quote) — 49
**Wilson, Gov. Malcolm**
Use of TV in election campaign —
134
**Wilson, Justice James**
Against slavery — 70
Considered equal to Madison — 41
Doctrine of law of nature — 41
Great political philosopher — 138,
194
**Wilson, President Woodrow**
Outstanding leader among Presidents
— 20
**Witherspoon, Rev. John**
Signer of Declaration of Independ-
ence — 141
**Writs of Assistance Case**
*See* Otis, James (Writs . . .)

**Yankelovich, Inc. (Daniel)**
Poll on changing attitudes of youth —
101f.